SINK OR SWIM

SINK OR SWIM

The Politics of Bilingual Education

Colman Brez Stein, Jr.

PRAEGER SPECIAL STUDIES • PRAEGER SCIENTIFIC

New York   •   Westport, Connecticut   •   London

Library of Congress Cataloging-in-Publication Data

Stein, Colman B.
   Sink or swim.

   "Praeger special studies. Praeger scientific."
   Bibliography: p.
   Includes index.
   1. Education, Bilingual—United States. 2. Educa-
tion, Bilingual—Political aspects—United States.
3. Education and state—United States. I. Title.
LC3731.S77 1986   371.97'00973   86-8196
ISBN 0-275-92161-1 (alk. paper)

Library of Congress Catalog Card Number: 86-8196
ISBN: 0-275-92161-1 (alk. paper)

First published in 1986

Praeger Publishers, 521 Fifth Avenue, New York, NY 10175
A division of Greenwood Press, Inc.

Printed in the United States of America

The paper used in this book complies with the Permanent
Paper Standard issued by the National Information Standards
Organization (Z39.48-1984).

10 9 8 7 6 5 4 3 2

Preface

This book grew out of a doctoral dissertation at the University of Maryland in 1983. It analyzes the political development of modern bilingual education – instruction in two languages.

The book is dedicated to the memory of my great-grandfather, Colman Brez, of Vilna, Poland, for whom my father and I are named, who came to this country and struggled for a better way of life for his family; and of my grandfather, Dunbar Aaron Rosenthal, of Southwest, Washington, D.C., who struggled just as hard for the same purpose. It is also dedicated to my parents and step-parents, Colman and Natalie Stein and Seymour and Bettie Mintz, and to my grandmother, Fannye Rosenthal, for their love and support; to my in-laws, Rojeria and Olga Leonor Martinez for their consistent love; to all the creative bilingual and ESL educators who impart a sense of the fascination and importance of learning to their students; to my academic mentor, Barbara Finkelstein; to my children Daniel and Claudia for their understanding, patience, and love; and most of all, to my wife Marlem for her love, and for everything.

Contents

Introduction

The development of bilingual education was first and foremost a response to political pressure rather than a carefully evolved and tested pedagogical strategy. . . .[1]

Fred Burke, New Jersey State
Superintendent of Schools

Bilingual education is many things: an instructional method, a means of teaching English proficiency, a dropout prevention technique, and a way to stimulate foreign language learning. But most of all it is a political force. It was born out of Lyndon Johnson's War on Poverty and grew to maturity in Congresses dominated by liberal Democrats. Its use as a civil rights measure was initiated and later reduced by federal government action amidst politically charged atmospheres. It brings to the surface a number of other political issues relating to immigration, official language policy, the future of the melting pot, demographic changes, and ethnocentrism.

Hundreds of other books have examined bilingual education's pedagogical aspects; this is the first to concentrate on its national, state, and local politics. Politics means the art of influencing or controlling policy decisions relating to the governance of public institutions. Politics is deeply interwoven into the bilingual education program from Congress and the White House to the U.S. Department of Education down to the local schoolhouse. Where the bilingual office or program is placed tells you a lot about its political importance. If the federal bilingual office is situated blocks away from the central command structure, it may be far less involved in the informal, but highly significant, internal communication system, than other programs are. If the principal decides to place the bilingual classroom in the back of the auditorium, while placing other classes in traditional classrooms, he has acted politically in terms of the bilingual programs' status and prestige. There are more subtle decisions affecting textbook content, funding, teacher tenure, access to information, and many other matters that also come into play politically, even if the decision-makers are not fully aware of the consequences of their decisions.

There are also political issues involved in larger policy decisions. When you change the curriculum, for example, from monolingual to bilingual you are making a political statement. When you label some students as linguistically sufficient and others as linguistically deficient you are saying something about how you view the world. When local and state school authorities acknowledge the growing presence of language minority students in the midst of declining majority enrollment, they are saying something that has political ramifications. The same is true when they offer professional jobs to members of ethnic groups that were once excluded or when they decide whether or not to follow the spirit or merely the letter of a federal directive.

Public education itself is a political venture. It was undertaken by eighteenth and nineteenth century U.S. leaders as a nation-building enterprise, a way to transmit a developing Anglo-American culture to children in disparate former colonies and new states. As industry boomed and non-Anglo-Saxon immigrants came to man the factories, cities mushroomed and people congregated in smaller and smaller spaces. Policy-makers decided that compulsory schooling was necessary. They wanted to train a new class of professionals, to end child labor, to prevent juvenile delinquency by keeping the young off the streets, and to inculcate in the students the Protestant ethic and Anglo conformity.[2] Anglo conformity means "the desirability of maintaining English institutions (as modified by the American Revolution), the English language and English-oriented cultural patterns as dominant and standard in American life."[3] The anglocentric curriculum is its educational expression.

The English minority in the Dutch colony of New York fought for the right to have English as an official second language, but the Dutch refused to grant them this right. Anglo-Americans in the U.S. were just as reluctant to grant language or cultural rights to the non-Anglo-Saxons, especially in the schools. These rights had to be fought for, and frequently were. The Irish Catholics under Bishop John Hughes deeply resented the use of the Protestant King James Bible in the public schools. They protested and got no change, so they created their own network of parochial schools and colleges.[4]

The Germans stayed and fought. They won over numbers of state and local school systems to German-English bilingualism, especially in the German Triangle: Cincinnati to Milwaukee to St. Louis. The U.S. Commissioner of Education observed in 1870 that German was the nation's unofficial second language. Louisiana's French speakers (Acadians or Cajuns) and New Mexico's Spanish speakers feared that public instruction would become English-only, and struggled to institutionalize bilingual education provisions within their states' legal structures.[5]

Language-of-instruction issues are inherently political. One can no more separate politics from bilingual education than separate politics from foreign aid, defense budgets, or public works. They all spring from and relate to political considerations. So does education, in spite of the prevailing myth that public education is somehow inviolate and unsullied and that miscreants are out to besmirch it by "politicizing it." Public education is run by governments, and governments are by nature political.

To best uncover the politics of bilingual education, it is necessary to focus on and delineate the experience of Hispanics, the group for which modern bilingual education has been designed. We will examine the Hispanic educational experience before and after the advent of bilingual education on the national scene in 1968. The experience of other language minority groups will occasionally be included for comparative purposes. Then the scene shifts to the years in which bilingual education arose and was put into practice. The last section explores bilingual education in the 1980s. The book will concentrate on the political themes involved in the events and incidents described. Evaluations of the effectiveness of various types of bilingual and non-bilingual instructional methods for students with limited English proficiency will not be included except in cases in which the publicity surrounding evaluation studies has had a political impact.

Several issues and themes will emerge from this examination. One is the center-periphery question. Bilingual education has moved into the schoolhouses and administrative offices, but how central is it to their operations? Another is the "melting pot-mixing bowl" controversy. Does bilingual education absorb non-English-speaking people into the Anglo conformist mainstream or does it by its very nature lead to a quite different type of outlook? To what degree has bilingual education uplifted Hispanics into the middle class, as many of its advocates claimed it would? What effect has the changing demographic presence of Latins, Asians, and other language minorities had on political and educational institutions?

Bilingual education is now a reality in schools from the Bering Sea District of Alaska to the Key West area of Florida; from the St. John's Valley of Northern Maine to Guam and American Samoa in the far-flung Pacific. Billions of federal, state, and local dollars have sustained it. Billions of words in over 150 languages are involved in it. Hundreds of thousands of learners, parents, and educators have been involved in programs. After two decades of a national bilingual effort, a political analysis is long overdue. This book analyzes the political process bound up in bilingual education.

SINK OR SWIM

1

Military-Style Assimilation, 1880–1945

Failing to realize that the general outlook of the people was Spanish, not Anglo-Saxon, . . . we crassly attempted to impose an alien culture upon them. The form that this imposition took was "a haphazard cultural attack," a compound of the Rotary, American educational practices and a ceremonial parliamentarianism.[1]

Carey McWilliams

When Colonel Teddy Roosevelt charged up San Juan Hill, he did more than defeat the Spanish. He helped to usher in an era of foreign adventurism and domestic ethnocentrism. As president, Roosevelt sent Samuel Lindsay to Puerto Rico as education commissioner to establish a U.S.-style school system in this newly acquired territory. Lindsay reported in 1902 that ". . . colonization carried forward by the armies of war is vastly more costly than that carried forward by the armies of peace whose outposts and garrisons are the public schools of the advancing nation. . . ."[2]

Roosevelt, in his own unique style, applied Lindsay's dedication to the advancement of the armies of peace to the domestic scene:

There is no room in this country for hyphenated Americanism. Our allegiance must be purely to the United States. For an American citizen to vote as a German-American, Irish-American or Italian-American is to be a traitor to American institutions . . . any man who comes here . . . must adopt the institutions of the United States, and therefore, he must adopt the language which is now the native tongue of our people, no matter what the several strains in our blood may be. It would not be merely a misfortune, but a crime

1

to perpetuate differences of language in this country ... we should provide
for every immigrant, by day schools for the young and night schools for the
adult, the chance to learn English, and if, after say five years, he has not
learned English, he should be sent back to the land from whence he came.[3]

This sort of outlook helped establish the educational tone for the
immigrant generations and their children and grandchildren from 1880 to
1945. This period was brought on by the tremendous expansion of
industry and its need for manpower to run the machines, build the roads,
bridges, and buildings, harvest the crops, and mine the minerals. This
period coincided with military-style assimilation. The immigrants'
children had to be assimilated rapidly, by force if necessary.

The crusade for Anglo conformity permeated education. Educators
frequently put forth their politics explicitly and zealously. They stated that
the schools were out to assimilate the newcomers. A teacher training
school director told the National Education Association convention that
immigrant parents "can no longer be depended on for safe guidance ...
hence our American schools must prepare these children for the new conditions."[4] She elaborated: "As Rome brought order, peace, and freedom
to the various nationalities in her borders, so today must the teacher
endeavor ... to bring them to the Anglo-Saxon standard. ..."[5]

The dean of Stanford's College of Education found the immigrants
from Southern and Eastern Europe to be "illiterate, docile, often lacking
in initiative and almost wholly without the Anglo-Saxon conceptions of
righteousness, liberty, law, order, public decency and government."[6]
The Texas state school superintendent warned Hispanics that they had no
right to speak Spanish in the state's public institutions.[7]

The theory of hereditary intelligence underlay this militant approach to
assimilation. The new arrivals from Europe, Latin America, and Asia
were classified as deficient in learning capacity because they had inherited
deficient genes. Psychologists tested thousands of immigrants using an
IQ test in English. They concluded that the newcomers were so backward
as to be "feeble minded" or "retarded." This view buttressed the common
schoolhouse practice of holding immigrant children in the same grade
until they both learned English and could advance to grade level in their
content subjects. This was called "retardation" and led to a high dropout
rate. A prominent sociologist found Portuguese, Mexican, and Italian
youngsters to be "retarded material." Heredity seemed to justify poor
attainment levels and high grade retention and dropout rates. After all, if
they can't learn, why knock yourself out? You can't fight nature. The

best you can hope for is to leave them with a dose of patriotism and a few basic skills.[8]

Mexican-Americans were one of the major groups to undergo this military approach to assimilation. About 70,000 Mexican-Americans became part of the U.S. when the Southwest was acquired in 1848. Many more emigrated in the decades after 1880 when the opening of the transcontinental railroad spurred the industrialization of the Southwest. Many came first to San Antonio, El Paso, and Los Angeles. Many stayed and many others moved on to other sites of the burgeoning industrial, mining, agribusiness, and railroad sectors. Some entered the steel, meatpacking, and railroad industries of Chicago and Kansas City, the auto factories of Detroit, and the steel works at Bethlehem, Pennsylvania, during World War I.[9]

Southwest schools were neither agencies of upward mobility nor centers of learning for Mexican children. Instead they were agencies of frustration and dashed hopes. Most children were segregated at the elementary level into semiofficial "Mexican Schools." This practice reflected the assumptions of many Southwest educators that Mexicans needed no more than a minimal amount of schooling because they were destined for low-level jobs. This assumption jibed with the prevailing economic and political outlook of the Anglo power structure. Economist Paul Taylor conducted extensive studies of Mexican-American areas of the Southwest in 1928-1934 and found the attitude of one Texas school superintendent to be typical:

> Most of our Mexicans are of the lower class. They transplant onions, harvest them, etc. The less they know about everything else, the better contented they are. . . . If a man has very much sense or education either, he is not going to stick to this kind of work. So you see it is up to the white population to keep the Mexican on his knees in an onion patch. . . . This does not mix well with education.[10]

The segregated Mexican Schools were often located in the shadow of the dominant industry. El Paso's Smelter School stood next to the giant American Smelter and Refining Company works. Los Angeles' Anne Street School lay at the foot of the massive Southern Pacific railyards.[11] The message seemed to be that industrialists and farmers needed Latin manual labor, but would provide only minimal public education for their children.

Puerto Ricans entering New York from 1917 to 1945 found similar, if less harsh, conditions. Many of the migrants took waterfront and factory jobs and sent their children to nearby schools only to discover the practice of automatic retardation. Since educators assumed that Puerto Rican schools were inferior to those on the U.S. mainland, they considered it natural that students should be placed one or several grades behind where they would have been in Puerto Rico.[12] Submerging the child in English-only classrooms was the common practice. As a graduate of the city system recalled:

> Historically, in New York City, we have had two school systems, one school system for those youngsters who are expected to achieve, and one for the youngsters who were not expected to achieve, and don't achieve. And most of the minority youngsters are in that second school system, and the system is pretty much set up to see that they don't suceed.[13]

As a comparison to the Hispanic experience, it is useful to briefly examine Italian immigrant schooling. Italy sent the largest number of early twentieth century immigrants. These newcomers labored in the factories, mines, mills, docks, and construction sites in much the same way as the Mexicans and Puerto Ricans. The Italians, like the Hispanics, came from small towns or rural areas and were largely illiterate and not conversant with school culture. Their children, too, were stigmatized by teachers' assumptions about genetic inferiority. Most were relegated to vocational tracks on the assumption that they had no capacity for intellectual development. They were stereotyped as gangsters-in-training. A Chicago principal accused them of trying to steal everything in the school. A Newark teacher believed that the neighborhood surrounding the school was crime-infested. A 1933 survey of school attainment in New York City found that students from Italian neighborhoods were at the bottom of all ethnic groups.[14]

Italian children were told to anglicize themselves, to jettison their culture and language, and to remove themselves from the influences of their families who represented the Old World. Jane Addams of Hull House decried this family-splitting tendency. Another prominent social worker blamed the school's inducement of shame for part of the problem. As Leonard Covello, an Italian immigrant who became an innovative educator, remembered it:

> We soon got the idea that Italian meant inferior and a barrier was erected between the child of Italian origin and his parents. This was the accepted

process of Americanization, we were becoming Americans by learning to be ashamed of our parents.[15]

New York City schools educated the children of the Jews, Italians, Puerto Ricans, and others and struggled to acculturate them in the ways of Anglo conformity:

> Thousands of middle class young women found themselves teaching the children of the newcomers and facing the enormous gulf that separated them from their charges. Many teachers, rigid and prejudiced, did not try to bridge the gap, but simply relied on discipline and drill to get them through the days or years. Many others, aware and sympathetic, tried to establish rapport, but found the barriers too high. . . . Even in the absence of hostility to the children themselves, most teachers were determined to eradicate all evidence of foreign background and substitute American ideas and ideals. . . .[16]

THE AMERICANIZATION CAMPAIGN

The high point of military-style assimilation occurred during the Americanization Campaign. This national movement of business and government leaders, social workers, and educators tried to ensure that the heavily immigrant industrial work force would be loyal to the U.S. instead of to their native country during World War I. Factory lunch periods were turned into giant Americanization sessions. Patriotism and English acquisition were on the agenda. The movement spread to the night schools and public schools. Cabinet officials, state school superintendents, YMCAs, and settlement houses joined in.[17]

The Ford Motor Company's Americanization School graduation ceremonies featured a pageant in which the graduates entered wearing signs stating their countries of origin. They were ushered into a gigantic simulated melting pot as the teachers cleansed them with huge scrub brushes. Finally, they emerged with new signs proclaiming that they were 100 percent Americans.

Southwestern school boards instructed superintendents to devise Americanization curricula for their Mexican-American students, regardless of how long the students or their families had lived in the United States. To be Mexican-American was seen as being less American than Anglos were. These curricula included:

1. Los Angeles' vocational workshops to train female students to become Americanized garment workers.
2. Miami, Arizona's plan to inject a larger measure of patriotism into the instruction of young males before they dropped out to follow their fathers and grandfathers into the copper mines.
3. Ontario, California's strategy to produce more literate and patriotic maids and factory workers.[18]

This nationalist crusade engendered resentment. Ethnic, political, religious, and labor groups voiced their opposition. It reminded some of the Russification campaigns carried out in Eastern Europe to try to Russify youth from non-Russian nationalities. It reminded an Armenian immigrant of attempts by the Ottoman Empire to remake him into a Turk. A number of leading intellectuals opposed the campaign, and some became the forerunners of the movement for cultural pluralism.[19]

By the early 1920s the Americanization campaign fizzled. Its leader, Florence Kellor, attributed its demise to the immigrants' tendency to congregate in colonies that were resistant to assimilation. But while the formal campaign died, the melody lingered. The next decade was prosperous and reactionary. "Normalcy" seemed to imply a return to a real or imagined past in which things were simpler and the population was more homogeneous. The resurgence of the Ku Klux Klan, the Palmer Raids, the forced deportations of thousands of Mexicans, and the Sacco-Vanzetti Case typified this harsh and xenophobic period that lingered into the 1930s. There was a general distrust of things considered "foreign" (non-Anglo-Saxon).

School systems continued segregating Mexican-Americans throughout the 1920s, 1930s, and the first half of the 1940s. Los Angeles used its newly established psychology department to examine the causes of low Mexican-American school attainment. They tested some students and determined that their educational deficiencies needed special treatment. This special treatment became the forerunner of the educable mentally retarded classes. Once a student was assigned here, it was hard to get transferred out.[20]

A theory of negative bilingualism permeated the schooling of Mexican-American and Puerto Rican youth. This theory held that students who knew two languages would have a harder time in either one than a monolingual student. The solution seemed obvious – snuff out Spanish and stick exclusively to English.

SCHOOLHOUSE APPLICATIONS – RE-FORMING THE CHILD'S LIVING HISTORY

Schoolteachers and administrators often set about removing the ethnic child's legacy of language and culture and substituting the Anglo-American world view. This world view approaches history and culture as if both began in England and came to fruition in the United States. Educators submerged the child in English-only classrooms, with no special language instruction.

Renaming the Child

Like immigration officials who anglicized immigrants' names on entry, teachers often changed children's names during the first week of school. Juan became John, Maria became Mary. These changes were usually made without consulting parents and were often entered into official school records. Some children took the hint and changed their own names. A Polish-American from Detroit remembered: "As young students we learned that Polish names were not prized possessions and we became ashamed of them."[21] Leonardo Coviello had his name changed to Leonard Covello. When he informed his parents, his mother responded, "A person's life and his honor is in his name. He never changes it. A name is not a shirt or a piece of underwear."[22]

Stamping out the Native Language

After changing the name, the next step would be to remove the influence of the native language. A New York City school official banned Italian and Yiddish from the schools of the heavily immigrant Lower East Side. She even instructed teachers to go into bathrooms and playgrounds to punish those caught speaking these dreaded languages. In the Southwest, Spanish was banned in the schools and on the grounds. When caught speaking, students were sent to detention hall, fined, and even beaten. Irene Ramirez of San Antonio remembered: "I was punished in elementary, junior, and senior high school for speaking Spanish. In junior high school you were held after school the first two times they caught you. But the third time they would take the stick to you."[23]

Reinforcing the Anglocentric Curriculum

After partially or wholly expunging the children's linguistic and cultural legacies, educators felt duty-bound to substitute the anglocentric curriculum. Most school officials "held a common set of WASP values, professed a common-core (that is pan-Protestant) Christianity, were ethnocentric and tended to glorify the sturdy virtues of a departed past."[24] Since Anglo-American culture was the standard, other cultures were seen as substandard. This was especially true of Latin American culture. Hubert Humphrey observed:

> The average North American lives in profound ignorance of Latin America. Most adults in this country were educated in schools where the overwhelming majority of textbooks and reference books either ignored Latin Americans or reflected condescending attitudes toward them.[25]

The textbook treatment of the Mexican-American War in Texas schools exemplified the politics of the anglocentric curriculum. The political message was that all virtue resided on the Anglo side and all evil on the Mexican side. Mexican-Americans were given the message that as the losing side they were supposed to be docile and deferential to Anglos. A perceptible rise in inter-ethnic tensions has been noted during the explication of this topic. In a few cases the tension led to violence.[26]

More common nationwide was curricular stereotyping. Latins were treated as defeated and inert people. Heroic figures were almost all Anglos. Those few Latins who were included in textbooks were almost always entertainers or sports figures. Stereotyping, one-sided histories presented as immutable fact, and failure to include the contributions of non-Anglo groups are important components of the anglocentric curriculum.[27]

Submerging the Child

Submerging the child in the English-only program without special language instruction produced two main results. First, it made it quite difficult for the child to keep abreast of content subjects while trying to pick up English by osmosis. Second, it left the student floating in a sea of Anglo conformity. He had to accept or even embrace the curriculum or get out. This is the essence of sink-or-swim politics.

This school culture led to a two-stage development in most Hispanic children. First came "retardation," the term used to mean grade retention or being held back. This retardation was "manmade . . . an educational artifact. The classification of pupils was not divinely inspired or imbedded in the order of nature."[28] It tended to confirm the educational and vocational horizons that had been largely predetermined for Puerto Ricans and Mexican-Americans. It said stay where you are, what you learn in school will not help you advance economically. While a small number of Latin youngsters made it up through the ranks of academia and the job market, the majority activated the second stage of the development. They dropped out of school.

Latin communities, although predominately poor and politically underrepresented, were far from passive in the face of these conditions. A Puerto Rican parents committee in New York organized to end the automatic retardation that their children experienced, and eventually succeeded. Educators and parents in Puerto Rico fought for decades against the anglicization of the school curriculum, including the use of English as the sole language of instruction. Eventually they won the right to retain Spanish as the language of instruction, with English as the second language. The League of United Latin American Citizens (LULAC) arose in Texas in the 1930s partly to combat segregated schooling. Dr. George Sanchez of the University of Texas waged a long struggle against segregation and the educational practices that flowed from hereditarianism. Many Anglo educators bemoaned the fact that so many Hispanics chose not to become anglicized. Hispanic dissatisfaction with, and refusal to succumb to, military-style assimilation led to the beginnings of change in the post-World War II era.[29]

2

Missionary-Style Assimilation, 1945-1968

The integrationist educators and writers of the forties still shared a common goal with their segregationist predecessors of the twenties and thirties, both groups looked upon the assimilation of the Mexican and Mexican-American in the "American Way of Life" as the ultimate goal.[1]

Charles Wollenberg

Just as missionaries move in after soldiers have pacified the terrain, educators of the postwar era gradually projected a softer approach to assimilation after decades of the harsh military approach. The strategy was to convert or lure the youngsters to Anglo conformity, not to beat them over the head with it. The missionary approach means the effort "to persuade working-class clients to develop middle-class patterns of behavior."[2] Hispanic dissatisfaction with the old ways and assertiveness in removing some of these practices helped to bring on the new era.

Returning Mexican-American soldiers looked at the conditions they had left behind and decided that things had to change. They formed the GI Forum, which along with LULAC supported the Mendez and Delgado desegregation suits in California and Texas. These suits forced school officials to admit the existence of the Mexican Schools and to admit that no legal sanction existed for them. Under court order both states removed this unlawful segregation and other states followed suit. These cases served as precedents for the landmark *Brown* v. *Board of Education* decision.[3]

The second stage of Puerto Rican migration to New York took place after 1945, when air traffic opened. This stage was much larger than the first, it encompassed hundreds of thousands of people, many of whom took low-wage jobs formerly held by Jews and Italians. As a New York State official observed:

> The Puerto Rican immigration has been a boon to employers, bringing in a rich supply of cheap labor. . . . Almost 20,000 Puerto Ricans, mainly women, have been absorbed by the garment industry and almost 10,000 men by hotels and restaurants, while tens of thousands of others have found factory work or employment in building or domestic service.[4]

Puerto Ricans also inherited the schools that had tried so hard to assimilate the Jews and Italians. The schools at first submerged the new migrants. Most youngsters were unable to keep up to grade level as they were learning the new language. Some concerned educators decided that submersion was no longer viable and pressed for reforms. School officials acquiesced in the absence of a clear policy and allowed local experimentation within the city's massive school system.[5]

The Association of Assistant Principals convinced a few schools to employ bilingual teachers' aides. Several other schools added the position of Puerto Rican Coordinator to organize the children and to teach them English. Unfortunately few coordinators knew Spanish. One school organized a group of students to serve as go-betweens. One school conducted special classes in Spanish; others obtained Spanish textbooks and instructional materials; still others set up vestibule classes. There were plans to lure the parents into the school. A special guidance section was established in the Bureau of Curriculum Research. Education journals brimmed over with ideas on the subject.[6] However, none of it worked. Puerto Rican students still experienced low attainment and high dropout rates. As Clara Rodriguez saw it: "A central point of conflict was the teachers' implicit insistence that I (all Puerto Ricans) conform to the norms of white middle class America . . . the schools were antithetical to my way of being."[7] The Board of Education mulled over the issue and arrived at a time-honored solution – they appointed a study commission. The commission investigated for four years and then issued its *Puerto Rican Study* in 1958. The study recommended several major reforms and was the first time that a major school system acknowledged the educational needs of language minority children.[8]

CULTURAL DEPRIVATION

New York City school psychologist Judith Krugman worked in this milieu. She took note of the large influx of minority students in her 1955 presidential address to the American Psychological Association. She heralded a new concept in education and psychology, cultural deprivation theory. It was an environmentalist theory that blamed poor school performance on deficiencies in minority culture rather than on the genetic inheritance of low intelligence. The solution was for the schools to intervene in the transmission-of-culture process to replace parental and community values with those of the middle class. The speech attracted wide attention and was reprinted in the New York City school system's journal.[9]

It paralleled earlier conceptualizations put forth after the demise of the Americanization campaign that were known as social disorganization and social pathology theories. They were supposed to offer newcomers a bridge to cross over from the Old World to the New. Originally formulated by sociologists at the University of Chicago, the concepts stimulated widespread interest in academic circles, but were not consciously operationalized until Krugman brought the issue down to the level of the school system.[10] Sociologist W. I. Thomas, an early adherent of these social disorganization theories, co-authored a major study of the Polish immigration to the United States. Thomas stated,

> The problem with the Poles on the Northwest Side of Chicago is not that they are biologically or racially inferior, they are culturally inferior. Their European peasant culture just is not going to be of any help to them. It is a terrible problem and they are not assimilating to urban industrial life. That is why we have the high crime rates, delinquency rates, homicide rates and that sort of thing. Unless we who are responsible for them come in and change their culture, they are never going to make it in America.[11]

This view also typifies the missionary approach to assimilation.

Educators began to classify Puerto Ricans, Mexican-Americans, blacks, and American Indians under cultural deprivation labels after Krugman's speech. The concept later became the battle cry of the War on Poverty, as we will see.

Like their New York City counterparts, Southwestern educators began to press for reforms. As segregation ended, they cast about for new ways to educate language minorities. Some hired bilingual aides, some tried English as a Second Language programs, some tried bilingual instruction, and others tried all of the above, none of the above, or pieces of the above. They were unclear as to how to proceed, and were poised midway between the old ways and an undefined future.

Cultural deprivation ideas began to pervade the region. Tucson initiated a demonstration program to overcome "language disability." "Language disability" meant that children could not speak English. The remedy was to teach a heavy dose of English and discard Spanish even in a city practically astride the Mexican border. Tucson educators did not understand that the retention of Spanish could be an asset rather than a liability.[12]

Social scientists characterized Mexican-American culture as a backward folk-culture. Some criticized the family structure for holding back the upward mobility of the young:

> Parents as a whole neither impose standards of excellence for tasks performed by their children, nor do they communicate to them that they expect evidence of high achievement. The parents' great love for the children is not conditional. . . . The Mexican-American child is not prodded to achieve or risk shame on himself and his family . . . this type of up-bringing creates stumbling blocks by stressing values that hinder mobility: family ties, honor, masculinity, and living in the present.[13]

This is the classic cultural deprivation prescription for change. It tells children: Remove yourself from the family, forget your language and culture, and climb upward on your own. It says to parents: Prod your children, make your love conditional on achievement, and raise children who are thoroughly detachable. Little thought is given to changing the schools; the fault lies entirely with the parents.

ENGLISH AS A SECOND LANGUAGE

As educators experimented with new approaches, some began to adapt English as a Second Language (ESL) programs for their students. ESL provides instruction in English acquisition. It is taught in English only – no native language instruction is used. Students from one or more language backgrounds may participate in the same ESL class.

Charles Fries of the University of Michigan developed ESL in the 1930s and applied it to the instruction of foreign diplomats, businessmen, and government officials. English language centers were set up in conjunction with U.S. diplomatic missions abroad, especially by

Franklin Roosevelt's Good Neighbor Policy for Latin America. ESL was later used on U.S. university campuses for incoming foreign students. ESL was designed and formulated to serve the needs of literate, educated middle- and upper-class adults who were conversant with school culture.[14]

Suddenly, in the 1950s and 1960s it was transferred to some Southwestern and Eastern school districts. It was used to instruct the children of poor and often illiterate Hispanics who were unfamiliar with school culture. The most common ESL model was the pullout approach in which students were taken out of regular classes for ESL classes daily or several times a week.

After several years, some parents and educators complained about its drawbacks:

1. Since it usually took several years to learn English, it was hard to learn the content subjects taught in English. Students fell behind and often had to repeat grades.
2. The pullout method exacerbated the problem by causing children to miss some of their content instruction.
3. ESL students were often taunted by their classmates for having to go into the "dummy" class.[15]

One example of this situation took place in Lancaster, Pennsylvania, where Hispanic children were discovered spending most of their time doing artwork in the back of their content subject classes. The ESL class had not equipped them with enough English to be able to understand what was going on in class. A New York City school provided a special homeroom that used ESL methods to acclimate 20 foreign-born eighth-graders each day before they entered their English-only classes. Only four of the students survived to the ninth grade.[16]

SCHOOLHOUSE PRACTICES:
LURING THE CHILDREN INTO ANGLO CONFORMITY

Educators of Spanish-speaking students implemented cultural deprivation theory in the context of assimilationism. They sought to convince language minority students to embrace majority culture.

Convincing Parents to Speak English

Educators organized campaigns to enlist parental support for ending or reducing the use of Spanish in the home. They sometimes visited homes to accomplish this goal, but were met with distrust or confusion. A Texas parent commented that a teacher "had rushed in here like a rooster ... to try to stop me speaking the language of my forefathers."[17] These campaigns achieved little, since teachers lacked empathy for their students. A Texas teacher's comments were typical: "Their only handicap is a bag full of superstitions and silly notions that they inherited from Mexico ... a lot depends on whether we can get them to switch from Spanish to English, when they speak Spanish they think Mexican."[18] These uninvited home visits and the none-too-subtle efforts to eradicate Spanish reveal a great deal about the mentality that underlay the missionary approach to assimilation.

Recognizing Ethnic Symbols

Educators became interested in presenting symbols of ethnicity. They encouraged the schools to celebrate Cinco de Mayo for Mexican-Americans and Pan-American Day for other Latins. A few Hispanic names appeared in textbooks and a few schools were named for well-known Hispanics. But the end result was little more than curricular tokenism.

Foreign Language Learning

With the 1957 Soviet launch of Sputnik, national attention turned not only to math and science, but to foreign language learning (foreign languages defined as those languages other than English). It was discovered that foreign language learning was lagging far behind learning in other industrialized countries. World War I xenophobia had reduced foreign language instruction. The federal government hoped to remedy this situation through its National Defense Education Act. This legislation provided grants for local language learning and for teacher training. Spanish and French replaced Latin as the most commonly studied languages.

But a strange dichotomy developed. Those who entered school already knowing Spanish were dissuaded from conserving and perfecting their language ability, while middle-class English speakers were geared toward learning Spanish. It was a classic mismatch.[19]

Vocational Tracking

Many schools classify and group pupils by ethnicity and class. Most Latins were placed in vocational tracks that led to blue-collar jobs. The most desirable blue-collar jobs, such as those in printing and carpentry, were set aside for the sons of Anglo trade-union members. Many Latins were dissuaded from seeking these desirable jobs or the training programs that led to them. They were also dissuaded from academic tracks on the basis that they were destined for low-level service or manufacturing or agricultural jobs and did not need to concern themselves about college.[20]

A California teacher chose Anglo children as classroom monitors because they could get practical experience in learning to supervise Mexicans. This experience would be useful in adult life. The whole culture of the town supported this ethnic stratification, and the school only affirmed it:

> Whether they are at home, in church, in school, on the playground, shopping with parents, attending scout meetings or watching the Harvest Festival activities, children are provided with examples of the social position they are expected to play. They are frequently shown that Anglos are best in everything and Mexicans are the worst.[21]

Educable Mentally Retarded Classes

The postwar era saw the rise of school-based psychology. No longer confined to merely testing and labeling children, educational psychologists now had the chance to operationalize their theories and classification schemes. Students with lower-than-average IQs who were not severely retarded were often placed in Educable Mentally Retarded (EMR) classes. Hispanics were often sent to these classes because they scored low on the IQ tests given in English. Educators and psychologists were committing political acts when they carried out this labeling and assignment syndrome. They were declaring that Hispanics and other non-English speakers were deficient learners who needed special psychological attention. Lack of English was indirectly equated with deficient intelligence. By the 1960s and 1970s a number of court challenges led to a reduction in this practice.[22]

Lowered Expectations

The expectation of failure often leads to the acting out of that expectation. Many teachers intended to aid their Hispanic students but were diverted by their adherence to cultural deprivation. If one believes that a child's lack of culture prevents her or him from learning anything more than basic skills, one can create a situation in which the child learns only basic skills. The prophecy becomes self-fulfilling. It becomes an excuse not to teach; after all, they won't get anywhere anyway. This message seeps through the schoolhouse walls and is absorbed by the learners:

> Chicano children begin to develop a sense of loyalty to their people, to their fate, that distinguishes them from the Anglo boys and girls of the same age. They become ... deferential to one another in school as opposed to their teachers, whom they tend to obey rather than respect.[23]

Grooming the Talented

Many educators prepare bright students for promising academic and professional careers. But their gifted ethnic students required special help to make them competitive with the Anglos they would encounter in college. This special help included heavy doses of instruction in character building, manners, and attaining civility to help them achieve a sort of facsimile WASP status. This special grooming is a familiar theme in ethnic autobiographies. Richard Rodriguez was carefully groomed by his Sacramento teachers to enable him to rise out of the working class and into a scholarly career. In order to do so, he had to weaken his ties to his parents; there was no other choice. Either you conformed to the rigors of the upward climb or you stayed in the low-status position you came from.[24]

Very early on teachers and principals select those whom they believe have a chance to succeed, and nurture and polish and cajole them into the proper patterns of behavior. They may base these selections more on physical appearance than on perceived intelligence. Richard Gambino felt that his light complexion made him more attractive to his teachers than his Italian-American schoolmates were. Clara Rodriguez in New York and "Carmen" in South Texas observed that the teachers chose the lightest-complected, most Anglo-looking children as their favorites and as the models for success.[25]

Norman Podhoretz's grooming process perhaps best typifies the situation. Podhoretz's teacher and mentor spent months trying to wean him away from the "Jewish barbarians" of his 1940s Brooklyn neighborhood. She made snide remarks about his working-class parents. She consciously sought to lift him out of his environment and into the more rarified world of the upper middle class. She promoted

> conformity to a highly stylized set of surface habits and fashions . . . which by design operated to set one at ease only with others similarly trained and to cut one off altogether from those who were not. . . . She was saying that because I was a talented boy, a better class of people stood ready to admit me into their ranks. But only on one condition: I had to signify by my general deportment that I acknowledged them as superior to the class of people among whom I had been born.[26]

Neighbors were proud of him, but at the same time they predicted that he would not even acknowledge their presence in ten years. Podhoretz later realized what he had done to himself: "It appalls me to think what a transformation I had to work on myelf. . . . there is a kind of treason in it; treason toward my family, treason toward my friends."[27]

School culture atomizes the talented students, separates them from those deemed less worthy and sends them on their solitary quests for higher status. Teachers, counsellors, and principals take pride in the ethnic student's achievement; it may make teaching in a low-status school a little less painful. They may bring the winner back years later to inspire the current students. Politically the grooming system serves as a transmission belt to keep the American Dream alive, even in the poorest areas. Educators and parents believe in this system, even after the evidence suggests otherwise. The evidence suggests that the grooming system holds out little hope for the overwhelming number of low-income students. But not believing in the system can be frightening, since there is little to replace it with.

Missionary-style assimilation modified the earlier military style, but did not break with it. The environmentalist concept of cultural deprivation replaced the hereditarian view, and there was large-scale experimentation.

The mere submersion of students was no longer politically viable in a democracy that had begun to offer civil rights to its minorities. But little had changed in the schooling of Hispanics or in their vocational prospects. Hispanic leaders increasingly looked to Washington for solutions.

3

Reinventing Bilingual Education

Unlike ESL, bilingual education was practically an unknown quantity in the late 1950s and early 1960s. This chapter describes how this program was resurrected in Miami and re-invented nationally as the War on Poverty's approach to Hispanic community improvement. We will see the role of cultural deprivation as a central organizing principle of the War on Poverty and as the motivating strategy behind the use of bilingual education as a compensatory or remedial program. Bilingual education (also called BE or the program) had a rich history during the height of the German immigration in the mid-nineteenth century. The political lessons were:

1. The program was localized in each city or state in which it operated; the federal government was not directly involved.
2. It was a symbol of German political clout.
3. Its capacity to endure depended on the strength of that clout. In St. Louis, for example, where it had been in existence for decades, it was voted out by an anti-German faction that won control of the school board.
4. It was not conceived of as a compensatory or remedial program.[1]

MIAMI RESURRECTS THE PROGRAM

The vast influx of Cuban refugees to Dade County, Florida, in the early 1960s provided the backdrop for the resurgence of bilingual

20

education. The refugees were from Cuba's middle and upper classes. Among them were many doctors of pedagogy who had administered educational programs, and school-trained teachers who had taught in them.[2]

The Dade County public school system, which included Miami, was anxious to aid the Cuban transition to American life. School officials also offered Spanish instruction to English-speaking children so that they could better participate in the trade and commerce that had begun to flow through Miami as a gateway to Latin America. The federal government had been providing several million dollars annually for refugee education. The funding program was formula based – certain sums were provided each year based on the number of refugee children that were attending school. Politically this program was an acknowledgement that the Cubans were in the United States to stay, as well as a recognition of a special federal interest in the condition of the Cubans. It was also a form of compensation for the Dade County school system. The funds helped the school system provide bilingual orientation teachers, secretaries, teachers' aides, and visiting teachers. The money also supported teacher retraining programs at nine universities. It is important to emphasize the unique quality of this federal support; no other Hispanic bilingual education program has received support of this magnitude.

School officials believed that a demonstration project was needed to awaken educators and the public to the needs of the Spanish speakers; they wanted one that would go beyond ESL. They applied to the Ford Foundation in 1962 and received $350,000 for a three-year experimental Spanish-English program to begin in 1963. The Board of Education added part of the federal money and supplied some of its own funds. Pauline Rojas, a disciple of ESL pioneer Charles Fries, had directed the English language center at the University of Puerto Rico. She was chosen as the director. Since there were no current U.S. bilingual programs and no profession to draw upon, she had to look to Latin America for a model on which to base the project. She chose the American schools in Ecuador and Guatemala that educated the children of U.S. diplomats and businessmen as well as the children of wealthy Ecuadorians and Guatemalans. These schools used both Spanish and English as media of instruction, both to teach fluency in both languages and to prepare the children in the content subjects. One of the main aims was to produce fully bilingual students; this became the main goal of the Coral Way Project.

The Coral Way Elementary School contained middle-class students, half Cuban-born and half U.S.-born. The Cuban families in the neighborhoods surrounding the school had already attained middle-class status by 1963. This was an unusual situation, because they had been in the U.S. less than four years. Parents were given the choice of whether to enroll their children in this new program, and most did. Many of the Cubans were familiar with the operation of this type of dual-language program in Cuba.

The University of Miami retrained 30 Cuban veteran teachers who earned temporary certificates and served as teachers' aides. Six taught at Coral Way. The majority of teachers were native English speakers who volunteered to participate. The project developed its own curricula and instructional materials. Coral Way implemented a "Two-Way" system in which children from both ethnic groups would learn each others' languages and the content subjects in both languages. The goal was to produce fully bilingual, well-educated children; there was nothing compensatory or remedial about it. There is no evidence that the Cubans were considered culturally deprived. Evaluators rated the program a success. At least some children became fully fluent in both languages, and the others achieved partial fluency. Educators from other Hispanic school districts toured Coral Way. The curricular and instructional materials were widely distributed. The word was out that bilingual education had been tried and it worked. Coral Way provided the political and pedagogical impetus to publicize bilingual education nationally.

Several Southwestern and Eastern school districts began experimenting with bilingual programs in the 1960s. Some were supported by funds from Title I of the Elementary and Secondary Education Act of 1965. Some used variations of the Coral Way model and sought to include all the children as recipients of the program. Most programs served Hispanics only. In Miami bilingual education spread to other schools after the Coral Way project ended in 1966. But nowhere was it as fully funded and supported as at Coral Way. After 1965, when poorer Cubans immigrated to Miami, bilingual education became a compensatory program.

Both Coral Way and the earlier onset of ESL programs set forces in motion that would affect the course of language education policy in the coming decades. Bilingual and ESL instruction were initially designed to serve middle-class students and then adapted later to serve poor students. Coral Way had begun the process of achieving political recognition for the needs of Spanish-speaking children.

CULTURAL DEPRIVATION ACHIEVES NATIONAL RECOGNITION

After Judith Krugman's speech, some educators and social scientists organized their curricula and research around the concept of cultural deprivation. Some applied it to New York City's Demonstration Guidance and Higher Horizons Projects, which later became models for the War on Poverty. Some applied it specifically to Hispanic students. Sophie Elam discovered that Puerto Ricans suffered from a variant of cultural deprivation known as language deprivation. A New York City assistant superintendent further developed the concept of cultural deprivation and publicized it to a wider audience through a 1962 *NEA Journal* article. The National Education Association (NEA) issued a report on the subject. The U.S. Office of Education (OE) sponsored conferences on cultural deprivation themes in 1962 and 1963 in collaboration with the NEA, the National Institute of Mental Health, and the federal Office of Juvenile Delinquency.[3]

Psychology professor Frank Reissman provided national exposure in his widely read book, *The Culturally Deprived Child*, in which he acknowledged the help of Judith Krugman. Scholars and educators organized a University of Chicago conference on the subject in 1964. Chicago School Superintendent Benjamin Willis stated his adherence to cultural deprivation that same year. Hundreds of articles, books, and dissertations would address the subject in succeeding years; it had become a growth industry.[4]

J. McVicker Hunt built his reputation as a leading cultural deprivation theorist with the publication of his article, "The Psychological Basis for Using Preschool Enrichment as an Antidote to Cultural Deprivation." He described the theory and explained how it differed from the hereditarian position. He argued that the primary strategy was to reach the child before he or she entered school, before the negative values of parents and surroundings had time to consolidate. Hunt became the chairperson of one of President Lyndon Johnson's three task forces on education, and influenced fellow scholars, educators, and federal officials.[5]

WASHINGTON ABSORBS CULTURAL DEPRIVATION

Johnson's field marshal in the War on Poverty was Sargent Shriver. Shriver had helped his brother-in-law, President John Kennedy, launch the Peace Corps and had served as its first director. Then he became Johnson's right-hand man in the legislative battle to institute the anti-poverty campaign. Later he administered a major component of the poverty war, the Head Start program.[6]

Before coming to Washington, Shriver had served as the president of the Chicago Board of Education. He had believed in the hereditarian concept of genetically determined intelligence. Under the influence of J. McVicker Hunt, Susan Gray, Benjamin Bloom, and Oscar Lewis, he later changed to the cultural deprivation view. He was attracted by the idea of early intervention to break the hold of poverty-induced values. He brought this concept into the public arena for inclusion in the War on Poverty in general and in Head Start in particular. The idea took root and can be detected in many federal education programs. Members of the education task forces used cultural deprivation to structure their recommendations for legislative and administrative action. There is no evidence of any opposition to the inclusion of the concept by task force members, congressional representatives, or members of the administration. It was the state of the art, the product of the leading minds of academia.[7]

DOUBTS ABOUT THE EDUCATION BUREAUCRACIES

Representatives in Congress interested in education and task force members doubted if federal and state education bureaucracies were capable of carrying out major reforms of the systems that they ran. These doubts have persisted and have caused Congress to intervene to defend or expand bilingual programs when they were under attack by these bureaucracies or their allies. U.S. Senator Robert Kennedy believed that school officials were more the problem than the solution to low attainment among the poor. Task force members viewed the U.S. Office of Education as weak and overly deferential to powerful interest groups. The local and state educational agencies were seen as stolid and impervious to change.[8] Commissioner of Education Francis Keppel blamed the state agencies for poor service delivery. Keppel stated in a 1969 interview that he and other task force members "felt that the state departments of education were the feeblest bunch of second-rate or fifth-rate educators who combined educational incompetence with bureaucratic immovability."[9]

Flowing from this distrust was an attempt to implement educational reform outside the school bureaucracies. It was led by the executive secretary of John Gardner's education task force, William Cannon. He devised a plan to undermine the bureaucracies' control of school reform. He patterned it after the Community Action Program that he had helped to formulate earlier in the War on Poverty. This community program was put together outside the control of the local political machines. In education, Cannon hoped that a network of research and development laboratories, regional demonstration projects, and supplementary educational centers would subvert the school establishment. But this was not to be. Too much was at stake, and the education lobbies fought tenaciously to maintain their traditional control. President Johnson took their side in his haste to have his Elementary and Secondary Education Act (ESEA) passed. He did not want disgruntled school officials to waylay his bill.[10] Johnson told his top operatives: "I want you guys to get off your asses and do everything posible to get everything in my proposal passed as soon as possible, before the aura and the halo that surround me disappear."[11] The congressional distrust of the educational bureaucracies has continued ever since.

THE ELEMENTARY AND SECONDARY EDUCATION ACT

Johnson believed that the ESEA was the cornerstone of his struggle to defeat poverty. He had often said that improved education would break the chain of poverty. After his huge 1964 electoral victory, he wanted to strike while he and the Democratic Congress were still in the honeymoon stage. He acted quickly to both compromise with and defeat the two historic roadblocks to federal aid to education, the southern and Catholic groups. Johnson was a master legislative strategist and he moved into overdrive.[12]

The all-out push for the ESEA produced some resentment. Senator Robert Kennedy feared that school bureaucrats would divert congressional reform intentions and disenfranchise low-income parents. He demanded that accountability measures be written into the new law. The administration, fearing that this demand could obstruct passage, agreed to institute a Pentagon-devised evaluation system that would satisfy both Congress' and parents' need for accountability. A new position of Assistant HEW Secretary for Planning and Evaluation was created to monitor this accountability component. Kennedy was mollified.[13]

With the southern, Catholic, and Kennedy objections removed, the ESEA was enacted in 1965. Title I (now Chapter I) programs were the key element. They provided $1 billion to schools that served low-income students to use as they saw fit. Compensatory or remedial education to combat cultural deprivation was the key strategy. The ESEA functioned politically in three ways. First, it gave federal funds to keep hard-pressed school systems afloat. Senator Wayne Morse called it "a back door to federal aid."[14] Second, it helped relieve some of the pressure on the federal government to do something about poverty. The pressure had grown intense after the first wave of urban riots in 1964. Third, it gave educators, scholars, and teacher-trainers a mechanism to begin applying and evaluating their cultural deprivation notions.[15]

HISPANIC PROTESTS

Hispanics were merely an afterthought in the ESEA. They were rarely mentioned in government and academic poverty literature. Hispanic organizations were not major participants in the campaign to enact the ESEA. There were only a few Hispanics in Congress, only a handful of other elected and appointed officials, and no single dominant national leadership organization.[16]

This semi-invisibility changed in the 1960s. A series of southwestern protests erupted, challenging the traditional pattern of Hispanic subordination. Part of this protest movement paralleled the black civil rights movement; some of it was unique to the conditions of the Southwest. Cesar Chavez's campaign to unionize farmworkers was the first round in this protest movement. Then came Reyes Tijerina's struggle for land grant rights, Corky Gonzalez's Crusade for Justice, and the La Raza Unida Party. The term *Chicano* came into popular usage among some Mexican-Americans. Chicano nationalists put forth demands for community control of social and educational policy.[17]

A series of blowouts hit the high schools in the region. These were walkouts demanding an end to the "no Spanish" rule, better facilities, bilingual education, more sensitive teachers and counselors, and the study of Chicano history and culture. There was no central leadership to these protests. Puerto Ricans also entered the school protest arena. Some Puerto Rican parents had been deeply involved in the New York City desegregation protests in the mid-1960s. A few years later there were specifically Puerto Rican protests over improved school facilities, better teachers, bilingual education, Puerto Rican culture and history, and other issues that approximated those of Mexican-Americans in the Southwest.

The Puerto Rican protests took place in school and college campuses throughout the East and Midwest.[18]

POLICY OPTIONS AND
HISPANIC CULTURAL DEPRIVATION

Hispanic protest intensified and political and education decision-makers were confronted by a need to respond. There were several policy options available. First, they could gear their programs to changing the child by continuing the compensatory program to combat cultural deprivation. Second, they could seek to change the schools by removing traditional discriminatory practices and democratizing the curriculum and teaching methods. Third, they could seek to change society by leveling the opportunity structure and removing the school systems' stratified approach. It became clear that school officials and their political allies would stay with the first option; there was little incentive to go off in radical directions. As this decision became clear, scholars and educators concentrated on ways to apply the precepts of cultural deprivation to Hispanic learners.

Cultural deprivation was an inexact theory and there was no unanimity about how Hispanics fit into it. A few analysts determined that poor scholastic achievement among Hispanics was caused by family instability. Others took the opposite approach and blamed the families and communities for being too strong and stable. Families were supposed to have exercised such a tight control over youngsters that individualistic upward mobility was impossible. Other analysts claimed that language factors were the chief reason for poor school performance. A California conference on Mexican-Americans concluded that lack of assimilation of American values was the prime culprit.[19] The NEA began publicizing cultural deprivation concepts as they related to Hispanics. Minority cultures were seen as "not compatible with modern life." Minority people were "too disadvantaged to develop sufficient regenerative forces from within . . . maladjustment continues to spread."[20] A NEA conference in 1966 promoted bilingual education as the compensatory measure to relieve cultural deprivation.

Oscar Lewis's culture of poverty concept was part of this stream. Lewis observed a Puerto Rican family in San Juan and New York and contended that it transmitted deeply embedded poverty characteristics from generation to generation. This transmission led to a culture of poverty. His observations were complicated by the fact that some members of the extended family were prostitutes, and an identification of prostitution with Puerto Rican culture was made by some Anglo-Americans.[21] Lewis's concepts produced strong reactions. New York City School Board member and later President Joseph Monserrat stated, "When I was a kid I used to be called a 'spic.' They do not have to call me a 'spic' now because that is too derogatory. Now they can refer to me as culturally deprived, socially disadvantaged or the product of a culture of poverty."[22] Education professor, Francesco Cordasco tried to counter Lewis's notions and feared that they would catch on in the body politic. Many others criticized aspects of this growing cultural deprivation movement. While some of these criticisms and refutations may have blunted the edge of cultural deprivation, and may have led to a change in nomenclature (to cultural deficits or educationally disadvantaged), the central thesis endured – the values of parents and communities account for the poor school performances of minority children.[23]

THE ESEA IN PRACTICE IN HISPANIC SCHOOLS, 1965-1968

ESEA's Title I allocated funds to schools that served poor students. In areas of Hispanic poverty, ESL instruction was subsidized by Title I. In other areas, bilingual instruction was tried out. This bilingual instruction usually meant the transitional approach in which only Spanish speakers were involved. Once they learned English, there was no more instruction in Spanish. A very few tried to emulate the Coral Way program with the goal of fluency in both languages.

Most of the bilingual programs were seen as compensatory measures to overcome cultural deprivation. Chicago, for example, launched such a program. Hoboken, New Jersey, set up a federally funded bilingual experiment whose goals were summarized in its title, "Assimilation through Cultural Understanding." The superintendent described the program's context:

A growing percentage of Puerto Rican children (3% in 1954 to 34% in 1967) coupled with a foreign-born group (9.4%) has produced a situation in which over 43% of our school population is culturally unassimilated and linguistically handicapped. The magnitude of the problem produced by the situation is such that it has affected the remaining 57% of our student population.[24]

The superintendent's assumption that Puerto Rican and foreign-born students were "culturally unassimilated and linguistically handicapped" reveals a lot about the mentality of those who launched such programs.

The United States Commission on Civil Rights discovered that many traditional school practices like the "no Spanish" rule and vocational tracking were still operative in many southwestern schools, even in districts that obtained significant amounts of Title I monies.[25] A study of federal and state-funded compensatory programs for Puerto Ricans in seven eastern and midwestern cities concluded:

> The programs are a mixed bag. There are after-school tutorials and before-school breakfasts; teaching English as a Second Language and teaching English as a First Language; bilingual approaches and non-lingual approaches; teacher visits to Puerto Rican homes and teacher "visitations" to Puerto Rico; efforts to make parents feel welcome and efforts to make parents feel guilty; seminars to convince teachers that Puerto Rican children have special needs and seminars to convince teachers that Puerto Ricans are "just like everybody else." Every program boasts its own point of view and every point of view boasts its own program. There is a considerable amount of random activity that creates an illusion of progress.[26]

This "mixed bag" did not satisfy advocates of improved Hispanic education. They pressed for special Hispanic-oriented programs.

THE NEA, THE TEXANS, AND THE BILINGUAL EDUCATION ACT

The National Education Association, as previously mentioned, promoted cultural deprivation theory as part of its overall school reform package. After the successful lobbying effort for the ESEA, some NEA leaders devoted their time and energy to Hispanic educational issues. They wanted to institute bilingual education because it was a more complete program than ESL and because it could be used as a compensatory measure. They sponsored several southwestern conferences on the subject in 1966 and 1967.[27]

Several prominent University of Texas professors joined forces with the NEA to try to obtain federal recognition for and funding of bilingual education. Among them, George Sanchez, Herschel Manuel, and Theodore Andersson had been promoting bilingual instruction and greater foreign language learning for many decades. They sponsored a

University of Texas Conference on the Bilingual Child. Texas state legislators Joe Bernal and Carlos Truan were also instrumental in the campaign. They had led a walkout at a 1966 federal Equal Opportunity Conference over demands for greater Mexican-American participation in the War on Poverty. Very soon afterward President Johnson appointed the first Hispanic commissioner to the Equal Employment Opportunities Commission and set up an Inter-Agency Committee for Mexican-American Affairs.[28]

U.S. Senator Ralph Yarborough of Texas attended the NEA's conference on bilingual education and became a convert. He became determined to secure federal sponsorship for bilingual education and introduced such a bill in the opening days of the 1967 congressional session, just a few months after his attendance at the NEA Conference.[29] Senators and representatives from southwestern and eastern states cosponsored the measure, which was known as the Bilingual Education Act (BEA), Title VII of the Elementary and Secondary Education Act. It was a new title that was added two years after the ESEA was enacted. Like the ESEA as a whole, it was designed to serve only low-income students. It specifically designated Hispanic students as the recipients of services under the act. The BEA did not prescribe dual language instruction, even though the title implied it. Instead, experimentation was seen as the way to devise "programs to meet these special educational needs."[30] Yarborough stated that "compared to the minor shot in the arm which most schools are receiving from Title I of the ESEA . . . the Bilingual Education Act will be a major transfusion of new blood."[31] Some advocates of bilingual education began proclaiming that the new act would be a Magna Carta that would liberate Hispanics. They approached it with "evangelical fervor."[32]

The BEA included all the assumptions about the usefulness of compensatory programs that ESEA contained. As a federal bilingual education director stated several years later,

> the legislation for disadvantaged children based on a "compensatory" proposition gave proponents a vehicle to promote an idea . . . if the advocates of bilingual education had not used the "disadvantaged" route, the role of our national government in supporting bilingual/bicultural education would still be in question.[33]

Yarborough wanted to end a tradition of poor Hispanic school attainment; he hoped bilingual education would increase Hispanic access to middle-class status. He also wanted to build a broad coalition of reelection supporters among Texas minorities, teachers' associations, and labor unions. He was appointed to head a special subcommittee that held hearings in the Southwest and elsewhere. He had done a good job of mobilizing support; there was no congressional opposition.

The opposition came from his fellow Texan in the White House. The administration did not want a separate title. They claimed that sufficient funding for bilingual programs was available under Title I. Commissioner of Education Harold Howe contended that the bill was politically and perhaps legally untenable because it applied to only one ethnic group. He also stated that the federal government had already done a lot for Mexican-Americans by creating the Inter-Agency Office for Mexican-American Affairs and that therefore the new bill was not needed to satisfy the aspirations of Hispanics. John Gardner, the Secretary of Health, Education and Welfare, affirmed Howe's views and added that none of the War on Poverty's education task forces had recommended instituting a special title for bilingual education.[34]

The word began to circulate in administrative and congressional circles that the real purpose of the BEA was to provide jobs for Hispanics and to give them a small piece of the action in ESEA. The claim about a jobs program has reappeared many times since. Howe later referred to the bill as "Hispanic community action" and "their hunk of the action."[35]

A deal was struck between Yarborough and the White House. Yarborough would drop the specific references to Hispanics and make the bill applicable to all non-English speakers. In return the White House would drop its opposition to a separate title. Congress passed the measure in December 1967 and the president signed it in January 1968. He took partial credit for its passage when he spoke to a coalition of Mexican-American groups.[36]

THE FUNDING DILEMMA

One task remained before the Bilingual Education Act could be implemented – Congress had to appropriate money to run the program. However, the mood in Washington was shifting; social and educational program funding was no longer as readily available as it had been in 1965. Charles Schulze, a Budget Bureau director, warned Johnson in 1966 that "we are no longer able to fund adequately all the Great Society programs."[37] Administration officials delayed making a budget request to Congress for bilingual education. Nothing at all was appropriated in the calendar year 1968. Johnson recommended only $5 million for the fiscal year that began in mid-1969. Yarborough denounced Johnson's move as "tokenism . . . an empty gesture, reneging on a promise. . . . We will be effectively dashing to the ground all the hopes we have raised."[38] He added later that "We passed the bill but the Office of Education and the Administration fought it. . . . They held down the funding all the time."[39] By the spring of 1968, Johnson announced his intention not to seek another term. The lame duck months of 1968 were "an ebb tide in the Johnson Administration's planning process and suggests a kind of pathological cycle that parallels the ebb and flow of presidential power generally. . . . The early euphoria of the Great Society had faded."[40] It appeared that the BEA might become enmeshed in this ebb tide and emerge stillborn. A compromise was finally reached and by mid-1969 the OE had $7.5 million to start the engines of bilingual education.[41] The BEA had become involved in what another Budget Bureau director would call "take it and run money":

> The President and Califano and Wilbur Cohen were of the school that you take what you can get and run. They would come back and say, "Oh just start with 5 million or 10 million, a foot in the door." And if you look at the HEW program, it's just loaded with little bitty programs. . . .[42]

With the passage of BEA, the federal government sounded a national call for something to be done about Hispanic schooling. Nobody was sure just what needed to be done. A new page in the history of Hispanic schooling had been turned, but those who proclaimed the new law as a Magna Carta were drifting into fantasy.

4

Creating a Program out of Thin Air, 1968–1980

Imagine trying to construct an impressive, majestic brick cathedral without bricks or mortar, with inexperienced workers and very limited resources for training them. Yet that is how most bilingual programs got off the ground.[1]

Maria Medina Swanson

Bilingual education's next stage was the attempt to translate intent into action. Office of Education officials employed two of their subagencies to administer and regulate the program. First, they relied on the Office of Bilingual Education (OBE) and its successor, the Office of Bilingual Education and Minority Languages Affairs (OBEMLA), to administer the provision of grants to school districts under the Bilingual Education Act, which was Title VII of the Elementary and Secondary Education Act. Second, they relied on the Office of Civil Rights (OCR) to enforce the 1964 Civil Rights Act's prohibition of national origin discrimination. These two agencies had to operate in the changing political realities of the late 1960s and 1970s. One change that soon became apparent was the declining status of the War on Poverty.

THE DIMINISHING WAR ON POVERTY

Educators, researchers, and others began to question whether the War on Poverty programs were likely to end poverty. Some said that social class position determined the status one would reach in life far more than schooling did. Others argued that genetic inheritance was the source of

33

intelligence. Both positions discounted the importance of formal education as an equalizer of opportunity.[2]

The Democratic-dominated Congress continued to sustain ESEA, but the law's credibility was weakened. A number of reports and studies cast doubt on certain cherished assumptions of the Great Society. A leading educator contended that after three years of compensatory programs, "not only had the child in the inner city not improved, he had retrogressed."[3] The War on Poverty's school reform program was in a precarious position as the Nixon administration assumed power.

> The fragile foundations supporting the educational components of the War on Poverty were now exposed. Studies suggested that the schools, as they were, did little to overcome poverty. Actual programs hardly appeared to effect children. The detachment shown by school boards and others in charge of educating poor children indicated how unrealistic it was to expect the school system to reform itself.[4]

Former OE official James Gallagher stated that "The credibility of federal programs is under severe and justified attack."[5] After the third year of many federal reforms, "their political glamor has worn off and their favored place in the administration was taken by bright and shiny new programs that are polished by hope and unsullied by experience. . . . New policies are thrown up like corks on the waves."[6] A cycle of excitement, frustration, and despair was being played out. Bilingual education entered the national policy arena just as the stages of frustration and despair were coming into being.

STARTING FROM SCRATCH

The OE was mandated to implement the Bilingual Education Act. But the OE was understaffed and underfunded and was not in favor at the White House or on Capitol Hill. It had expanded by waves of categorical or specifically targeted legislation. The Bilingual Education Act was seen as just the latest in a long string of categorical laws.

The OE created the OBE and appointed Albar Pena, a Texas educator, as its first director. Pena set about assembling a staff, reviewing grant requests, and coordinating efforts with state and local school systems. There was no guarantee that the program would survive.

OBE dispensed its first series of grants to school districts to support bilingual programs in 1969. OE official Bruce Gaarder reviewed these projects and found

1. A severe lack of trained teachers.
2. Little or no project evaluation by OBE or by local school officials.
3. Confusion over goals because "Congress couched its legislation in terms that permit both ethnocentrists and cultural pluralists to see what they want to see in this Act."[7]
4. Heavy dependence on teacher's aides who were neither bilingual nor fully literate in their native language.
5. Little commitment to dual language instruction.[8]

These conclusions pointed out the major obstacle to administering bilingual programs: there was no infrastructure in place or in formation. The OBE had to start from scratch, it had to create an infrastructure from thin air. The shortage of trained teachers was the most glaring need. Without trained teachers no new program could come into being.

But who would train them, what colleges of education would undertake this task? Who would finance these training programs? How would the teachers be certified? Even by the mid-1970s, OBE had no solution to these problems and no plan to arrive at a solution. The United States Government Accounting Office castigated OBE for this lack of vision in a report entitled *Bilingual Education: An Unmet Need.* Other unmet needs included textbooks, research, evaluation studies, curricula, and a whole range of other weak links in the infrastructure. As mentioned earlier, a small teacher training program had been built to serve the Cuban refugees; but there seemed to be no inclination on OBE's part to build on what went before. They muddled along trying to create a program without a real plan and without any real notion of how to develop one.[9]

PROGRAM SHORTCOMINGS

Bilingual advocates criticized the federal program for its shortcomings. Some were attributable to inadequate funding. Other shortcomings were caused by poor planning and implementation. It soon became clear that the Bilingual Education Act by itself would neither uplift the Hispanic community nor would it emphasize dual fluency programs. Some supporters claimed that the hope that this program alone would bring a vastly improved socioeconomic status to Hispanics had proven to be unwarranted.[10]

Many bilingual advocates criticized the predominance of transitional bilingual programs among those funded by the government.[11] Transitional programs are usually one- to three-year instructional efforts that employ native language instruction as a bridge to learning English. Once English is learned there is no more native language instruction. Transitional programs are subtractive because they discard the native language from the curriculum. Additive programs, on the other hand, teach and preserve both languages. Supporters of additive programs claim that dual language learning as in Coral Way or in the Canadian immersion experiments help students learn English and the content subjects better and help them obtain the skill of bilingualism.

OCR ENTERS THE BILINGUAL ARENA

The OE's Office of Civil Rights (OCR) came on the bilingual scene as part of the federal government's response to the Chicano school walkouts. OCR arose as the education enforcement arm of the 1964 Civil Rights Act. It ignored Hispanic educational concerns in its first years of existence. Political pressures generated by the Hispanic protest movement forced OCR to get involved with Hispanics during the school walkouts under its authority to act against national origin discrimination. In 1970 it issued its May 25 Memorandum which required that school districts devise integrated educational plans that were geared to the needs of Spanish speakers. It sent this notice to over 100 districts that were 5 percent or more Hispanic. OCR's leverage was the threat to cut off all federal funds to those districts that did not comply with their mandates. Legal defense groups followed up this memorandum with a number of suits demanding that specific districts provide bilingual or other special programs to their non-English-speaking students.[12]

Few fundamental changes occurred. In Beeville, Texas, for example, the school superintendent responded to the memorandum by merely changing the name of his vocational track to career education. Hispanics were still relegated to this dead-end track. As a former OCR staffer commented, "Words and formulations in Washington take on a new dimension when they reach Beeville, Texas."[13] The longer-range implications of OCR's entry were perhaps more significant than any short-term changes that were made in school districts. The OCR action set the stage for future litigation which would result in the landmark Lau Decision and it established a precedent for more enforcement action after 1975.[14]

THE SUPREME COURT AND OCR
SHAPE ENFORCEMENT METHODS

Chinese parents in San Francisco brought suit in 1970 against the school district for the failure to do anything special to instruct their non-English-speaking children. They acted in the legal climate initiated by OCR's entry into the arena of national origin discrimination. The parents contended that, as language minorities, they were protected by the ban against national origin discrimination. The Supreme Court agreed with them in 1974. The Court removed the submersion mode as a legally permissible way to educate non-English-speaking children. The Court stated in its Lau Decision:

> The failure of the San Francisco school system to provide language instruction to approximately 1800 students of Chinese ancestry who do not speak English, or to provide them with other adequate instructional procedures, denies them a meaningful opportunity to participate in the public education program.[15]

Justice William O. Douglas, the Court's spokesman, added, "There is no equality of treatment merely by providing students with the same facilities, textbooks, teachers and curriculum."[16] The Court declined to specify a remedy. Other state and federal courts ruled on similar cases in specific localities. Some courts directly prescribed that bilingual education be instituted, others did not.

LIBERAL CONGRESSIONAL REPRESENTATIVES
EXPAND THE PROGRAM

The Title VII bilingual program survived its first five years, and it penetrated the OE, some state departments of education, and various local districts. But it was still weak and tentative. It only received $35 million in 1974 and served only about 6 percent of the LEP students nationwide. It was still hidden in bureaucratic backwaters.

Senator Yarborough lost his bid for reelection in 1970 and his role as Congress's bilingual advocate was assumed by liberal Democrats such as Senators Edward Kennedy, Alan Cranston, and Walter Mondale and Representatives Henry Gonzalez and James Scheuer. When the Bilingual Education Act came up for reauthorization in 1974 and 1978, these lawmakers and their allies expanded the program and brought it into the national policy arena. The poverty provision was dropped and the target population was broadened from limited English speaking ability (LESA) to limited English proficient (LEP). This meant that those who could speak English but could not read or write it were eligible. A local program could now consist of up to 40 percent English speakers to increase integration. The participation of a number of non-Hispanic groups was facilitated. A support network was created that consisted of a clearinghouse; regional support centers; materials development, assessment, and evaluation centers; a research agenda and grants for teacher training and graduate study.

The legislation added a provision requiring participating school districts to include bicultural components in their instructional programs. The term bilingual/bicultural soon caught on. The bicultural addition became controversial. Some felt that it would lead to a divided society like Canada's in which adherents of Spanish and English would battle for dominance. The liberal legislators added funding increments that brought the program a fivefold increase in the years 1973 to 1980. They were also instrumental in providing bilingual program funds through other education acts such as vocational education, adult education, and refugee education.[17] Although these congressional supporters expanded the program, they did not change its basic function – as a remedial measure to compensate language minority children for the deficient cultural values that their parents and communities supposedly transmitted to them. As a federal bilingual director stated: "The public policy formulations – administrative, judicial, and legislative – have tended to support only those programs of bilingual education which are transitional/compensatory/remedial/assimilationist in nature. . . ."[18]

PROFESSIONALIZATION

The National Association for Bilingual Education (NABE) arose in the mid-1970s as bilingual education's organizational expression. It is a professional association that also represents parents of LEP children. Most of its leaders have been or have become local, state, or federal bilingual officials. NABE worked with state and local educators to develop program models, curricula, instructional materials, and teacher certification standards. It published a journal, participated in research seminars, and generally professionalized the developing field of bilingual education.

NABE generally adhered to an incrementalist legislative approach; they tried to get a little more funding each year, but lacked a long-range strategy. Their lack of a strategy or a vision can be seen in many of their activities. They often had to fight rear-guard actions against opponents who gained the initial momentum. Many NABE members tried to fight critics armed with standardized test scores of academic performance. They tried to out-quantify the numbers crunchers, instead of emphasizing the valuable nonquantifiable record of programmatic success. They failed to stress often enough that LEP students have not been acclimated to standardized tests and often perform poorly on them, even if their overall progress is quite good.[19] They did not realize that studies done by friends or foes are left to gather dust unless politicians or the media publicize them. They should have fought for studies based on ground rules that would have examined the program's intangible qualities. Then they should have moved heaven and earth to get these studies widely distributed and used in the political debate surrounding bilingual education.

One reason for the political ineptness was the lack of a Washington presence in the 1970s.[20] NABE relied too heavily on sympathetic representatives in Congress whose agendas were multifaceted and had only a limited amount of time for bilingual education. NABE fell asleep in the late 1970s thinking that President Carter's Lau Regulations would become operative and that bilingual education would become an entitlement program like social security and Medicare. They were rudely awakened when the regulations were junked and Ronald Reagan came into office.

They partially remedied this weakness in the 1980s when they established a Washington presence and helped prepare a significant 1984 reauthorization package that became law. They began to alter their technocratic approach when some bilingual advocates began stressing all the program achievements, including reduced dropout rates, lower grade retention, more identification with the school, and increased parental participation instead of merely dwelling on standardized test scores.

A POLITICAL OPPOSITION ARISES IN THE 1970s

Opposition to bilingual education arises primarily in times of congressional consideration of the program. It also surfaces when bilingual education makes headlines nationally or locally. The opposition had no single organizational embodiment in the 1970s. Opponents included liberals and conservatives; most were journalists, politicians, scholars, and union officials. There was virtually no opposition from 1968 to 1974, when the program was tiny and its survival was questionable.

As liberal supporters in Congress broadened it in 1974 and after, attacks on the program came from Washington *Post* columnist Stephen Rosenfeld, *Post* writer Noel Epstein, New York City principal Howard Hurwitz, American Federation of Teachers leader Albert Shanker, and *Harper's* writer Tom Bethell. Some opponents denounced the program altogether, others only attacked aspects of it. The opposition would coalesce and gain a measure of strength in the debates over the Lau Regulations, as we shall see.[21]

THE WHITE HOUSE AND
THE POLITICS OF AMBIGUITY

Administration officials, both Republican and Democratic, have tended to ignore or downplay bilingual education; only a few have been enthusiastic about it. As far back as 1973, an internal memo at the Department of Health, Education and Welfare (HEW) stated that "we have not had a coherent and consistent policy for our bilingual education program."[22] While President Ford's officials were expressing a similar dissatisfaction, his education commissioner Terrel Bell was devising and implementing the Lau Remedies, which sought to more firmly implant the program. This duality was not too surprising for Republicans who were generally only lukewarm toward this largely Democratic-sponsored measure. More surprising perhaps, was the ambivalence or even conflict that permeated the Carter administration.

Carter's HEW secretary Joseph Califano had supported the program since the Johnson years, during which he had been a key presidential assistant. But in 1978 he took the unusual step of publicly questioning bilingual education: "I am not happy with that program . . . you can't put your finger on it. There is not a clear sense of purpose."[23] Califano's qualms seemed to mirror those of his boss, Jimmy Carter, who told his cabinet, "I want English taught, not ethnic culture."[24] HEW and OE officials scrambled to try to figure out how to adhere to the president's wishes. The officials created an intra-departmental task force of the leaders of education-related agencies. The task force discussed management issues but avoided policy matters. Califano proposed placing the bilingual program under the much larger Title I program, thereby abolishing its autonomy. Hispanic advocacy groups, Vice-President Mondale, and Senator Edward Kennedy challenged him on this proposal and caused him to back down. Things remained pretty much as they had been, and the OBE kept its autonomy.[25]

Kennedy's view was, according to assistant education commissioner Marshall Smith, that bilingual education "can't do bad, or is at least neutral. . . . You don't really know how to make a difference . . . so why not do it in a way that advocacy groups can feel good about?"[26] Vice-President Mondale's staff defended bilingual education as "one of the few things these groups have." They urged the president to "let them run their own program."[27] The Ford and Carter administrations were less than enthusiastic about bilingual education. Congress and a few federal officials like Commissioner Bell and Vice-President Mondale sustained it, but no clear policy direction emerged. The program floated in a sea of ambiguity.

THE EDUCATION DEPARTMENT'S CONFLICTING POLICY DIRECTIONS

Like the White House and other administration officials, the Office of Education and its successor the Department of Education conflicted over the value and future of bilingual education. While the commissioners and secretaries were usually in favor of the program's survival in the 1970s, many of their subordinates were not. Some researchers in the Office of Planning, Budgeting and Evaluation (OPBE) have been part of this opposition. OPBE sponsored two national studies on the effectiveness of the program as measured by standardized test data. The first was conducted by the private A.I.R. firm and released in 1977. The second was conducted by departmental staffers, and was never officially sanctioned or released; however, the media obtained and printed parts of it in 1981.[28]

Both studies cast doubt on the program's worth much as earlier reports had questioned the efficacy of Chapter I and Head Start. Opponents used these studies as rallying cries to attack the program. Bilingual advocates criticized the authors' methodologies and their claims of objectivity. Many educators and politicians were confused by the whole process. Many of the issues are ensconced in labyrinths known only to full-time education researchers. While it is not within the scope of this book to deal with the merits of these studies, it is important to look at the political points involved.

First, these studies always provoke controversy over the ground rules. What you choose to focus on and how you choose to approach the selected topic often determine the results you will find. Second, as mentioned earlier, studies will lie dormant unless they are brought into the political arena. Once they are, the study findings may become so enmeshed in controversy that their substance is lost. How a study is packaged is politically far more significant than what it actually says. Finally, the Department of Education's lack of a policy framework within which to place bilingual education seems to doom any study to a departmental graveyard, so that the department can get on with the task of grinding out its programmatic mandates.

OBE-OBEMLA carried out this policy of muddling through. As a Hispanic-led agency it was expected to be an advocate for Hispanic education within the constellation of Washington power centers. It was often unable to do this because it had to spend so much time and energy justifying its existence. By the late 1970s the program was almost constantly embattled. There was enormous pressure from ". . . bureaucratic government agencies, from teacher unions, from universities, from jingoistic writers, from a sloganeering press, from congressional spokespersons for the 'good old days' when minorities 'knew their place. . . .'"29

THE LAU REGULATIONS CONTROVERSY

The Office of Civil Rights tried to apply the 1975 Lau Remedies as if they were formalized regulations until a federal judge told them to either go through the process of formalizing them or to drop them altogether. Finally in 1980, more than six years after the Supreme Court's Lau Decision, the Education Department was ready to float provisional regulations. They picked the worst possible time. The country was in the midst of the Iranian hostage crisis and had recently experienced the Mariel Cuban influx. Anti-foreignism was probably at its highest point in decades. But it was also an election year, and President Carter badly needed a heavy turnout and vote among Hispanics in crucial states like Texas, California, and New York.

The Lau Regulations stated that if districts wanted to retain their federal funding of all kinds, they must institute bilingual programs in schools with 20 or more LEP students from the same native language groups. Districts would have to determine the language dominance of all their students, not just those who had previously been classified as LEP students. While there were some escape hatches, it was the first time that the federal government prescribed bilingual education on a nationwide basis.[30]

Predictably, the national associations representing school officials were furious. The last thing they wanted was a welter of new prescriptive regulations. They particularly disliked the "unfunded mandates," costly federal rules with no federal reimbursement. The National Education Association and NABE supported the regulations, but were practically the only national education organizations to do so.[31]

Secretary of Education Shirley Hufstedler ignored the entreaties of the majority of organizations and published the proposed regulations on August 5, 1980. A torrent of protest surfaced. Hufstedler called in OBEMLA leaders to help her defend these regulations. In so doing she set the stage for the popular misconception that the new regulations and the Title VII program were one and the same. Few educators, journalists, politicians, or ordinary citizens were able to distinguish between Title VII as a discretionary grant-giving program and the new regulations as a civil rights enforcement measure. They lumped them together. The opposition made the most of it and was able to weaken both the grant-giving and enforcement aspects of bilingual education.[32]

American Federation of Teachers President Albert Shanker and several national education organizations pressured Congress. Even some bilingual advocates who were state or local school officials joined the chorus of opposition. The battle cry was "Stop unwarranted federal intrusion." The opponents gained when Secretary Hufstedler waffled on how much these new regulations would cost to implement; she estimated somewhere between $29 million and $239 million. This time the bilingual supporters in Congress were unable to rescue bilingual education.[33] Enough senators and representatives were disturbed by the regulations to form a majority that postponed the implementation of the regulations until June 1981. By 1981 the new education secretary, Terrel Bell, now in a conservative mode, scrapped the regulations altogether and returned to the standard of the May 25 Memorandum of 1970.

The bilingual movement's, OCR's, and OBEMLA's lack of clear policy direction had rendered the program vulnerable to attack. In this case the attack succeeded in weakening the program, but not in ending it.

A national program was created from nothing in 1968. Its weak infrastructure wobbled. It lacked trained teachers, instructional materials, administrative support, and almost everything else. It was beset by enforcement entanglements and by hostile attacks from a vociferous band of opponents. It had to confront antagonistic local and state establishments. And yet it survived, and in some places flourished. The wonder was that it survived at all.

5

The Fight for Power

It is not unusual for anti-bilingual tirades to degenerate into old-fashioned fear and racism, fueled by census statistics showing Hispanics to be the fastest-growing ethnic group in the country. Just as the prospect of a black mayor frightened legions of white voters in Chicago, the proliferation of bilingualism poses the threat of one group of Chicagoans losing power to another.[1]

Chicago journalist, Alfredo Lanier, 1984

Once Congress passed the Bilingual Education Act and grants became available to school districts, struggles developed over whether to put bilingual programs into practice and how to do so. State legislatures became embroiled in fights over state bilingual laws and funding issues. Interest groups within school districts grappled with school boards over whether the program was needed and/or whether the program should be more than a minimal effort, a symbolic gesture. Interest groups fought among themselves: teachers, parents, various Hispanic groups, administrators, and teachers' unions. The situation was wide open and the battle lines were quickly drawn.

STATEHOUSE STRUGGLES IN COLORADO AND TEXAS

Colorado has had a substantial Hispanic population for over a century, but it waited for more than seven years after the federal law's enactment to pass one of their own. The political establishment was

45

reluctant to grant any decision-making power to Hispanics. A Chicano Caucus in the state legislature lobbied hard for a bilingual law. After a protracted fight, they prevailed. Funding was another matter. It took another period of intense negotiations and implied threats to secure monies.[2]

The governor recommended an allocation of $1 million, and the Chicano Caucus declared that unacceptable. The governor then offered $1.5 million and the Caucus demanded $8 million. The two sides finally agreed on $2.55 million. Colorado later became one of the first states to rescind its bilingual law during the downswing after the defeat of the Lau Regulations in 1981.

Texas too was beset by political infighting. Several Mexican-American legislators and their allies had been organizing for bilingual education since the mid-1960s. A law was finally enacted in 1973 in a form different from that desired by bilingual advocates. Hispanic legislators wanted a law that provided improved social and political prestige for Mexican-Americans through Spanish language instruction. Anglo legislators were split between those who agreed to support some sort of bilingual law and those who opposed it altogether. The Anglo supporters favored legislation that stressed English acquisition as a remedy for the socioeconomic plight of poor Chicanos. This version eventually won out and has helped shape bilingual schooling in Texas ever since.[3]

THE FIGHT FOR RECOGNITION IN MICHIGAN

Port City is the pseudonym of a middle-sized Michigan city with a 5 percent Hispanic population. Latins first came there 60 years ago as skilled factory workers. More recently others filtered out of the migratory labor stream that worked on nearby farms. In 1973 the Hispanic community waged and lost a campaign to retain the job of the only Hispanic teacher at a local elementary school. Three years later the state's passage of a bilingual law stimulated local interest. Community leaders organized meetings and rallies demanding that the school system institute a bilingual program. In the face of school board silence, they organized a protest at the school board meeting. School board members were surprised at the large turnout and by the intensity of the feelings expressed, but they failed to act.[4]

The elementary school principal stated that his Hispanic students had no school problems. Community pressure increased and peaked when a study was released that revealed that almost half the Hispanic students had been held back at least one grade. These results and the furor surrounding them helped soften the board's opposition. The board acquiesced reluctantly and a program was instituted. It had taken more than two years.

THE AFT, THE SCHOOL BOARD, AND HISPANICS IN NEW YORK CITY

Minority communities and the American Federation of Teachers (AFT) had a long tradition of confrontation in New York City, especially in relation to community control of schools in Ocean Hill-Brownsville and on the Lower East Side. As these tense dramas were being played out in the late 1960s and early 1970s, bilingual education entered the city on little cat's feet. An assistant superintendent approached a group of Puerto Rican ESL teachers with the prospect of starting a small program now that federal funds had become available. At first the group resisted, in the belief that bilingual instruction was detrimental to non-English-speakers. They later came to agree with the concept and with the idea of a local program, and they enlisted the aid of other Hispanic educators. They jointly formed the Puerto Rican Educators Association (PREA) and lobbied the state and local school boards to expand the skimpy programs that existed at that time. They also joined two other community groups, Aspira and the Puerto Rican Legal Defense and Education Fund, in suing the school board for failing to provide an adequate education for LEP children. In 1974 the judge brought both sides together in a compromise known as the Aspira Consent Decree. Hundreds of new teachers and support personnel were hired, many of whom were Latins. Latins had previously constituted only 2 percent of the teachers in a system whose student population was over 20 percent Latin.[5]

Albert Shanker, the local and later the national president of the AFT, was generally opposed to bilingual education. He had entered school speaking only Yiddish and acknowledged the need for someone who spoke the children's native language to be on duty in the schools. But he felt that dual language instruction retarded the acquisition of English. He believed in the melting-pot concept of assimilation and feared that bilingual educators threatened both the melting pot and the jobs of many of his union members.[6]

In 1975, just as the Aspira Decree teachers were entering the school system, the city suffered a fiscal crisis (remember the headline FORD TO CITY; DROP DEAD!). The school board decided that it had to lay off 1,600 teachers. The expectation was that the last hired would be the first fired. Aspira, however, obtained an injunction from the federal judge that prevented the layoff of the bilingual teachers. Shanker and the AFT were furious. They issued strongly worded statements, demonstrated, and launched mini-strikes; but in the end they acceded to the court order. Tremendous bitterness between regular and bilingual teachers built up. They worked side by side in an atmosphere of mutual distrust. The school board did little to support the bilingual program. The deputy chancellor stated that "the city hasn't made up its mind whether it is going to proceed with bilingual education.[7]"

The PREA continued its pressure to expand and institutionalize the program, but the New York *Times* editorialized against these activitists for "misinterpreting the goals of bilingual education as a means of creating a Spanish-speaking power base." The editorial raised the specter of a "misguided linguistic separatism"[8] similar to what was occurring in Québec. This view would gain national currency within a few years. A PREA leader observed that bilingual education "was born at a traumatic time and is now in its postnatal stage, no one is sure whether it will survive."[9]

CHICANO MILITANCY IN SOUTH TEXAS

Chicano militancy found a fertile base in South Texas. This region of fruit and vegetable cultivation and cattle raising had long been dominated by Anglo ranchers and growers. Chicanos have occupied subordinate positions in the socioeconomic and political structures. A wave of protest sprang up in Crystal City, the "spinach capital of the world," in the mid-1960s. Chicano union leaders and students launched the La Raza Unida party and challenged Anglo dominance. Traditionally a Democratic party bastion, the region had provided the margin of victory in many statewide political races. Local political leader Archie Parr had allegedly fixed Lyndon Johnson's first senatorial election many years earlier.[10]

La Raza Unida electorally defeated the Crystal City school board establishment and later made important inroads into the city council. There were charges and counter-charges of vote fraud, racism, separatism, and violence. La Raza Unida put forth bilingual education as one of its principal demands. The movement spread throughout the area. Traditional power brokers resisted this movement at first, but eventually accepted the inevitable and came to terms with it. The growers and ranchers retained their economic power, but relinquished part of their control over political, social, and educational institutions. The region's schools were shaped by this political struggle and its resolution. Bilingual programs proliferated. Chicano teachers, administrators, and superintendents became a part of the new reality. Many Anglo teachers confined their negative remarks about Chicanos to teachers' lounges and stated that it was no longer possible to ban Spanish from the school grounds.[11]

While reforms abounded, the millenium was nowhere in sight. The small town of San Diego, Texas, was a case in point. This overwhelmingly Chicano town's bilingual program was centered in the Archie Parr Elementary School. It helped Chicanos attain professional positions in the school system. Most of the students advanced through the bilingual program and went on to secondary school with far less problems than they had had during the days of the explicitly anglocentric curriculum. Their attainment levels rose and the number of dropouts fell. There was, however, little upward mobility. The schools had not prepared the students to compete in the universities or in the professional job market, and only a handful were able to succeed in these milieus. The rest entered the armed services or the technical schools or went to work in agribusiness. With the exception of school system positions, there were few avenues of advancement. The schools had changed, but the opportunity structure had not.[12]

AN UPHILL BATTLE IN INDEPENDENCE, OREGON

This small agricultural town had a growing Mexican-American minority whose advocacy of bilingual education frightened school officials. As community pressure increased and federal funds became available, the superintendent relented and started a small bilingual program. Deeply committed to military or missionary-style assimilation, school officials made it clear that the program would last only so long as federal funds did. Bilingual advocates continued pressing for a more extensive program. Bilingual education provided a forum for a developing Anglo-Hispanic power struggle.[13]

PRESSURING POWERFUL SUPERINTENDENTS IN SOUTHERN COLORADO

Southern Colorado's San Luis Valley was the center of the state's Chicano population and the center of Anglo school officials' resistance to the new state bilingual law. One superintendent commented, in words reminiscent of the Deep South, "We've always gotten along with our Mexican parents, until these outsiders started coming in and stirring things up." Officials finally agreed to permit bilingual programs, but reverted to subterfuge to derail them. State law required that there be an elected parents' advisory committee. The officials scheduled the election on a weekday. Hispanic parents were angry because most were farmworkers and had to work daytime hours. They pressured state authorities to intercede on their behalf, which they did, and the election was rescheduled to a better time.[14]

NEW JERSEY'S GEOGRAPHIC DETERMINISM AND INTERNECINE WARFARE

New Jersey's bilingual program presented a landscape of conflicting interests. The state program arose and expanded in response to intense community unrest. The unrest was generalized, and was not specifically tied to educational issues. A number of Hispanics were hired to administer bilingual programs in New Jersey's local school districts, but they had only ceremonial authority. Local school boards and superintendents were highly resistant to bilingual education and instituted programs only when community pressure forced them to. The results were predictable. The state bilingual director surveyed the 17 districts that had bilingual programs and found that there were none "whose curriculum and instructional program connected with the needs of the Spanish-speaking children in the program."[15] Program directors often hired poorly trained teachers. School boards refused to authorize the hiring of support personnel (for example, counselors, librarians, and social workers). Bilingual classes were frequently held under stairwells, in hallways, in storage rooms, and in the back of auditoriums. This was a kind of geographic determinism that illustrated the program's low status. The state bilingual director concluded that local superintendents had programmed bilingual education to fail.[16]

There was also an ongoing power struggle between Cubans and Puerto Ricans. This conflict first surfaced when the Teacher Corps program provided the state with 70 teacher positions for Hispanics. Cubans got 66 of them, even though they were far less numerous than Puerto Ricans. The two groups battled over state and local school board nominations, bilingual program positions, certification provisions for bilingual teachers, and almost everything else. To complicate matters further, there was hostility between bilingual and ESL teachers. The latter were in place before the bilingual programs arrived. They resisted the onset of bilingual programs, but lost. They later changed and merged their professional organization into that of the bilingual teachers, and they have cooperated since.[17]

PARENT-TEACHER DISCORD IN STOCKTON

Stockton's bilingual program, one of California's first, took everyone by surprise. Suddenly an elementary school was chosen to initiate the program. Parents were not consulted. A nearly total staff change was put into effect over the summer. The school year started with all new faces in the classrooms and in the office. The parents and teachers kept their distance from one another. Each viewed the other through a prism of "functional myths." The teachers believed that the parents were unstable and irresponsible toward their children. This view enabled teachers to justify putting forth only a minimal effort. Parents viewed teachers as unfeeling and unapproachable bureaucrats. Both sides settled for the view that the situation was inevitable. No one seemed to notice that the administrative maneuverings that launched the program seemed to have set up a situation of mutual antipathy.[18]

FIGHTING THE STATE AUTHORITIES IN IDAHO

The small number of Hispanic permanent residents in Idaho was augmented from spring to fall each year by thousands of migrant laborers. Some families filter out of this stream every year and increase the state's Hispanic population. State and local authorities in such cities as Nampa, Boise, and Burley apparently feared that introducing bilingual education into the migrant education programs would lead more Hispanics to stay permanently in Idaho. They forbade this type of instruction. The Idaho Migrant Council tried to negotiate, got nowhere, and took the case to court. The court decided in their favor and ordered the state education agency to conduct bilingual programs for migrants and to undertake an accurate count of the LEP students in the state.[19]

CONFLICT WITHIN BOSTON'S HISPANIC COMMUNITY

In 1971 Massachusetts became the first state to enact a bilingual education law. Hispanic activists nudged a liberal coalition of legislators into action to pass this law. Several years later Hispanics declared that their concerns should be heard in the ongoing and bitter federal desegregation case. A Denver judge in a desegregation case had ruled that Latins were entitled to separate representation as a distinct ethnic group. The Boston judge followed this precedent and called on the Latin community to provide its own representation.[20]

The question became What kind of representation? A coalition of Hispanic professionals had assumed that their leadership role was a foregone conclusion, even though most of its members lived in the suburbs and few had children in the Boston schools. A group of working-class parents of Boston students challenged the professionals. "How could these outsiders represent us and our children?" the parents asked. After acrimonious debate, the parents won and the professionals agreed to testify to the judge as experts, not as community leaders. The parents' group had the major say in desegregation matters. But, because of credential requirements, most of the bilingual program's jobs went to members or friends of the professional group. Several years later, the superintendent planned to diminish the bilingual program's funding and change its organizational structure. The superintendent chose to deal exclusively with the professional group. The parents' group marched and rallied against the superintendent's planned changes. In the end they were able to preserve the program and to achieve greater recognition from the school system.[21]

School systems often appear to be closed bureaucracies. But as most of the above cases demonstrate, the systems are subject to pressure as are the state legislatures. Bureaucracies and legislative bodies usually move in small steps. They rarely do more than they have to. They often provide less than adequate funding and resources, thereby forcing bilingual programs to continue to rely heavily on federal support. Currently only about 20 states provide any funding at all, some of these provide only token amounts. Bilingual laws were passed and programs were undertaken at the urging of Latin communities, as well as at the urging of courts and the federal government. The struggle to initiate and broaden bilingual programs often became a test of whether Hispanic communities could achieve a measure of political power.

6

The Blunderbuss Approach to Federal Enforcement

Bilingual education programs became the object of federal civil rights enforcement when the U.S. Office of Civil Rights entered the arena of Hispanic schooling in 1970. Federal interest increased when the Supreme Court rendered its Lau Decision in 1974 and when the U.S. Commission on Civil Rights became concerned about compliance with the Lau Decision. Thus Uncle Sam now had two faces on bilingual education: the kindly grant-giver and the stern enforcer.

OCR'S LAX AND STRINGENT ENFORCEMENT

OCR enforced the Office of Education's Lau Remedies by sending out letters to 333 local school districts in 1975 and more in succeeding years. The letters suggested that the districts might be out of compliance with the Lau Decision as interpreted by the Lau Remedies due to the absence or inadequacy of bilingual education programs. A suggested timetable for submitting and implementing compliance plans was attached. The potential threat of federal funds cutoffs for noncompliance underlay the enforcement effort. OCR regional offices were given the responsibility for follow-up.[1]

There was a sort of yin and yang quality to the enforcement effort. Some regional offices tried to stick to the letter and spirit of the Remedies, some only to the letter, and still others accepted any half-baked plan as compliance and abandoned both the letter and the spirit. The exact meaning of the Remedies was not easy to discern. According to a former Education Department general counsel, the Remedies "were poorly drafted and ambiguous and were applied in piecemeal fashion across the country."[2] OCR's uneven enforcement pattern seemed to reflect the unclarity of the Remedies and the reluctance of the Office of Education to go through the process of issuing formal regulations.

THE NUMBERS GAME: NEGLIGENCE AND DOUBLE-ENTRY BOOKKEEPING

Before OCR could get into gear, it needed accurate counts of the number of LEP students in school districts. Districts often hesitated to carry out counts for fear that the numbers that were revealed would increase pressure to start or expand bilingual programs. There was no nationally accepted test of English proficiency. Some districts chose tests according to whether they wanted higher or lower LEP numbers. Some districts practiced double-entry bookkeeping. They used a high set of LEP figures when they applied for state or federal bilingual grants; they used a lower set when they communicated with OCR to show that there was no need to expand bilingual programs. When the 1973 international oil crisis occurred, the federal government had to rely on oil industry figures on energy matters. By the same token, OCR had no independent means to compile or even verify LEP figures; it relied totally on the good faith, or lack thereof, of local districts.

The Chicago regional office tried to pin down Saginaw, Michigan officials. It ordered them not only to test students for English proficiency, but to determine which language was dominant. There was more. The determination had to involve finding out which language the student spoke in the classroom, in the lunchroom, and at home.[3] Strict adherence to this directive would have necessitated employing a corps of language monitors to roam around the school and the community checking on speech patterns. With orders like this, it is little wonder that so many school officials and their national organizations strongly opposed the Lau Regulations.

The OCR ordered Nashville to submit LEP figures. Nashville responded that its LEP population was minuscule and that it did not need special programs. It took a survey and found 200 LEP students. It took another survey soon after and discovered 1,200 students. Under the threat of being sued in court, Wilmington, Delaware officials began a count and found several hundred LEPs after claiming that there were only a handful.[4]

SCHOOL DISTRICT COMPLIANCE

Once some sort of LEP figures were available, the regional offices sent out directives requiring districts to prepare compliance plans. The OCR then either accepted these plans or sent them back to the districts for revision. Some school districts made every effort to comply with OCR directives; some made every effort not to comply and submitted paper plans. A Tampa area school district had a hard time complying because agreements reached on the phone with the Atlanta regional office looked quite different when Atlanta committed them to paper. Tampa had to submit three different versions of its compliance plan. The first was rejected, the second was classified as partial compliance, and the third was conditionally accepted.[5] Youngstown, Ohio officials made a "mad dash" to comply with OCR directives to begin a kindergarten through twelfth-grade program in one year. Neither Youngstown nor the state of Ohio had many bilingual teachers, so Youngstown raided other districts. Overall they opted for a time-honored tradition – they winged it. They cut and pasted together a program.[6]

In addition to the poorly conceived programs that resulted from this hasty program creation, many districts merely went through the motions. The U.S. Office of Education undermined OCR's credibility when it allowed districts that had been judged to be out of compliance to continue obtaining federal grants, including bilingual education grants. This allowed districts to engage in dilatory tactics without risking anything. OCR never did cut off any district's federal funds. Its enforcement effort was uneven and sometimes counterproductive. A University of Texas investigation found that "the total effect of OCR's compliance activities is to send out a message of noncreditability – a double standard in which discrimination is tolerated in some programs and not in others."[7] The effects of this enforcement effort were probably far less than advocates hoped for. A study of 96 Southern California districts that had been under scrutiny by OCR concluded, "Most school districts complying with the Lau Decision met compliance requirements through minimal efforts that have little effect on the existing district curricula."[8]

THE AFTERMATH OF COURT DECISIONS

Once court decisions are rendered, judges have difficulty determining whether school officials have complied with court orders to institute, upgrade, or expand bilingual programs. After several years there may be an erosion of the court's standards. San Francisco, for example, was the site of the case that culminated in the Lau Decision. If strict adherence to court decisions would take place anywhere, it would seem that this liberal, multicultural city would be the place. However, most of the post-decision expansion in the program seemed to take place at the administrative level. The administrators were consumed in jurisdictional and perquisite fights. They hired a cadre of experts who spent their time trying to "monopolize the system's bewildering jargon and statistics."[9] Neither the administrators nor the experts offered much support to the teachers and paraprofessionals whose dedication held the program together.

In another major case, *Serna* v. *Portales, New Mexico*, the court-ordered bilingual education program was allowed to lapse into an ESL-only program within a few years. The judge was unable to effectively monitor the situation after several years had passed.[10] In New York City's Aspira Consent Decree case the Puerto Rican Educators Association became increasingly frustrated at the mismatch between the judicial and educational systems. They felt that New York officials were making mere cosmetic adjustments to the program. The judge could and did intervene in the teacher layoff situation and in several other aspects of the case, but could not be expected to ensure the quality or substance of the program.[11]

Relying on judges to monitor programs is risky. Judges are not educators and may not understand or appreciate the differences between ESL, bilingual education, or immersion programs. Even if they do, they rarely have the time to conduct lengthy inquiries into the inner workings of school systems in order to gauge the level of compliance. They can intervene in open breaches of the decision, but they are reluctant to intervene if the district *appears* to be acceding to court orders.

THE U.S. COMMISSION ON CIVIL RIGHTS

The U.S. Commission on Civil Rights declared itself in favor of bilingual education in the mid-1970s and uncovered important information on program operations in its hearings and research efforts. The commission had the power to subpoena witnesses and could obtain contempt citations for those who refused to testify. During a 1976 hearing in Denver, they found the local bilingual program to be a disappointment to bilingual supporters. Bilingual teachers' responsibilities were stretched to ridiculous lengths in the five bilingual elementary schools. Many teachers had to run from class to class just to get the children together for an abbreviated class period. These schools were supposed to provide a curriculum that was fully bilingual. Instead the resource room model was used. This meant that the bilingual classes were really pullouts as in ESL, in which students went into resource rooms for brief periods. The state bilingual director observed:

> There was no program at all. It made a lot of words, a lot of statistics, a lot of something that was out there somewhere . . . the resource room concept would bring the kids to an area and have something, maybe tortilla making sessions and they spoke a few words in Spanish.[12]

A university president who was a bilingual supporter, commented that the program was "ineffective, fumbling and weak . . . lip service. I don't think that you can solve the bilingual-bicultural program by singing a few songs and celebrating a few holidays."[13]

The commission's state advisory committees did not have subpoena power and had to rely on persuasion to get school officials to attend. The Texas advisory committee had no luck in persuading the Corpus Christi superintendent to testify at their hearing. The commission itself later held hearings in Corpus Christi, and this time the superintendent appeared, with his lawyer. His answers to questions were formalistic. He described his bilingual program as functioning "to remove any youngster from his native tongue to English."[14]

Kenosha, Wisconsin's superintendent behaved similarly. He failed to attend a state advisory committee hearing and sent a principal instead. The superintendent ostensibly feared that the hearing would be conducted in Spanish; but he sent a principal who did not speak Spanish either. The committee found that Kenosha bunched LEP students into four-grade clusters and disregarded their grade-promotion or graduation requirements. They found similar problems with programs in Milwaukee, Racine, and other Wisconsin cities.[15]

A state advisory committee hearing in California revealed similar sorts of complaints. The state office was understaffed and underfunded and incapable of monitoring state-funded programs or reviewing applications for federally funded programs. A majority of the teachers in the bilingual program were actually monolingual. Parents were angry about shoddy program performance.[16]

The commission and its state advisory committees played an important role in bringing program deficiencies to light within a constructive context. They wanted to strengthen bilingual education rather than scrap it. The information that they uncovered was often used by parents and other bilingual advocates to push for strengthened programs.

Taken as a whole, the federal enforcement effort failed to produce either substantial compliance with the Lau Remedies or much change in the instructional offerings in cases in which the courts ordered improvements. This failure flows partly from the weakly drawn Lau Remedies, the inability of judges to monitor compliance over time and the uneven character of OCR enforcement. Uncle Sam fired a blunderbuss at school officials. He scared some into action. But many others took the tried and true course of inaction, they merely outwaited the federal pressure and took the heat off by submitting plans that were not intended to be applied. It is not that federal officials have short attention spans, it is that they have short policy spans. Policy changes often, and local officials may be able to ride out the flurry created by the latest wave of policy.

7

Business as Usual:
The Missionary Style Revisited

It is not enough to appropriate money for programs and label them "bilingual" when nothing in fact has changed in the classroom.[1]

A California legal assistance attorney

Bilingual education deeply affected some school districts. Many other districts added some aspects of bilingual education to their repertories but kept the program at arm's length. The districts added a thin veneer over the same old patterns, a facade that masks a stubborn reality. Many of the school officials are like dinosaurs in swamps – they do not move much, and when they do, they move very slowly. The closer one looks at the bilingual programs in operation, the clearer the outlines of the traditional missionary-style assimilation become.

RETARDED CLASSES AND CULTURAL DEPRIVATION

Manchester, New Hampshire relegated language minority children to the category of Specific Learning Disabled students and assigned them to special classes in the school for the mentally retarded. There was no testing mechanism to determine which students needed English proficiency classes. Once they were in these classes, there was no objective measurement to determine when they would be able to graduate from them. Everything was left up to teachers' subjective judgments. Manchester officials indicated to federal authorities that they would institute a full bilingual system, but they merely maintained the fragmentary pattern that they had had before. A report on this situation in Manchester was entitled *Shortchanging the Language Minority Student*.[2]

Other studies of bilingual programs in New England discovered cultural deprivation theory operating, as well as other features of the missionary approach. The school districts set up bilingual programs on a tear-out sheet. They were almost totally marginal to the everyday functioning of the school system. As far as officials were concerned, they were a necessary evil. The compensatory strategy to remedy cultural deprivation was in evidence throughout the program. Those children who attended bilingual classes were labeled stupid by their peers and, by implication, by the non-bilingual teachers. The bilingual teachers projected low expectations for children from working-class backgrounds. The bilingual teachers devoted most of their time and energy to the LEP children from middle-class backgrounds.[3]

REGALIA AND ACCULTURATION

Several California studies found other reincarnations of missionary-style assimilation operating in bilingual programs. One was the substitution of regalia for serious instructional programs. In a 60 percent Chicano school the bilingual teacher spoke Spanish less fluently than most of the students and was unable to effectively teach either Spanish or English proficiency. The teacher and the school culture compensated by instituting cultural programs. Serapes tacos, and piñatas were often in evidence. Yet neither Mexican-American nor Anglo culture were ever discussed in any depth. They were simply presented and children were supposed to ritualistically absorb them. Anglo culture was assumed to be the standard, and Mexican-American culture was an afterthought.[4]

Another facet of missionary-style assimilation was the clear intention to acculturate the children into being anglicized Chicanos. This took place in an 80 percent Chicano school that was widely known as a bilingual school. The principal regularly sent Latin youngsters to the speech therapist to straighten out what were regarded as pathological patterns of speech. The bilingual program was treated as nothing more than a bridge to Anglo culture. Hispanic culture was treated as a curious artifact. The school's administrators were functionaries carrying out the assimilation policy set by higher levels of officialdom. The teachers and administrators pictured the ideal student as Anglo and middle class. Since there were none in the school, they chose the next best thing, the children of the Anglo working class. They devoted extra time and effort to these children, in the hope that they would succeed. The Hispanics, who were all working class, were guided toward vocational tracks. The Hispanic children were expected to go to work in low-paid, blue-collar jobs and not to succeed in school.[5]

MENTAL WITHDRAWAL

The Dallas neighborhood of La Bajura had an elementary school that housed one of the area's first bilingual programs. The curriculum was a mere Spanish translation of the traditional anglocentric curriculum. Children entered the program well dressed, well scrubbed, and enthusiastic. A noticeable drop-off in enthusiasm took place as the children progressed through the early grades. The school culture seemed to say to the children: No matter what you do here, the chances are that you will end up doing the society's dirty work. Stay where you are and be satisfied. The children seemed to absorb the message and gradually distanced themselves from the teachers and the school culture.[6]

LOWERED EXPECTATIONS

Pueblo, Colorado school officials used the bilingual program to hire Hispanic teachers and administrators. But in every other way, the bilingual program demonstrated the subordinate position that most local Hispanics lived in. The bilingual teachers did not expect much from their students. The low expectations became part of the program's atmosphere and no one expected that it would do much to advance the childrens' education or their vocational prospects. The bilingual program did not create the socioeconomic situation, it just tried to survive within it.[7]

THE SCHOOLS' RIGHT TO UNDERPERFORM

Business-as-usual bilingual programs were the result of school system resistance to change. School officials seemed to subconsciously proclaim their right to underperform; to go through the motions of the teaching and learning process without getting anywhere. They placed the onus for learning on the minority language child. It is the same as stating that defective school systems are not to blame for school failure, defective children are, and they and their parents had better understand this fact. As a former OBEMLA director put it:

> When children are painfully ashamed of who they are, they are not going to do very well in school whether they be taught monolingually, bilingually or trilingually. But it's worse if the bilingual education that these children receive is predicated on having them change out of who they are into something else.
>
> It's worse when their bilingual education has poorly trained teachers, poorly prepared materials and classes conducted in poor facilities.
>
> It's worse when use of their language is viewed as transitional: as an unfortunate necessity rather than an opportunity for academic and psychological growth.
>
> It's worse when their language is used only when there are special funds from the government; else we go back to the "regular" program.
>
> It's worse when they realize that no one else is being taught Spanish or in Spanish and they see that their language is not valued in the larger society.
>
> How can we evaluate programs fairly under these conditions? They are not atypical. I have personally seen bilingual teachers working on the landing of stairs in New York City and in hallways in Chicago.[8]

Bilingual programs can be made to fit neatly into the school systems' traditional structures. These programs often become domesticated and marginalized so that school systems can carry on business as usual. Educators are left free to promote their missionary assimilationist notions in the classroom and throughout the culture of the school. Yet to depict this as the whole story would be inaccurate and unfair. Bilingual education affected some areas dramatically; some things would never be the same. The South Texas case mentioned earlier exemplifies this phenomenon. Creative programs have arisen in plenty of districts. These programs point the way to future possibilities.

8

Creative Programs and the Politics of Pluralism

While it is important for the child to learn a second language, it is equally important that they learn to function in our multicultural society and to interact with other ethnic groups. . . . The program fosters patriotism by pointing to the past efforts of members of diverse backgrounds in the building of this country as well as encouraging students to follow the same path. Integration, not assimilation is practiced in this program.[1]

Evangelina Diaz on her
multicultural school in Buffalo, 1983

Pluralist philosophy underlies the formation and development of creative bilingual programs. Pluralism is an informal philosophy or approach that values different cultures and traditions; it is the antithesis of ethnocentrism. Pluralism rose to prominence as a reaction against the World War I era Americanization campaign. Horace Kallen, an early adherent, described it as an appropriate philosophy for a multicultural, multilingual democracy. Jane Addams of Hull House was an early practitioner; she created a Labor Museum to display the Old World and New World work conditions and life styles of Chicago's immigrant communities. The immigrants' children and grandchildren learned to appreciate their families' struggles and to take pride in their accomplishments.[2]

Several urban school districts began to practice various aspects of pluralism in the 1930s as the Americanization fervor was dissipating. New York City's Bureau of Intercultural Education convinced local schools to institute tolerance assemblies and intercultural teacher training seminars. This type of program grew after incidents of Nazi anti-Semitism, especially the infamous *Kristallnacht* ("The Night of the Broken Glass"). School officials in Cleveland, Detroit, Buffalo, Pittsburgh, and elsewhere carried out similar multicultural efforts. Officials in many school systems became aware of the adjustment problems of ethnic youth. A sociologist attributed the growth of organized crime in part to the profound alienation of many ethnic youth. Educator George Sanchez traced the growth of the Mexican-American *pachuco* gangs to the segregated and impositional schooling that students received. The schools had taught the youngsters to be ashamed of themselves and their families, but society provided little or no opportunity to realize their aspirations. In desperation, many turned to lives of petty crime. Interest in pluralism and multicultural pedagogy intensified after the Detroit race riots and the Zoot Suit riots in Los Angeles during World War II.[3]

LEONARD COVELLO, PLURALIST EDUCATOR

Leonard Covello was one of the most significant pluralist educators. As a child he had emigrated from Italy to East Harlem, the largest Italian settlement in the country. He underwent Americanization — the teachers changed his name and made him feel ashamed of his family. This provoked family arguments, after one of which he felt that childhood had become a heavy burden. He vowed not to let these things happen to future generations.[4]

As a young teacher in the New York City schools he helped to win the right to have Italian taught as a foreign language. Thousands of Italian-American youth used these classes to get in touch with their roots. Covello wrote the definitive description of the social background of the Italian public school student.[5]

As the principal of East Harlem's Benjamin Franklin High School, he initiated a community education program in which the school served East Harlem residents of all ages. When the large Puerto Rican migration to East Harlem occurred, Covello saw many parallels between the Puerto Rican and Italian experiences. He moved to bring these two groups together, always reminding Italians that they were in the same situation a generation earlier. He set up Spanish-language orientation classes, but kept the Hispanic newcomers in mixed classes most of the day. He worked to overcome the potential for tension between his black and

Italian students during Mussolini's invasion of Ethiopia. He influenced future leaders, including Joseph Monserrat, the first Puerto Rican member and later president of the New York City Board of Education, and an unrelenting foe of cultural deprivation theory. Covello did everything in his power to carry out a pluralist worldview.[6]

CREATIVE BILINGUAL PROGRAMS

Leonard Covello's spirit lives in creative bilingual projects. Many cities have launched projects that serve language minorities and other students in an atmosphere of mutual respect. San Diego's program involves a number of elementary schools that provide intensive Spanish instruction to English speakers alongside intensive English instruction for Spanish speakers. Both language instructional programs work together; the languages are given equal status and cultural deprivation is nowhere to be found. The goal is for native speakers of both languages to achieve dual fluency by the time they graduate from this kindergarten to sixth-grade program.[7]

Buffalo's Public School 33 is located in a Polish neighborhood and contains a 25 percent Hispanic enrollment. Every child in this elementary school learns Spanish and English together – there are no special class-rooms for Hispanics only. The curriculum promotes understanding of the multiethnic contributions that have been made to the United States.[8]

Cincinnati's program features French, German, and Spanish instruction for 2,500 Anglo, black, and Hispanic students in magnet schools that are designed to promote desegregation. Students begin intensive language instruction in elementary school and continue in the Bilingual Academy middle school and the International Academy high school. New York *Times* education editor Fred Hechinger viewed the program as an antidote to linguistic chauvinism.[9]

West Palm Beach, Florida's Southboro Elementary School parents decided to transform the transitional bilingual program at the school into one in which all students could study together in Spanish and English. The transition program had separated the Spanish-speaking and English-speaking students; the new program unites them. All subjects, including computer courses, are taught in both languages for part of the day. Parents are aware that benefits other than student unity will accrue to their children. First they will have better career opportunities in the South Florida job market, which is thoroughly bilingual. Second, the likelihood of passing required high school language courses is greatly enhanced.[10]

Los Angeles' Ramona School is trilingual. Half of its students are refugees, Armenians from Lebanon, and Salvadorans. The school has Armenian-English and Spanish-English bilingual programs. All students take some classes together and PTA meetings are conducted in all three languages. El Paso's Ysleta School is only five blocks from Mexico. The principal attended school during the no Spanish era and has created a bilingual program that makes students fluent first in oral and written Spanish and then in English. A teacher reports that once grammar is learned in Spanish, it is easy to transfer this knowledge into English. Children learn to move back and forth naturally between Spanish and English.[11]

Model bilingual schools are designed to serve as models that can be replicated elsewhere. P.S. 25 in the Bronx was New York City's model bilingual school. It's low-income Puerto Rican students progressed in both learning English and in staying abreast of their content subjects in Spanish and then in English. Its guiding light, Hernan LaFontaine, later became the superintendent of Hartford, Connecticut's schools.[12]

Washington, D.C. converted its Oyster School in the 1970s into a model bilingual school. Formerly a white school in the city's pre-1954 segregated system, Oyster is located near a major Hispanic neighborhood. Like only a few other cities, Washington's sizable Hispanic community is neither Cuban, Mexican, nor Puerto Rican. The majority are recently arrived Salvadorans and other Central Americans. The school ministers to this community as well as to Anglos and blacks. Oyster used and modified the curriculum that was developed at Coral Way. It conducts a modified two-way program. President Jimmy Carter visited this school and tried out his Spanish on a bilingual group of Hispanic, black, and Anglo youngsters who recommended that he take more intensive instruction.[13]

Chicago established the 85-year-old Seward Elementary School as a model program. This school serves the Back-of-the-Yards neighborhood that was the home of longtime Mayor Richard Daley. Latins make up two-thirds of the school; Lithuanians, Irish, and Poles the other third. The program began with a popular parent-child bilingual preschool. Over 160 three- and four-year-olds graduated and became the nucleus for the elementary program.[14] Another Chicago model program teaches in four languages: Polish, English, Spanish, and Italian. Located in a predominately Polish neighborhood, the school is across the street from St. Stanislaus Church, where the masses are held in Polish. Still another Chicago program was described by a Harvard professor: "I have never seen such a well-functioning first grade society. By this I mean the extent to which children know where and when and what to do. . . ."[15]

Boston's Rafael Hernandez School also serves a polyglot low-income population. Boston's Hispanics are about half Puerto Rican; the rest are mostly Dominicans, Colombians, and Central Americans. The school also has significant Irish and black populations. The instructional program offers English and Spanish classes for speakers of both languages. A team of British educators spent many months investigating the school and observed that "Schools like the Hernandez have demonstrated the extent to which caring and committed institutions can stabilise student attendance and even parental residence."[16] Supportive school environments like this one can go a long way in preventing mental and physical withdrawal and in strengthening students' self-images.

Lowell, Massachusetts' Project Hand-In-Hand is a preschool learning center for speakers of Spanish, Portuguese, and English. Children are instructed in their native languages and in English. They learn about their neighborhoods, the country, and the world. They are equipped with the academic skills and understanding to negotiate either monolingual or bilingual elementary schools. Head Start officials aid the development of this sort of program. A number of innovative Head Start bilingual programs are under way and others are being planned.[17]

Another type of creative innovation is evident in bilingual gifted and talented programs in which LEP students are given an accelerated infusion of dual language fluency instruction. The participants are frequently identified in preschool or kindergarten. In these classes pupils read in one language and then in another; and then they count and work math problems in the same sequence. Union City, New Jersey has a program of this type.[18]

Charlotte, North Carolina has another type of significant program for its 2,000 LEP students. Along with an intensive ESL program, this district provides individualized native language instruction in math, reading, and writing. Personalized instruction is also provided to migrant students in their home base in Texas and at two sites in the state of Washington, where their parents travel each year in search of work. The three centers serve students year round, and a corps of teachers travels with groups of families to ensure that the learning sequence is uninterrupted.[19]

There are many creative bilingual programs in other languages besides Spanish. One is in Hamtramck, Michigan, an industrial city near Detroit that has traditionally been heavily Polish. Recent immigrants from Albania, Yugoslavia, and some of the Arab countries helped persuade the school district to institute multilingual programs in the languages of these countries as well as in Polish and English. Among other significant bilingual programs are the Navajo-English Rock Point School in Arizona, the Portuguese-English Fox Point School in Providence, Rhode Island, the Cherokee Cross-Cultural Bilingual Center in Oklahoma, and the Crow-English Lodge Grass School in Montana. Seattle has an Indochinese languages multilingual program in several secondary schools. French-English exemplary programs exist in Lafayette Parish, Louisiana; Madawaska, Maine; and Richford, Vermont.[20]

ENRICHMENT IMMERSION

Another series of related projects, enrichment immersion programs, began in the United States in 1971. Patterned after successful experiments in Canada, they have been designed to immerse majority students in minority languages instruction. In Canada, English-speaking students were immersed in French in the early elementary grades and later received instruction in English as well. Upon completing sixth grade most of the students had achieved dual-language proficiency and were at or above grade level in their content subjects. The parents of these 114,000 Anglo participants want their children to be fully conversant with their French-speaking peers. Since English is Canada's majority language there is little fear that the Anglo youngsters will lose their English or become forced to sink or swim in French. Elementary school students are eager to learn languages and learn more quickly than secondary or college students.[21]

Enrichment immersion programs can be conducted by themselves or in tandem with programs for LEPs as they are in San Diego. Immersion educators warn that immersion in the majority language is not an appropriate course of study for language minority students. Parents who want their children to learn Spanish are the largest motivating force behind U.S. immersion programs. This movement has caught on particularly in Southern California where demographic considerations and proximity to Mexico provide a supportive environment. A California-based parents group advocates dual language programs for both the majority and minority students. Patterned after the Canadian Parents for French, the group has the support of the California State Department of Education. The first U.S. program sprang up in Culver City, California, and several other cities have followed suit. They also exist in Milwaukee; Baton Rouge; Orem, Utah; Montgomery County, Maryland; Tulsa; Rochester; and Pittsburgh. French or German as well as Spanish are taught in some of these programs. Ames, Iowa pioneered evening classes in which parents and children learn Spanish together. Detroit is providing Spanish immersion opportunities to black inner-city youngsters. The University of Indiana-Northwest is training teachers for immersion programs. Some of this experimentation is aided by federal or state bilingual funding; other districts go it on their own.[22] Enrichment immersion has aroused considerable interest among language educators. A professor of Spanish observed the Rochester program and reported:

> In June 1982, it was my pleasure to observe math, science and social studies classes conducted in Spanish. I was particularly impressed with the simple explanation of the life of a butterfly by a first grader in simple, clear Spanish. . . . What I witnessed was an uncommon accomplishment.[23]

Variations on the enrichment immersion theme have developed. One of these is the FLES (Foreign Language in Elementary Schools) which teaches languages as subjects before, during, or after school rather than immersing the students in the second language. The President's Commission on Foreign Languages recommended in 1979 that regional high schools be established that would be devoted to language and area studies. Illinois has four such schools. Atlanta's North Fulton High School Center for International Studies is a magnet school composed of equal numbers of black and white students. Like other similar schools it concentrates on the functional attainment of a second language as well as specialization in the culture and area studies of the region where that language is used. North Fulton offers instruction in Arabic, Spanish, and French. Some of the other similar schools also require mastery of a third language.[24]

Louisiana is perhaps the most advanced state in promoting second language learning. This is largely due to the commitment to French and English learning by the state's French-speaking minority, the Acadians or Cajuns. The state legislature set up the Council for the Development of French in Louisiana (CODOFIL) in 1968, which has arranged for the importation of several hundred French teachers from Québec,

Switzerland, France, and Belgium. Spanish and German are also taught in public schools. A new law requires that instruction in a second language be provided for all academically able fourth-, fifth-, and sixth-graders.[25]

The programs described in this chapter are full of life. They create stimulating multicultural atmospheres in which learning takes place. While not immune to the negative influences described in earlier chapters, these programs represent some of the best efforts of our educational systems. Instructional goals are bound up with integration goals. Language learning is tied to content learning and cultural understanding. English, Spanish, and other languages are put forward on the basis of equality, not the superiority of one and the inferiority of the other. These programs point the way to what could be accomplished if energies and resources were channeled in these directions.

The bilingual program experience presented in the last few chapters indicates that some school districts have achieved a qualitative change, at least in some schools, from assimilationist to pluralist. Many other districts have made some moves in this direction, but are still mired in assimilationism. Concerned parents and/or educators are the motive force behind creative programs; these programs do not arise spontaneously. Usually these programs exist only in one or a small number of schools within a district, and do not represent district policy. Bilingual advocates would be well-advised to try to transform district policy in the direction of the philosophy underlying these creative programs. Critics of bilingual education would be well-advised to examine these programs carefully.

9

The Reagan Years

As governor of California Ronald Reagan signed the state's first bilingual bill into law. As president he denounced the program in 1981 and then supported it in 1983 and 1984. He appointed Terrel Bell to be his Education Secretary. As Commissioner of Education in the Ford administration, Bell had issued the Lau Remedies and had been a steadfast bilingual supporter. Under Reagan he scrapped the Lau Regulations and returned to the standard of the May 25 Memorandum, which his Lau Remedies had been designed to replace in 1975. At other times he spoke highly of bilingual education. These ambiguous policies came to characterize the Reagan administration as they had those of his predecessors. Other developments on the bilingual front also occurred during the Reagan years.

THE OPPOSITION

The bitterness that resulted from the Lau Regulations controversy seemed to embolden the opposition. While the opposition comprises various strands of opinion, some common themes emerge:

1. The program is divisive, it threatens the national unity that is reflected in a common core of public school values.
2. It encourages separatism and segregates students.
3. It encourages the continuance of an ethnic subgroup by slowing down their ability to learn English, absorb mainstream culture, and

blend into society. It impedes the acculturative process that earlier immigrants underwent.

4. It is a federal intrusion into state and local prerogatives.
5. Language and ethnicity belong in the home, the church, and the private school, not in the public school.

Besides the AFT leadership, other critics and opponents include the American Legion, U.S. English, and individual journalists, educators, and scholars. Their viewpoints are sometimes buttressed by editorials in major newspapers and magazines that criticize aspects of the program rather than the program as a whole. Most of the national education organizations favor the continuance of the program, but resist increased federal regulation of it. Columnists like Tom Bethell and Neal Pearce and scholars like Abigail Thernstrom and Nathan Glazer have been sharply critical.[1] Glazer mourns the weakening of the assimilationist ethic. He holds bilingual education partially accountable for this development:

> Assimilation has already proceeded so far with some groups, specifically with European ethnic groups, that it is not an unreasonable hope . . . there is no reason why it cannot still be held up as an idea. Instead it has been driven from the field of discussion of ethnic issues. The "melting pot" is now attacked not only on the empirical ground that it really did not melt that much or that fast, but on the normative ground that it should not have been allowed to do so. . . . Americanization becomes a dirty word, and bilingualism and biculturalism receive government support. . . . I doubt that this is wise.[2]

U.S. English is the only national group specifically established to oppose government-sponsored bilingualism. A spokesperson, former U.S. Senator S. I. Hayakawa, testified in a Congressional hearing on bilingual education that

> All of this rigamarole was unnecessary during the great wave of European immigration that hit this country between 1870 and 1930 when millions and millions and millions came over and no one showed a bit of concern for them. They said, "Well these foreigners better hurry up and learn English" and they did hurry up and learn English.[3]

The organization helped promote a successful California referendum that removed the bilingual ballot. It also backed the unsuccessful English Language Amendment that would have amended the U.S. Constitution to declare that English is the country's official language. The Constitution makes no mention of an official language. Bilingual education was not specifically forbidden by the amendment. However, anti-foreign-language sentiment may surface during debate over this amendment and rebound against bilingual education.

Aspects of this anti-foreign-language sentiment have already arisen as part of the debate over national and local English Language Amendments. U.S. English and the American Legion have been actively organizing this sentiment across the country. The issue strikes a responsive chord among some people. It seems particularly intense among some earlier immigrants who suffered for their lack of English proficiency when they arrived. Instead of urging reforms to make the transition smoother, they urge a return to the old days. A letter exemplifying this sentiment was reprinted in the *Congressional Record*. The writer, an immigrant from Italy in 1946, states that "I cried many times because I felt inadequate. . . . Do I sound resentful because I did not have it easy? Maybe to a degree I am but I also feel the better for it."[4]

Opponents seek to substitute English-only instruction for bilingual programs. A few want to return to submersion, others propose ESL, and still others believe that a program known as structured immersion would be best. This latter method places LEP students in an English-only learning environment and teaches them English and the content subjects simultaneously. Those who support this program trace its lineage to the Canadian immersion programs; but the Canadian immersion educators deny any connection. They say that Canadian programs are designed to teach minority languages to majority students. Immersion for language minorities is seen as harmful and subtractive. Wallace Lambert, a leading Canadian immersion educator, states that for language minorities, "Their personal identities, their early conceptual development, their chances of competing or succeeding in schools or their interest in trying to succeed would all be hampered by an immersion-in-English program."[5] Some advocates of bilingualism say that immersion for language minorities is only warmed-over submersion. Others contend that it may have some value for those LEP children who can read and write in their native language because they have the confidence to immerse themselves in the second language without losing the first. These children may be graduates of bilingual programs or immigrants who spent several years in school abroad learning to read and write before moving to the United States.[6]

Bubbling just below the surface of this debate is the question of control. Many opponents of bilingualism resent the fact that Hispanics or other language minorities control many of the bilingual programs. Bilingual advocates often favor this control because it provides Hispanics with a long-overdue role in educational decision-making, or because it provides jobs to both language minorities and empathetic Anglos, or because bilingual Hispanics may be seen as being in the best position to plan the language instruction of language minority children. The issue is usually couched in code words and rarely comes up directly.

TEACHER POLITICS

The pro-bilingual stance of the NEA contrasts with the anti-bilingual stance of the AFT. The two teacher unions have been competing for decades. The NEA broke its historic nonpartisanship by supporting the election of Jimmy Carter in 1976. Their major reward was the creation of the U.S. Department of Education. The AFT endorsed Reagan's opponents in 1980 and 1984, but unlike the NEA, it has supported him on many issues. One of these issues has been merit pay for teachers. Reagan appointed an AFT official to be staff director of the U.S. Commission on Civil Rights.

The NEA has 1.5 million members in school districts nationwide. The AFT has 500,000 members clustered in metropolitan areas. In some areas like Los Angeles, locals of the two organizations have merged and jointly represent teachers. Nationally the two teachers' unions are locked in combat for the hearts, minds, and dues money of U.S. teachers; bilingual issues are one of the major areas of contention between them.[7]

Another teacher struggle has been between ESL teachers and bilingual teachers. ESL was the basic program for LEP students before the advent of the Bilingual Education Act in many areas. Local chapters of the two national organizations have skirmished over staffing patterns, certification requirements, and seniority rights. Some ESL activists regretted their diminished role. Some bilingual activists believed that ESL teachers were promoting Anglo conformity rather than transmitting knowledge and skills to language minority students. Most of NABE's officers have been Hispanics, most of TESOL's have been Anglos. The power to control or influence the program was the political theme of the confrontation: ". . . the strife and acrimony . . . has its origins not in disagreements over methodology, but rather in the vested interests of the two groups, most clearly seen in the struggle for access to jobs and rewards."[8]

ORGANIZATIONAL UNITY

TESOL and NABE national leaders got together in the 1970s and declared peace. They did not merge their organizations, but agreed to work in concert. Both agreed that bilingual programs must contain an ESL component in order to fully instruct LEP students.[9] The two organizations joined with national groups of language educators and linguists to form the Joint National Committee for Languages that leads the fight for government support for the expansion of language learning. The Joint Committee supports bilingual programs for LEPs and for native English speakers. It has tried to unify legislative initiatives dealing with languages, instead of the each-man-for-himself pattern that currently prevails.[10] This pattern includes the following laws and proposed laws:

1. The Bilingual Education Act.
2. The Higher Education Act provisions that fund university language programs.
3. Various international programs administered by the departments of State, Education, and Defense that subsidize language and area studies programs for adults.
4. Chapter 1 (formerly Title I) programs which support ESL and bilingual instruction for low-income students.
5. The Education for Economic Security Act which mainly supports math and science instruction, but also funds foreign language learning.
6. The proposed American Defense Education Act which would fund foreign language learning amid a welter of educational programs.
7. The proposed Foreign Language Assistance for National Security Act, the brainchild of Senator Paul Simon of Illinois, would substantially upgrade foreign language instruction and teacher training.

Some of these measures overlap or move in contradictory directions. For example, the Higher Education Act promotes foreign language learning in universities, while subtractive bilingual or ESL programs pressure language minority students to discard their native languages. This situation parallels the federal policy on cigarettes. The surgeon general warns people not to smoke while the Agriculture Department is subsidizing the tobacco growers. The Joint Committee aims to overcome these discordant thrusts as well as the pigeonholing mentality that places each language program into its own airtight box. While there is some opposition to equating bilingual education with foreign-language learning among some members of constituent groups, the Joint National Committee's clarity and commitment may eventually obtain a unified language law that serves its various constituents while it serves the nation as a whole.

THE REAGAN ADMINISTRATION'S INITIAL RESPONSE

In the first three years of the Reagan administration, bilingual education was on the skids. The president spoke against the program and his administration reduced its funding by about 20 percent, reverting to the May 25 Memorandum of 1970 in civil rights enforcement. It tried to place bilingual funding in a block grant of unspecified funds that would have been sent to the states. This would have eviscerated the program. Congress opposed it and it was dropped. The administration supported a bill to transform the program from a native language instructional effort to an English-only program. Congress killed this too.[11]

The low point in relations between the administration and the bilingual community occurred in 1982 when Secretary Bell sent his auditors into Texas. The auditors found that six districts had not produced the desired educational results with their bilingual program and ordered them to repay more than one million dollars in federal bilingual funds. Congressional leaders were outraged. House Education and Labor Committee Chairman Carl Perkins of Kentucky demanded that Department of Education officials appear before his committee. There he berated them for singling out bilingual education, challenged the criteria used by the auditors who had no background in education, and demanded that they rescind the repayment order. Shortly thereafter, Bell complied. He reduced his demand to the token level of $40,000 and exempted several of the districts. Two years later, several districts had paid nothing and another had paid $9,000. House Government Affairs Committee Chairman Jack Brooks of Texas ordered the U.S. Government Accounting Office (GAO) to investigate the matter. The GAO refuted the department's claim for even this token amount. Once again powerful congressional representatives had rescued bilingual education from hostile administration officials.[12]

THE 1984 REAUTHORIZATION AND
SHIFTING REPUBLICAN POLITICS

In 1983, no one believed that NABE had a chance to get a pro-bilingual reauthorization of the Bilingual Education Act through Congress. The last reauthorization was due to expire in 1984. The administration was still trying to transform the program into an English-only program. Democratic congressmen Dale Kildee of Flint, Michigan, and Baltasar Corrada of San Juan, Puerto Rico, encouraged NABE and the National Council of La Raza to draft a new bill. They drafted a measure that both strengthened and expanded the Bilingual Education Act. The congressmen introduced the bill in March 1984 and got it enacted just seven months later. Its success depended on skillful maneuvering through treacherous terrain. Favorable responses by Republicans on three separate occasions secured the victory.

The first came from the White House. Reagan, Vice-President Bush, and Secretary Bell made several forays to the Sunbelt in late 1983 and early 1984 and proclaimed that bilingual education was a winner and should be preserved. Could this be coming from the same president who earlier stated that it was "absolutely wrong and against American concepts to have a bilingual education program that is now openly admittedly dedicated to preserving native language and never getting adequate in English"?[13] It was the kickoff of the 1984 reelection campaign, and as a Washington *Post* headline had put it earlier, AS THE HISPANIC VOTE EMERGES, REPUBLICANS SEEK TO CHRISTEN IT.[14] This was the tried and true method of electioneering – promising the voters what they wanted.

The second favorable Republican response came from an unlikely group, conservative Republican congressmen. Reps. Steve Bartlett of Dallas and John McCain of Phoenix joined with Kildee and Corrada to push the bill through Congress. These newly elected Education and Labor Committee members exacted a high price; an historic breach was made in the Bilingual Education Act. The new reauthorization permitted 4 to 10 percent of the funds to be spent on programs that did not need to use the native language. Known as Special Alternative Instruction, the new provision required special programs for LEPs that included specially designed curricula and instructional materials. Submersion was unacceptable. Preference would be given to those districts that could not serve all or some of their LEP students within bilingual programs. Districts could use this program, for instance, to instruct those students for whom no bilingual teachers were available.[15]

Bartlett became aware of the inadequacies of the submersion method during his own schooling in Lockhart, Texas. Many of his Spanish-speaking peers had dropped out or performed poorly because they were unable to attain English proficiency. He favored unleashing the creativity of local districts to design programs that met their needs, but he also wanted to ensure that there would be no backward steps to the old days of submersion.[16] Politically this compromise partially defused those who argued that the act was too prescriptive because it mandated only bilingual methods among the many that were available.

Finally, the third Republican response came again from the White House. In spite of Office of Management and Budget opposition, Reagan signed the omnibus-education bill that included bilingual education just two weeks before the election. The bilingual measure contained several new provisions besides the Special Alternative Instruction section mentioned above:

1. Preschool, family literacy, developmental, academic excellence, and gifted and talented programs.
2. The requirement that OBEMLA and state and local school systems conduct accurate counts of LEP students.
3. The mandate that programs had to meet students' promotional and graduation requirements.
4. The option to permit up to 50 percent native English speakers to participate in the developmental program.
5. A restructuring of the national bilingual network, the advisory council, and the university fellowship program.
6. A requirement that the first six months of grant-funded programs be devoted to preservice activity. This is to avoid school districts' having to operationalize programs within days of discovering that they had won a grant.[17]

THE UNDERLYING FEAR OF FOREIGNERS

In spite of the fact that bilingual education was designed in 1968 mainly for non-English-speaking U.S. citizens, many people equate the program with foreigners, especially with the undocumented (also called illegal aliens). Immigration issues have become bound up with bilingual education issues in the public mind. The national debate over the Simpson-Mazzoli immigration bill inevitably affects bilingual education, even though the bill has little to do with education.[18] Its main purpose is to stem the flow of the undocumented.

Some of the anxiety over this issue grew out of Texas' effort to bar the children of the undocumented from the schoolhouse, or to charge them tuition. Hispanic legal defense groups and others successfully challenged this Texas law and made it possible for all children to attend U.S. public schools regardless of citizenship status. Certain educational and political interests feared that Latins would soon become the dominant element in certain school districts and threaten the control of vested interests.[19]

To compensate school districts for the added expense of educating immigrants, Texas congressmen, led by House Majority Leader Jim Wright of Dallas, pushed through an immigrant education law that provides money to districts that have at least 3 percent immigrants among their school population. The Reagan administration did not openly oppose this bill. Neither did they openly oppose Simpson-Mazzoli. The White House began to waiver as the Simpson-Mazzoli bill debate intensified. Reagan later let it be known that he was leaning against it, based on the cost factor involved in the provision that would grant amnesty to some of the undocumented. He was probably swayed more by Hispanic fear that the employer sanction provision would lead to the indiscriminate harassment of Hispanics whether they were in the United States legally or not. The election was only weeks away and the Latin vote was a major factor in such large states as California, Texas, Florida, and New York. Reagan's lack of support for Simpson-Mazzoli helped lead to its demise in 1984, but similar immigration restriction legislation may eventually become enacted.

OBEMLA'S FUTURE AND HISPANIC CLOUT

Late in 1984, a Department of Education task force led by Undersecretary Gary Jones examined the options for departmental reorganization. One suggestion was to merge OBEMLA into another departmental office. This would have diminished bilingual education's autonomy. The task force considered the possible repercussions and decided against the merger because "pursuing this strategy now would undermine the President's attempts to reassure the Hispanic community and jeopardize legislative reform proposals already before Congress."[20]

Political considerations dominated Reagan administration actions just as they did those of his predecessors. Congress has been the program's steadfast supporter. The Senate took the lead in the original Bilingual Education Act and in the 1970s reauthorizations; the House initiated and sustained the movement that resulted in the 1984 reauthorization. Both chambers of Congress have shielded the program and expanded it when they could. Hispanic electoral clout accounts for part of this phenomenon. There are only 11 Hispanic congressmen out of 435 altogether, but 80 to 100 other districts have significant numbers of actual or potential Hispanic voters. But beyond this, many congressmen realize that bilingual education is the only national program in which Hispanics have a major or decisive role. If the program were to be scrapped, the Hispanic community might revert to the status of semi-invisibility it maintained before the War on Poverty. This Hispanic role involves *both* the Hispanic students who participate in the program and the Hispanic educational personnel who conduct it. Congressmen know about the politics of providing programs to ethnic groups. They also know that until something better comes along, bilingual education is the best hope that many Hispanics have going for them.

10

The Struggle for Control of the Department of Education

What was extraordinary about Secretary Bell's achievement is that one did not have the sense day by day, that he was caught in the middle of irreconcilable differences.[1]

Former Health, Education and Welfare Secretary
Eliot Richardson, 1984

These irreconcilable differences between left and right are acted out in scores of different ways. The political drama is often intense and confrontational, and it inevitably sucks in bilingual education. Bilingual education needs a favorable climate in Congress and the administration in order to function smoothly. When a liberal Congress battles a conservative administration, some OBEMLA staffers recede to the sidelines, huddle together, and pray for personal and programmatic survival. The issuance of program regulations, the letting of contracts, the obligation of grant funds, and even the dissemination of important information are delayed or put on hold for an extended period. This occurred during part of the first year of Reagan's second term, when the fight for control of the Department of Education was particularly bitter. Liberals and moderates in Congress, the education establishment, the media, and the administration itself confronted conservatives in and out of government over the policy direction that would control the department.

THE BACKDROP

The department arose in 1979 in an atmosphere of contention. Jimmy Carter had exchanged a promise to create a separate department for the NEA's endorsement in the 1976 election. The AFT wanted education functions to stay within the Department of Health, Education and Welfare – partly because they had close ties to the Health, Education and Welfare bureaucracy and leadership and partly because anything the NEA is for, the AFT is against.

Organizations representing education professionals were split; some favored the creation of a new department to give education more prominence at the national level as well as more funding. Others feared that a new department would bring on more regulations and more federal intrusion into heretofore local and state prerogatives. Conservative groups were even more fearful of federal intervention into local education. They were afraid that Uncle Sam would end up dictating the curriculum in local schoolhouses.

THE POLITICS OF LOCALISM

A strongly held localism has pervaded education ever since the founding of the republic. School districts in the older states usually follow township or borough boundaries. The country's 16,000 school districts (over 100,000 at the end of the nineteenth century) grew from an agrarian economy in which you knew only your immediate neighbors and had a healthy distrust for county, state, or federal school officials. This localism parallels our presidential voting system, which evolved from the same set of circumstances. In our electoral system we actually vote for local electors whom we are supposed to know personally, rather than for some distant politician. Our elector then casts his vote in the electoral college.

State constitutions call for establishing school systems; the U.S. Constitution does not mention education. State systems control the local districts within the state to some degree, even though most state systems are feeble. Hawaii has one statewide district. All the other states are divided into local school districts by counties or by two or more districts within counties. Los Angeles County has more than 85 districts. The state of Texas has 1,100. Some states have separate districts for high school and others for elementary schools. The duplication and waste are enormous. Some states allow wealthy enclaves to split off from poorer surrounding school districts. Weak and understaffed state education agencies typically busy themselves in issuing procedural regulations. Many expend a great deal of energy trying to decide, for example, whether local districts need to have 180 or 185 days of school annually in order to qualify for state aid. Few state agencies provide pedagogical or political leadership. Few go to the public to argue for the importance of education. When they are criticized about poor quality teachers, low test scores, fluffy course requirements, or other matters they retrench. They may re-emerge with a new competency test or merit pay for teachers, but little substantial change seems to occur.

The federal role in education has been debated for over a century. Just after the Civil War a federal department of education was created and later downgraded to an office in the Department of the Interior.[2]There it remained until President Eisenhower created the Department of Health, Education and Welfare in the 1950s. This move gave education more exposure, especially in the wake of the Soviet launch of the Sputnik satellite, when soul-searching went on in the U.S. about our deficient educational system. But the increase in exposure did not lead to an increase in prestige. Administration leaders and many others viewed the Office of Education as little more than a collection of unenlightened paper-pushers.[3] Public opinion has only recently begun to swing toward a view that education is an asset and an investment in the present and the future in spite of the low esteem in which the public holds federal education bureaucrats or federal bureaucrats as a whole.

Despite the greater interest in education, the antipathy to federal control continues. Congressional or administration attempts to create national curriculum models or national educational standards or national anything always run afoul of entrenched localism. Congress could only carve out a role that related to aiding the underserved, including the non-English-speaking, rather than a role that relates to educating the whole student population. Districts will seek or accept federal aid for a variety of purposes, but they will resist federal regulations as cumbersome and intrusive.

THE CURRENT BATTLEFIELD

When Reagan assumed power, rightists presumed that they would be given effective control of the department, which presidential counselor

Edwin Meese had labeled a "ridiculous bureaucratic joke."[4] If they could not get control of the departments of State or Health and Human Services, they could at least control the destiny of this minor outfit with little budget or staff and either have it dismantled or use it for conservative politics. But they were initially frustrated by the president's appointment of Terrel Bell as secretary. He was an old-line establishment figure. Bell had been Ford's commissioner of education and Utah's state school superintendent. He wanted to preserve the department and most of the Great Society programs. He agreed to funding reductions at first, but was able to partially restore the budget in later years. He gave lip service to dismantling the department and to promoting the Conservative Agenda. This agenda included:

1. Promoting tuition tax credits, vouchers, and other pro-private school measures.
2. Removing or weakening most regulations.
3. Placing most categorical programs into state block grants that are not specified as to which programs they must be used for.
4. Encouraging school prayer, discipline, and family values as against what are seen as liberal values (often referred to as *secular humanism*).[5]

Bell was first and foremost a consummate politician. He knew how to walk the line between conservative and moderate politics. He devoted most of his energies to the Excellence Agenda, which was designed to build a culture of high-quality and high-technology learning in the schools. He replaced the Carter administration emphasis on equity and civil rights with an emphasis on rigor and excellence. Never mind, he seemed to say, about the poor and the minorities that needed more help before they could develop their intellectual capacities to the fullest.

Congress, with liberals and moderates in most of the key education roles, defeated the attempts to dismantle the department as well as most of the Conservative Agenda. It simply refused to legislate the agenda and forced the administration to decelerate its deregulation binge. Bell, like the good soldier, in 1981 and 1982 took the administration's political baggage up to Capitol Hill and argued for it. But there was no fire; his heart was clearly not in it.

He did, however, make gestures. He dispatched auditors to Texas and demanded that six districts pay back their Title VII funds. After being chastised in Congress, he gave it up and seemed to settle down to other tasks. Two years later he was back in Texas, only this time he was praising bilingual education. He spoke at Pan American University and posed for pictures with university President Miguel Narvaez and Congressman Kika de la Garza while he presented a $349,000 OBEMLA grant to the university. He told the TESOL convention that language minorities were growing rapidly and that bilingual education was a major way to educate them. Conservatives began to criticize him as a "caretaker . . . the instrument of professional educators"[6] or as an outright obstacle to the achievement of their goals.

Bell dismissed conservative ideologues like Larry Uzzell, but kept others on like Gary Bauer. He froze out most of those who disagreed with his methods and went about his business in a quiet, methodical way. In reality he was carrying out a "constant behind-the-scenes battle to prevent right wing ideologues from shaping education policies."[7]

An important conservative inroad was made by Gary Jones and Gary Bauer, as high officials just below Bell. Jones came from the American Enterprise Institute and Bauer from the Republican National Committee and the White House. Bauer's self-defined mission was characterized by the New York *Times* as "Reading, Writing and Roping Liberals."[8] The two men often argued between themselves, but were able to inject some minor elements of the Conservative Agenda into the department, although they never could get Bell to do their bidding.

The Arrival of William Bennett

Conservatives became hopeful again when Bell resigned in late 1984. The search for a successor narrowed to William Bennett of the National Endowment for the Humanities and John Silber of Boston University. Both had to be inspected by a coalition of conservative organizations. This was something new and it disturbed some liberal and conservative educators. It seemed to suggest that a certain ideological cast or mentality was necessary for nomination. Bennett prevailed and elevated Bauer to his nominee for undersecretary while excluding Jones. Conservatives argued for an Office of Educational Philosophy and Practice that would unofficially promote the Conservative Agenda. Bennett agreed and staffed the new think tank with scholars and ideologues led by Larry Uzzell, now of Learn, Inc., and Elaine Gardner of the Heritage Foundation. Both wanted to dismantle the department and weaken the advocacy network that supported the federal education programs.

Gardner antagonized the special education organizations in a 1983 draft of an article in which she stated that the handicapped "falsely assume that the lottery of life has penalized them at random. This is not so. Nothing comes to an individual that he has not, at some point in his development, summoned."[9] She further contended that "there is no injustice in the universe. As unfair as that may seem, a person's external circumstances do fit his level of inner spiritual development. Those of the handicapped constituency who seek to have others bear their burdens and eliminate their challenges are seeking to avoid the central issues of their lives."[10] She also criticized the special education program for having too many and too strict regulations and the special education lobby for being too vociferous in seeking to advance its cause.

Senator Weicker Blindsides the Secretary

Senator Lowell Weicker (R.-Connecticut) would not countenance this type of argument. The father of a Down's syndrome child, he abhorred this kind of attack. He refused to reduce the budget on the backs of the poor and the weak. As the scion of a wealthy and well-connected Connecticut family who has been reelected by large margins in recent years, Weicker has had the political and financial wherewithal as well as the inclination to stand up to the administration on many occasions. He personally filibustered the school prayer amendment to death in the summer of 1984 and held up agreement on the 1986 Republican Senate Budget bill until the rest of the party agreed to a major increase in special education funds. As chairperson of the Senate Appropriations Subcommittee on the Departments of Labor, Health and Human Services and Education, Weicker, in collaboration with the liberal-moderate majority of both parties on the subcommittee, has been able to preserve most of the Great Society programs. Weicker sees his subcommittee as "the last bastion of moderate political philosophy in the Senate. It's a very difficult forum in which to practice Reagonomics."[11] He accused the Reagan administration of "trying to beat up on the frailest elements of our society. . . . I'm not in a budget-cutting exercise here."[12] His particular adversary has been David Stockman, director of the Office of Management and the Budget. Weicker has refused to accept deep cuts in social security that were based on "whether David Stockman has to get x amount of dollars out of the Social Security Administration so he can give it to the Defense Department."[13] Weicker also said, "I think education, health, the handicapped and mentally retarded are important and I've prevailed rather well. . . . The almighty God of this administration is how to save a buck and we aren't going to save any bucks at the expense of the mentally retarded and handicapped. Not when I'm the guy that receives their budgets."[14]

When Bennett entered Weicker's hearing chambers he was undoubtedly prepared to defend his views on the need to reduce the student loan program, but he was not prepared for Weicker's onslaught. Weicker berated him for hiring Gardner and Uzzell, while reading damning quotes from their writings. He decried the creation of an Office of Education Philosophy at the same time the department was scaling down federal education programs. He claimed to be completely mystified as to how advocates of dismantling the department could be on its payroll.[15]

Bennett, caught off guard, could only make a gesture of defending his actions. He stated that Gardner and Uzzell would not be in charge of departmental programs, only of research on issues like parental choice in education, discipline, and tuition tax credits. He contended that Gardner's views were unknown to him, were put forth before she entered the department, and that they flowed from her theological beliefs, which should not be questioned by the senator. Gary Bauer accompanied Bennett and tried to assure Weicker that he and Bennett often talked about the needs of the handicapped.

Weicker would have none of it. He kept pressing his advantage. Bennett's head drooped closer and closer to the table. Weicker demanded that Bennett produce Uzzell and Gardner for the next day's hearing. He belittled the notion that Gardner's views were theological. His criticisms of the department, and at least indirectly of Bennett, were echoed by other subcommittee members: Republicans Mark Andrews of North Dakota and Arlen Spector of Pennsylvania, and Democrats Lawton Chiles of Florida, William Proxmire of Wisconsin, and Daniel Inouye of Hawaii. Each criticized aspects of Bennett's budget proposals; no one was happy with his performance or his future plans. As a prominent conservative commented, "Bennett walked into a congressional ambush. . . . As sometimes happens when you are ambushed, he ran."[16]

Gardner and Uzzell testified the next day. Uzzell began by celebrating the fact that Yale, his own and Weicker's alma mater, was enlightened enough not to have a college of education. He continued in this vein, blasting the education establishment. Weicker shoved his rhetoric back at him and wondered aloud how Congress would be justified in paying over

$50,000 a year to such an enemy of education. Weicker had to maneuver through Uzzell's defenses for over ten minutes before he got Uzzell to admit that he still favored eliminating the department. Gardner also tried to sidestep the questions. She was no paragon of ideological purity. When pinned down, she did admit to believing in higher and lower forms of human life, but passed this view off to her religious convictions.

Weicker began his questioning of her by stating that he had just received a call from Sarah Brady, wife of presidential press secretary James Brady, who had been severely wounded and left permanently disabled in the 1981 attempt on the president's life. Sarah Brady, according to Weicker, was outraged at Gardner's remarks. The room became hushed, Weicker had won the day with a masterful display of political theatre. He had disarmed Uzzell and Gardner and put them on the defensive.

Bennett wrote Weicker, distancing himself from his two aides, claiming he did not know of Gardner's views on the handicapped, which he now called "insensitive and repugnant."[17] He asked for their resignations, and soon received them. His press spokesman, Thomas Moore, wanted Bennett to take the offensive, to state that his aides were being persecuted because of their conservative views. Moore wanted Bennett to assume the aggressive posture that "we could not afford to establish the precedent that Reagan appointees must assent to liberal orthodoxy in order to hold office."[18] Neither Bennett nor his chief of staff would even meet with Moore. They later passed the message that they wanted Moore's resignation and he soon complied.

Bennett began to clean house. He got rid of some conservative hangovers from earlier years, several of whom were ardent foes of bilingual education. He dismissed the National Advisory Council on Bilingual Education that contained several members who had vigorously attacked the program. The council had just issued a report blasting the program and recommending a reduction in funding.[19]

Eileen Gardner later complained that Bennett did know what her views were. She felt that she was pressured to resign by department officials who feared that Congress would retaliate by holding up the nomination of Gary Bauer to be departmental undersecretary. She contended that

> Bennett had just been through a major blow-up over his statements on student financial aid, he is brand new in his job and here was another controversy and I think he just felt he couldn't withstand it. . . . If he capitulated as soon as

he did, I would think that he would send a signal to those who oppose any changes in the department that they can bully him from here on out.[20]

The Fallout

Bennett's troubles had just begun – the media would soon join the fray. The Washington *Post*, the New York *Times* and several commentators took Weicker's side; the *Wall Street Journal* and the Washington *Times* took Gardner's and Uzzell's. The *Post* went after Bennett's plan to set up an Office of Education Philosophy and Practice, calling it a "pretentious boondoggle"[21] that would be used for "cheerleading, speech writing and time serving."[22] The *Wall Street Journal* focused on several aspects of the fracas. First, Gardner was thought to be under liberal attack because she was a black conservative: "Inside the Beltway, all blacks are required to believe that the answer to the problems of the disadvantaged is a big federal government. When a black like Ms. Gardner runs around preaching self-help, the whole immune system reacts to destroy this heresy."[23] Second, liberals were supposedly out to get Bennett and ultimately Reagan and they had tried to trash Bennett in the same way they had tried to beat down other Reagan appointees. Third, the White House had recently been unwilling to defend its own officials when they were under attack: "When there are rumors of resignation, someone near or at the top should have the brains and nerve to call and say 'Don't you dare.' "[24]

Columnist Haynes Johnson lambasted the Reaganites for appointing Gardner. Like other liberals and moderates in Congress and the media, Johnson portrayed the appointment as a microcosm of Reagan's second-term policies. He stated that the appointment represented "intellectual zealotry" and that the administration had allowed "its ideological impulses to run amok."[25] It was part of a throwback to social Darwinism, which Johnson characterized as

> The discredited cast of mind that permitted the robber barons to celebrate the crushing of the little people by claiming it was all the workings of God's immutable laws. In that reasoning you measure success by the survival of the fittest. What counts is strength and power. Sink or swim. If you fail it's your fault.[26]

Bennett had alienated himself from most members of Congress and leading media decision-makers on this issue as well as on student loans and other matters. He had remarked that students spent their loan money on cars, stereos, and trips to the beach. He later told parents who were having tough times financing the education of several children in college that they should have practiced family planning. He stated that good school systems have no trouble attracting good teachers. He promoted better history teaching in the schools on the premise that better instruction would lead students to see the correctness of the administration's policy in Central America. He said that high schools should create two tracks, one for college-bound youngsters and the other for the non-college bound. He proposed this as if it were a new idea. He was apparently oblivious to the widespread existence of tracking in many areas and to the struggle of many parents and community groups to remove it.[27]

Republican and Democratic members of Congress concerned with education matters were distressed at his performance. Senator Robert Stafford of Vermont, the second-ranking Republican on the Labor and Human Resources Committee and a subcommittee chairman, commented, "He's managed to alienate in one way or another most of the education constituencies."[28] Democratic Representative Augustus Hawkins of California, chairperson of the House Education and Labor Committee, commented, "I've seen Republicans on the Education Committee not being willing to defend him in his appearance before the committee. This is almost unheard of."[29] Representative Silvio Conte of Massachusetts, the ranking Republican on the House Appropriations Committee, told Bennett that he "seemed to be trying to see how many days in a row he could make the front page of the New York *Times* or the Washington *Post*"[30] and that "you will reap what you sow."[31]

At the same time conservatives were starting to lose patience with Bennett's compromises with the liberals. George Roche, a college president who chaired the National Council on Education Research, resigned in May 1985 in anger over the lack of departmental support. Roche had several times attacked bilingual education and had used his position to try to inject conservative politics into the department. After being stymied by Secretary Bell and Congress in 1984, Roche sought Bennett's help in freeing the council to carry out what it saw as its political mandate; they got the opposite. Bennett ordered the council not to meet until further notice. Bennett's chief of staff said that the order was a tactic to avoid controversy that might hamper the Senate confirmation of Gary Bauer and other departmental nominees. Roche left his post with a blast at the department for "showing contempt" for the idea that local school personnel and parents have the best idea of how to educate their children.[32]

More ominously, Burton Pines, Heritage Foundation vice-president, and Paul Weyrich, president of the Free Congress Research and Education Foundation and an architect of the Conservative Social Agenda, raised serious doubts about Bennett's commitment to the triumph of conservative politics. Pines and Weyrich had hoped that Bennett would be the leader of a cultural conservatism in the administration: "He was one of the few heroes in a government devoid of heroes."[33] They denounced his decision to accede to Weicker. They had urged him to mobilize conservatives nationwide to protect his appointments and the administration in general. They contended that by seeking peace with the liberals, Bennett had emboldened the liberal will to defeat him. The "Washington lynch mob" attack not only weakened Bennett and the department, but it put the confirmation of Gary Bauer in jeopardy, they claimed. Bennett, they stated, must rebound from his defeat and devise a strategy of victory.

> To succeed, however, he must learn to play politics Washington-style. He must understand that the fight against Mr. Uzzell and Ms. Gardner was not about them but about him and his plans to reorder the federal education agenda. He must staff his inner circle with those who understand the nature of the battle and can craft a counteroffensive aimed not simply at survival but at victory.[34]

THE LARGER POLITICAL STRUGGLE: A STERILE DEBATE

These skirmishes reveal a bitter struggle between liberals and conservatives over the future of the department. Conservatives believe that liberal mentality as embodied in most federal education programs must go before any progress in education can be achieved. Liberals believe that conservative ideologues must not be permitted to tamper with the Great Society programs. They feel that it is necessary to slap down moves to insert conservative politics into the day-to-day workings of the department.

The sterility of the debate is shown in its lack of effects on education nationwide. Education is in a crisis, and the country suffers from a terribly weak knowledge and skills infrastructure, the language aspect of which has been delineated elsewhere. Confronting a complex and challenging world without a well-educated populace dooms the United States to an eventual position of political, economic, and military inferiority. Conservatives at their best can raise provocative questions and the liberals at best can conserve and improve important programs. But neither has an agenda to mobilize public opinion and resources to overcome what Bell's Commission on Excellence in Education called "a rising tide of mediocrity." Partisans may lurch left and right, but the problems are nowhere addressed.

11

The Latin Presence and Opportunity Structure

During the six year period from 1976 to 1982, the number of language minority children increased by 27 percent, while the number of all other school-age youngsters declined by 13 percent. If the same trends would continue to operate for the next six years, nearly a quarter of all school-age children will be language minority in 1990.[1]

Secretary of Education Terrel Bell, 1984

We still maintain and speak Spanish despite the second and third generation youths. No other cultures preserve that here. It's a sore point because they say we want to be different. To this I say, "Vive la difference."[2]

Puerto Rican women in New York City, 1980

The public has only recently become aware of the national presence of Latins in the United States. No longer are they a small minority group confined to the Southwest and New York City; they make up a sizable and growing segment of the overall population and they are distributed more widely. Examining their demographic presence, social characteristics, and opportunity structure sets the stage for understanding bilingual education in the 1980s.

THE VOCATIONAL CONDITION

Hispanics continue to occupy the bottom sectors of the vocational hierarchies. The National Commission for Employment Policy issued a

1982 report entitled *Hispanics and Jobs: Barriers to Progress*. The commission is federally supported and consists of cabinet secretaries, other government officials, and economists. The report concluded that many Hispanics

> have problems finding good jobs and earning a decent income even in prosperous times. . . . For some, finding work is a severe problem. For others low pay is the major issue. Hispanics generally experience common barriers to labor market success: lack of proficiency in English, low levels of formal schooling and discrimination. . . . Hispanics fare almost as badly as blacks in the labor market judged by unemployment and wages. . . . [3]

Hispanic males are overwhelmingly blue-collar workers, 59 percent as opposed to 46 percent for non-Hispanic white males. Their median income in 1979 was $9,200, about $3,000 less than the median for non-Hispanic whites. Their unemployment rate is considerably higher. The only important exception is Cuban-Americans, an immigrant wave containing a very high percentage of people with professional or managerial backgrounds. Cuban-Americans comprise about 1 of every 20 Latins in the United States. Few other Latins come to school with the educational and financial advantages of the Cubans.[4]

The U.S. Commission on Civil Rights reported in 1982 that a third of all Hispanic males were overeducated for the jobs they held. This meant that they "were in jobs requiring substantially less education than they had attained." Forty-five percent of Latin males experienced intermittent employment, involuntary part-time work, marginal jobs, and inequitable pay. In all these categories, Latins had qualifications far above the average for non-Hispanic white males.[5]

This unpromising employment situation leads to a bleak outlook for young Hispanics about to enter the labor market. The overeducation phenomenon means that high school or college diplomas are no guarantee of acquiring better jobs. As both commissions cited in this chapter demonstrate, discrimination is still operative, even though it may be subtle. Young people often become aware of this lack of opportunity from parents or peers. Frequently school advancement is seen as a disincentive: "No matter how far I go I'll still end up in the same kind of dead-end job." Educators often respond that there is no absolute barrier to achieving a middle-class standard of success, plenty of Hispanics have done so. While this seems to be true in many individual cases, it does not offer a mass solution for the great majority of the hundreds of thousands of Hispanics who enter the labor market each year.

A DEVELOPING TWO-TIER ECONOMY

The high-technology future that looks good in some quarters poses serious questions about the prospects for language minorities. Eighty percent of New York City's new jobs require high school or college diplomas. Most Latins lack these credentials and will be forced to compete for the other 20 percent of the jobs. Traditional light and medium industrial jobs are disappearing in New York City as they are in most of the Frost Belt. Even Sunbelt industries are starting to shrink as competition with foreign producers intensifies. The Carolinas, for example, have lost a significant portion of their textile-producing capacity and California's electronics factories are providing fewer blue-collar opportunities.

The movement toward high technology stratifies the labor force.

> As the computers and robots take over more and more functions in the factory and office, a two-tier work force is developing. At the top will be a few executives, scientists and engineers, professionals and managers. . . . At the bottom will be low paid workers performing relatively simple, low-skilled, dull, routine high-turnover jobs. . . . If the nation continues losing its heavy industrial capacity as many as 6 million of the nation's jobless may become a permanent "labor surplus underclass."[6]

Torsten Husen, a Swedish comparative educator who has conducted many major studies of advanced industrial economies and their schools, arrived at similar conclusions. He contends that as these nations gear their schools to the production of technocrats to serve this stratified economy, school systems will increasingly become the domain of the elite. A new underclass will be formed from those who

> from the very beginning tend to be school failures. They also tend to (rephrasing Orwell) be less equal than the others, by coming from underprivileged homes. . . . Their parents often have lower levels of education and are suspicious of the school as an institution. Very early during the school careers, these children give up competing for success. . . . Those that are from the beginning (to quote Orwell correctly) "more equal than others" by virtue of coming from proper backgrounds with better-educated and more school-conscious parents, tend irrespective of the school system to have an advantage. A formally equal treatment in competitive milieu does not lead to a greater equality of outcome.[7]

Following this line of reasoning, it seems clear that neither bilingual education nor any purely educational program is likely to alter the

Hispanic opportunity structure by itself. Educational reform must be a part of expanded vocational opportunity that is accessible to language minorities before the equality of outcomes that Husen refers to could become closer to being a reality.[8]

The standardized test is the measure of academic and vocational success. As part of the minimum competency movement, more than 40 states have instituted standardized testing procedures to determine promotion, graduation, and/or placement in tracks or ability groups. The tests were first confined to senior high school students, but have been increasingly used for junior high and elementary school students. Minorities have usually done poorly on them. Initially this poor showing was attributed to genetic inheritance. Later it was felt that bias toward the culture of the middle-class majority skewed the test results. More recently, some educators have emphasized the quality of education, especially the learning of the skill of taking tests, as the major variable. Inner-city children rarely receive adequate instruction in test-taking.

Whichever explanation is chosen, the fact remains that these tests tend to certify Hispanics for failure. Most educators expect that they will not do well. When 18 Mexican-American students from a poor district of Los Angeles scored quite well on an advanced placement test in physics, the Educational Testing Service disallowed the scores and made them retake the test. The assumption seemed to be that so many students from a poor, minority school could not possibly do so well. The students took the test and passed again with the same range of high scores. They had an enlightened teacher who did not believe in low expectations. Hispanics must both master test-taking skills and overcome the doubts and low expectations of the educational establishment before they will be able to advance in school and compete for high-technology professional jobs.[9]

THE DEMOGRAPHICS

Latins are 7 percent of the U.S. population, according to the 1980 census. Many demographers believe that the census undercounted Hispanics and that the numbers in 1986 are close to 10 percent. Some consumer surveys estimate the Hispanic mass market at 12-14 percent of the population. Hispanics are a young and urbanized population, about seven years younger than the national average. The population is ethnically diverse. About 60 percent are of Mexican descent, about 10 percent mainland Puerto Ricans, about 5 percent Cuban, and the other quarter are Dominicans, Central Americans (principally Salvadorans and Guatemalans), and South Americans (mainly Colombians, Ecuadorians, and Peruvians).[10]

Settlement patterns vary. The southwestern Hispanic community is overwhelmingly Mexican with growing enclaves of Central Americans in Los Angeles, San Francisco, Houston, Tucson, and Phoenix. In most major southwestern cities Hispanics are the largest single ethnic group; in some, like San Antonio, they form a majority. In others they are the second largest group, and Anglos predominate.[11]

South Florida's Dade County is almost half Latin. Most of the Latins are Cubans, but 40 percent are a combination of other Latin groups. Cubans are still clustered primarily in Florida, although no longer exclusively in Dade County. Secondary areas of settlement include the New York and Chicago metropolitan areas.[12]

Puerto Ricans no longer live exclusively in the New York City area. Many live in northeastern cities and Chicago. Some middle-sized cities in New Jersey, Connecticut, and Massachusetts are heavily Puerto Rican. New York City's Hispanic community is about 50 percent Puerto Rican; the rest are Dominicans, Colombians, Cubans, and other Central and South Americans. Like Los Angeles, New York has more than 2 million Hispanics. Chicago's large Hispanic community has a majority of Mexicans, with significant numbers of Cubans, Puerto Ricans, Salvadorans, and Colombians. A number of cities that had small Hispanic communities 10 to 15 years ago now have much larger ones. These cities include Tampa, Seattle, Minneapolis-St. Paul, Charlotte, Providence, Wilmington (Delaware), Atlanta, Milwaukee, Detroit, Kansas City, Las Vegas, Cheyenne, New Orleans, Boston, Hartford, and Buffalo.

Some cities' housing patterns are characterized by all-Latin barrios or by mixed neighborhoods. Many larger cities have both kinds of neighborhoods. Many newly arrived Hispanics live in all-Hispanic neighborhoods or in neighborhoods that contain blacks or Asians as well as Hispanics. Many longer-term residents also live in all-Latin barrios, but many live among working-class or middle-class non-Hispanic whites as well. Chicago's example is instructive. About 45 percent of the Hispanic population in 1980 lived in two of the 20 school districts. Another 18 percent lived in two other school districts. In these four districts they made up 30 percent of the population. Another 28 percent lived in four other districts where they constituted about 20 percent of the population. Four other districts had not Hispanics at all.[13]

About one in five Hispanics marry non-Hispanics. The trend is most prevalent, naturally enough, among those Hispanics whose schooling, living, or working situation includes the opportunity for contact with people from other ethnic groups. There is no indication that intermarriage necessarily means physical, cultural, or intellectual withdrawal from the Hispanic community. The Hispanic culture is maintained in one form or another in most U.S. cities, and those who are interested have ample opportunities to participate in, or get to know something about, this enduring culture.[14]

This culture is probably best exemplified by the persistence of Spanish. In a recent national survey, the great majority of Hispanics aimed to become bilingual; they wanted to preserve or improve their Spanish as they learn English. Large and small Spanish language newspapers and radio and television stations help promote language preservation. Another survey found that both Hispanics and Anglos support bilingual education. Anglos generally view bilingual education as a way to learn English; Hispanics want to foster bilingualism.[15]

SCHOOL SYSTEM DEMOGRAPHY

The Hispanic presence is most clearly visible in the school systems. As births decreased markedly among Anglos in the 1970s, they tended to increase among Hispanics. This is due to a greater percentage of Hispanic women of childbearing age, larger families, and immigration. Many Anglos moved to the suburbs or sent their children to private schools; blacks have done so to a lesser degree. Most Hispanics live either in central cities, industrial suburbs, or smaller industrial or agribusiness cities.[16]

Of the nation's six largest school districts, five are 20 to 50 percent Latin. New York City's schools are about a third Latin, Los Angeles' over half. A Los Angeles school board member commented in 1981 that "current enrollment trends suggest that the city's school system will become nearly all Hispanic in the next decade." In 1981 there were 5,000 fewer non-Hispanic whites than there were a year earlier. Chicago's schools are 20 percent Latin; Dade County, Florida's are approaching 50 percent and Houston's are 34 percent. Among the top six urban school populations, Detroit's is below 20 percent. Nationally there were about 8 percent Hispanics in the schools in 1984. This could be far below the actual situation. An analysis of school-age children reveals that in 1980

17 percent were language minority, which would make about 13 or 14 percent Hispanic in 1980; there has clearly been a significant growth since then. Of the statewide systems, California and Texas schools were 30 percent Hispanic, New Mexico was 47 percent, and Arizona 25 percent. Since the percentage of Hispanics in the population up to age 14 is much higher than its percentage of the population in general, there is every reason to expect that the numbers will continue to grow. When you add other language minorities you find more states and cities that are in need of educational programs like bilingual education. Language minorities are those whose native language is other than English. The majority of language minority students are in the limited English proficient (LEP) category.[17]

As the Latin presence increases rapidly, the opportunities for advancement are still moribund. Educational attainment is more and more dependent on the mastery of certain technological skills and the ability to perform well on certain standardized tests. While a minority of Hispanic youth will attain success in business and the professions under this emerging school-to-work transition, the majority will be relegated to the low-level service jobs unless basic structural reforms are made in schooling and in access to careers.

12

The Politics of Provincialism: The Legacy of the Anglocentric Curriculum

A widely held claim has it that Anglo-Saxons are poor learners of other languages, and that among them the Americans are the poorest.[1]

Defense Department-sponsored report, 1984

There is just a tremendous amount of ignorance about where places are in the world. I have met a number of students who think Canada is a state.[2]

Geography Professor
University of Georgia, 1985

The results of many decades of public schooling using the anglocentric curriculum are evident in the weak national knowledge infrastructure in such subjects as foreign languages, area studies, geography, and U.S. history. Parochial or isolationist politics has led to a set of assumptions that permeate education:

1. The U.S. has been formed, developed, and maintained by a few prominent leaders, most of whom were Anglo-Saxon males.
2. The U.S. is insulated from the world and has only a minor need for international relations.
3. Those relations can usually be conducted in English or through translators.
4. When necessary, adults can learn languages in brief intensive courses. Elementary and secondary school language study is important, but not a necessity.

5. Area studies and geography are the preserve of experts and are not a necessary part of school or college instruction.

This set of assumptions leads to a public education policy that either neglects the study of these subjects or allows them to stagnate in traditional modes.

THE LANGUAGE DEFICIT

During the 1960s and 1970s school systems and colleges removed foreign language requirements because the languages were considered irrelevant. In many ways they were; at least in the way they were taught as useless appendages. Terminal boredom reigned. Language teachers' perspectives helped to shape this situation: "The whole idea of using a second language for a purpose, for learning content, for negotiating internationally is foreign to our foreign language teachers."[3] Students soon get the idea that languages are for rote learning and memorizing for tests. What is learned in these classroom exercises stays in the classroom.

Prior to World War I and during the post-Sputnik era about a third of high school students enrolled in language classes. Currently about 19 percent do. This is far behind most other highly industrialized countries even though it is up slightly from recent years. The consequences of this instructional deficit are visible in commerce, diplomacy, intelligence, and elsewhere. An advertising executive stated that ". . . Americans doing business abroad are significantly disadvantaged by poor and insufficient training in foreign languages. There is always a subtle, but distinct, loss of the 'upper hand' when one cannot make oneself understood."[4] U.S. firms frequently cannot even compete for procurement or training contracts let by Japanese and other foreign companies or governments because their staffs lack foreign language capabilities.

In diplomacy a similar pattern prevails. Diplomats may have had the rudiments of language training, but they rarely practice it. According to Foreign Service Officer Moorhead Kennedy, one of the Iranian hostages,

> Language training is only part of it. You must practice it once you get into the field. . . . But in the Foreign Service we often see the phenomenon repeated in the American media abroad, our international lawyers stationed abroad, of Americans who . . . have not enough knowledge to get to know the people, even if they have been technically trained in the language.

They sort of draw the linguistic wagons in a circle . . . within the comfort of people who speak only English and a few token foreigners.

You notice our Dutch colleagues, Dutch diplomats, Italians, Germans particularly are much more prepared to become . . . part of the life of the country simply because they have been learning foreign languages all their lives and because they do not have what Admiral Inman referred to, the kind of arrogance that others should be expected to know English.[5]

Admiral Bobby Inman, the former National Security Agency director and CIA deputy director, described the intelligence deficits that resulted from this arrogance. On working in Islamic countries: "I think the classic example is the slowness in recognizing the threat to our interests of the Islam situation. Much of it was simply not understanding the fervor that lay behind the words in a different language." On Iran in particular: ". . . you ended up not having people with a language skill present to follow the conversation in the bazaars or on the campuses, in the universities or in the mosques . . . to detect long before it ever reached the state where it was in the streets."[6] On Central America:

I think it impacted on the slowness with recognizing what was happening in Central America, where in a great many cases, lack of representation, lack of language skills, lack of raw reporting that ought to have been detected, the efforts to ship arms, build guerilla movements, long before it became the problem that it is now.[7]

National Security Agency Director Paul Larkin added that intelligence agencies also suffered when articles or books were translated mechanically or incorrectly because the translators had no knowledge of the idioms or nuances involved in the languages they were dealing with.

AREA STUDIES AND GEOGRAPHY

Not surprisingly a large percentage of area studies specialists in the government, academia, and research also lack language proficiency. A 1970 survey found that 21 percent had no language competence at all in the major language of their area, and only 41 percent could speak and read the language easily. This trend filters down to the graduate student level. A 1983 Rand Corporation survey of government-funded fellowship students in foreign languages and area studies found that 25 percent could not understand native speakers of the language they were studying and that 64 percent could not teach in the language. A Defense

Department report stated that it would be desirable if our area specialists were never called on to provide more than name, rank, and serial number.[8]

Our geographic knowledge base continues this pattern. In 1951 the country was surprised to discover that only 78 percent of college students could correctly answer rudimentary geography questions. In 1984 only 27 percent could answer the same questions correctly. Less than 50 percent knew the two largest states in area, only 21 percent knew the two smallest. Twenty percent of sixth-graders could not find the United States on a world map. Geography has been dropped as a separate subject of study, and geographic knowledge has been allowed to seep out of the social studies curriculum. We are, the geographers tell us, a nation of geographic illiterates.[9]

The foregoing examples in foreign language, area studies, and geography are not the whole story, however. While they reflect the situation in most schools, there is a counter-trend in the political and business realms. Pragmatic internationalism, like pluralism, counterposes creative programs to the anglocentric curriculum. This pragmatism promotes a more global view of knowledge and skill acquisition.

PRAGMATIC INTERNATIONALISM: AN ANTIDOTE TO PROVINCIALISM

Various political and business leaders have proposed alternatives to isolationism as ways to bolster their local economy's ability to compete in the international trade arena. Seattle's Mayor Charles Royer, for example, presents the case for this approach. Boeing, the area's dominant employer, was forced to reduce its work force by 80,000 in the late 1960s and early 1970s. The company and the region stayed afloat only through the expansion of its foreign trade. Royer emphasized that well-trained human resources are as important as sophisticated technology and machinery for doing business abroad. He stated that Seattle and other cities must make better use of their citizens' multilingual and multicultural backgrounds. Native languages must be used as assets. Many more people must be trained in languages and in international business.[10]

A leading Texas banker contends that many people in the U.S. are

terribly provincial in the fear so many Americans have, English Anglo-Americans have of a second language of a foreign language and the attitude that so many businessmen have that "If you don't speak English you simply can't do business with me." Even when they go to a foreign country, so many have this attitude. . . . Bilingual education is a critical issue in the southwestern area of the United States. . . . The south Texas economy is very dependent on the south of the border business community. It is necessary to know both Spanish and English to transact business in an efficient way.[11]

Governor Bob Graham of Florida also aims to increase his state's business ties to Latin America. These ties include serving as a regional center for the sale and distribution of U.S. goods and serving as headquarters for Japanese, Middle Eastern, and European companies that want to do business in Latin America. It also means providing facilities for Latin tourists, consumers, and investors to come to Florida to spend their money. Graham noted that most of Miami's restaurants, shops, banks, and municipal government offices have had to become bilingual in order to attract or serve this Latin clientele. He believes that all Floridians should "look upon linguistics not as an issue of self-pride and national patriotism, but of pragmatism and good sense."[12]

South Dakota's Governor William Janklow believed that the state's ability to export its grain will determine the future of the economy.

Look at the market we have potentially with just Mexico. We can feed its people with our agricultural food stuffs. But we can't communicate with them. . . . One of the reasons we can't sell our agricultural products is that we can't deal with other people on their own cultural and language levels. If there is anybody in all the world that ought to insist that their people learn foreign languages, it's the people of rural America. It's the farmers. The biggest foreign trade we have in America is agricultural produce.[13]

Former U.S. Senator Paul Tsongas of Massachusetts is primarily concerned about the export of his state's advanced technology.

With 40 percent of our high-tech production exported each year, there is no reason why the people of our state should not share directly in this fast-growing sector of our economy. I want to see people from Massachusetts work in Massachusetts. I think that foreign language training is a smart way to prepare for a career with an export-oriented future.[14]

Finally Oregon's Governor Victor Atiyeh established a Commission on Foreign Languages and International Studies that was funded largely by the Exxon and Hewlett-Packard foundations. The commission recommended increased school and college language and international business programs to train career professionals who would aid in the expansion of the state's Pacific trade, foreign investment, and tourism.[15]

Regions that are highly conscious of foreign trade opportunities have been among the forerunners in instituting language and area studies programs at the elementary, secondary, and postsecondary levels. With this awareness of mutual self-interest as a backdrop, majority parents are more likely to find a climate conducive to establishing effective second language programs, and language minority parents are more likely to encounter a climate conducive to the creation of effective additive bilingual programs.

THE STRUGGLE FOR HISTORY

A final legacy of the anglocentric curriculum is the content of U.S. history instruction. History teachers, politicians, researchers, and school officials have been reassessing the traditional method of teaching U.S. history.[16] This method glorifies great personalities, usually Anglo males, and downplays the contributions of ethnic and racial minorities and women. This method influences the context in which bilingual education operates

1. By underemphasizing the contributions of language minorities it renders them either invisible or marginal to mainstream culture. If language minorities are so peripheral, why should governments expend so much energy and money for special programs to upgrade their schooling?

2. By giving the impression that earlier immigrants adjusted smoothly and willingly to Anglo conformity, it leaves the notion that the melting pot is the only way to deal with newcomers or non-English speakers. The traditional method omits the harsh realities of the schoolhouse in the days of military-style assimilation, especially the clash between the home and the school over the child's loyalty.

A number of schools and colleges have experimented with two main alternative methods. The first breaks down history into constituent segments (e.g., women's history, labor history, black history, etc.). The second pays deference to the constituent groups while continuing in the anglocentric mode. The struggle to find a history that is both common to all and that treats the contributions of all groups fairly is an ongoing process.

Colleges of education have grappled with a variant of this question as they decide how to teach required history or foundations of education courses to education majors who will in turn transmit what they learn to their students. The traditional glorification of the public school method was attacked by revisionists who contended that the schools have been riddled by racism and sexism. Another group, the culturalists, has stressed the importance of non-school influences in educating the populace. All three groups, with some exceptions, ignore or marginalize Hispanic school history and thereby rob bilingual education of its historical context. If one does not understand what came before, it is very hard to understand why so many Hispanics and others are such partisans of bilingual education.

Most historians of education treat Hispanic school history by either ignoring it or devoting a simplistic paragraph or two. They usually imply that Hispanics have been passive or inert or they lump them together with blacks and others into a general category of minorities. They treat immigration as a phenomenon that ended in 1924 and rarely consider the situation of more recent immigrants. They rarely deal with discrimination; many have referred to Mexican-American education without ever mentioning segregation or the "no Spanish" rule.

A few general historians of U.S. educational history like Butts and Tyack have been sensitive to these issues. So have historians of minority education like Weinberg, San Miguel, and Wollenberg.[17] Some of those who have written histories of Hispanic communities have covered schooling as an integral part of the community's development. As the history of education profession awakens to the existence and special circumstances of Hispanic communities, historians will either continue with the celebratory, revisionist, or culturalist models or they will search for new ones. The perspective from which history is taught in the public schools and in the colleges of education affects the public perception of bilingual education.

13

The State of the Schools

The public policy arena has become saturated with the debate over how to remedy the crisis in the schools. National education commission reports and studies add new layers to the pyramid of doom: discipline, math and science, test scores, computer learning, writing skills, humanities content, and teacher competency are declining. These reports are politely quoted in the media and then forgotten. Several reforms have emerged that have been instituted in several states; merit pay has been chief among them. Texas and a few other states have made significant changes in the state education agencies' delivery systems, but fundamental changes are still in the future.

The preceding chapters described the bleak Hispanic opportunity structure and set the scene for an examination of school conditions by delineating the precarious national knowledge base in foreign languages, area studies, geography, and U.S. history. This chapter discusses the relationship of school systems to their Hispanic students in light of the developing role of bilingual education.

THE MENTAL WITHDRAWAL-GRADE RETENTION-DROPOUT SYNDROME

Latin youngsters frequently confront a school culture that purports to objectively instruct them in the ways of the world, but actually blends into this instructional process an Anglo cultural overlay. First the child's enthusiasm wanes, and he mentally and spiritually removes himself from the lesson plan. He then finds himself being held back a grade, and finally, several years later, he is apt to withdraw physically.

The mental withdrawal stage is visible through participant observation and it has been widely noted by ethnographers and other social scientists.[1] The rate of grade retention is quantifiable, as the following statistics demonstrate:

At age 9, 75 percent of all students are in the fourth grade; only 69 percent of Hispanics are.

At age 13, 72 percent of students are in the eighth grade; only 53 percent of Hispanics are.

At age 17, 73 percent of students are in the eleventh grade; only 54 percent of Hispanics are.[2]

Many educators are unaware of the magnitude of the situation. In the Port City, Michigan case described earlier, school officials were shocked to discover the number of Hispanics who were one or more grades behind their age level. Social promotions may be used as an alternative; students are promoted for good attendance and behavior. But a number of functional illiterates may be merely passed on from one grade to another. If youngsters are not taught to read or write properly, it does little good to advance them. With some exceptions, children either absorb the school's teachings in the elementary grades or do not acquire them during their academic careers.

Physical withdrawal often follows several years of staying behind grade level. It is a type of vicious cycle in which the longer a student stays in school, the further behind he gets. Pedagogical or vocational goals seem further and further away, less and less attainable. The lack of achievement fuels frustration and hope for progress is extinguished. Hispanics drop out at three to four times the national rate.[3]

Of those who graduate, some go on to higher education, usually to a community college. Some obtain associate degrees. Only a small fraction obtain bachelor's degrees (about 7 percent), compared to 25 percent overall. The significant spurt in college attendance in the 1970s has fallen back. Part of the cause lies in the reduction of student loan funds and Pell grants.[4]

Michigan Hispanic high school dropouts reported that a lack of communication with teachers and counselors helped lead to the decision to withdraw. Parents complained of unfair treatment. Most dropouts had been placed in the general education track. Those who succeeded in high school were largely in the more prestigious college preparatory track or in the vocational/technical track, which was more related to job acquisition. The successful students had better relations with teachers and parents than did the dropouts. A national study of Hispanic secondary students found that school personnel who were able to create an environment of caring in which students and parents felt comfortable and identified with the school were most likely to successfully encourage students to graduate.[5]

As New York City's minority dropout rate reached 60 percent, educators and political analysts assessed the possibilities for reform. Hunter College President Donna Shalala urged that radical surgery be performed on the entire city school system. School should start at age three, special services should be provided for children with special needs, and the business and political leadership must actively involve itself with the schools. New York *Times* columnist Sidney Schanberg agreed with the spirit of many of Shalala's suggestions and publicly questioned the school system as to why this great waste of potential human talent should be taking place.[6]

THE ABANDONMENT OF THE CENTRAL CITY SCHOOLS

Many of the public school supporters who are disturbed at the high dropout rate are also alarmed at the willingness of political and business leaders to allow urban school systems to decay. Buildings are old, classrooms are ill-equipped and understaffed, textbooks are scarce, and teachers are poorly paid and often ill-trained. Funding crises are becoming part of the landscape. The federal funding reductions since 1981 to 1984 have exacerbated this crisis. San Jose, California's school system actually declared bankruptcy in 1983. All this occurs as Blacks, Hispanics, and Asians have become the urban school majority, while most Anglos living in the city send their children to private or parochial schools.[7]

A former New York City school superintendent observed:

> The condition of municipal and educational overburden has had a catastrophic impact on the educational systems of the larger cities. As the cities became poorer, their needs became greater; the demands upon the schools for vital services increase, while the capability to meet these demands declines. The result − a steadily rising rush to abandon the cities for the safer richer middle class suburbs, leaving the desolation of the inner urban areas to the minority

poor, who become more isolated and more paralyzed as the process moves relentlessly toward total abandonment of the inner cities.[8]

In some cities this abandonment has led Hispanic parents to send their children to the parochial schools when they can afford it. In New York City large numbers of Hispanic students are now in ESL classes in the parochial schools. Not too long ago urban school systems set the pattern for innovation among the nations' districts. Now they are looking more like the equivalent to the role urban public hospitals play in the health care system: the last resort, the preserve of the minority poor.

THE EDUCATIONAL CONSEQUENCES OF BEING POOR

Most Hispanics are among the working poor. This low-income way of life often affects their children's schooling. One consequence of urban poverty is the frequent need for the family to move from residence to residence, often forcing a change of school. These moves may be caused by eviction, gentrification (the transformation of poor neighborhoods into middle-class areas), fires, or other causes. P.S. 62 in the South Bronx typifies this condition. It is one of 26 New York City elementary schools with annual turnover rates of more than 70 percent. Twenty percent of the families in the area are living in temporary shelters and will move in the near future. A teacher commented that "there is no consistency of instruction. They come from another school and you don't know what they know or how they have been taught. And by the time you find out they have moved on . . . ."[9]

Other facets of low-income life that affect schooling include malnutrition, improper clothing, and inadequate health and dental care. Overcrowded living conditions may limit the ability to complete homework. Households are often led by a single parent. Many parents are illiterate and many lack the ability to help the children with school work. Books, newspapers, and other reading material may be in short supply. Poor parents are usually more hesitant to become involved with the school than are middle-class parents. Finally, the urgency of making money to help support the family compels many young people to leave school to work full time.

Creative bilingual programs staffed by empathetic teachers can keep some of these young people in school and help some of them achieve a higher status in life. But neither bilingual education nor any instructional program can, by itself, remove poverty conditions. Bilingual programs are no panacea, only a significant approach toward aiding in the achievement of academic success.

THE SCHOOL-TO-WORK TRANSITION

The process in which the acquisition of educational skills and credentials leads to meaningful jobs is well recognized. The question is, Does it work for most Latins? The answer in Boston and probably elsewhere is, rarely. The Boston schools' 16 percent Latin population rarely ends up with decent jobs because they lack the education, training, and skills to obtain them. Poorly conceived, funded, planned, and staffed Chapter I and bilingual programs never help most of them stay abreast of their Anglo peers. The vocational programs are designed to supply firms who want "job ready" high school graduates. Most Latin youngsters are unable to fit into this category. At best they can qualify for dead-end service jobs as the economy increasingly moves toward the two-tier economy mentioned earlier.

Boston is a prime example of this bifurcated economy. Ringed by research and development firms that work in tandem with the area's large number of major universities, the city has steadily lost its manufacturing, public sector, and port-related jobs. The service sector provides low-level jobs in hospitals, laboratories, fast-food chains, and hotels. There are professional jobs here too, but the scarcity of college credentials greatly reduces the likelihood that many will be filled by Latins. Those young people who leave school to blend into the service economy are likely to encounter long periods of unemployment and underemployment in the midst of changing economic realities.[10]

BILINGUAL TEACHERS

Bilingual education has always limped on one leg because of the teacher shortage. National estimates of the unfilled openings for teachers vary from 20,000 to over 100,000. Bilingual program administrators, social workers, psychologists, and counselors are also in short supply. Colleges of education have been reluctant to undertake bilingual teacher training programs. Some will include the program only when federal funding covers the costs. The training program may end when the grant from Washington runs out. Professors in these training programs are often held at arm's length. They are less likely to be on a tenure track and are rarely involved in central departmental decision-making. Few get promoted to leadership positions within colleges of education. Without a trained corps of bilingual teachers, programs will never be fully effective.[11]

Opponents of bilingual education often dismiss the program as nothing more than a Hispanic jobs program. It has been – it has aided the entry of thousands of Hispanics and other language minorities into the education profession. But this is not the whole story. Nationwide, Hispanics comprise about 33 percent of bilingual teachers, 12 percent of ESL teachers, and 3 percent of teachers overall. In California, the state with the largest Hispanic population, only 10 percent of the bilingual teachers were Hispanic in 1982. This is less than the percentage of Hispanics in white-collar and professional levels of the state civil service.[12]

Half of all U.S. teachers have taught LEP students, even though only a small fraction had any professional preparation. The same holds true for ESL teachers. Only 40 percent had even one course in teaching English to non-native speakers. Only 6 percent of all teachers had any coursework in ESL. These figures reveal that large numbers of LEP students are being taught by professionally unprepared teachers, which is probably in violation of the Lau Decision.[13]

BILINGUAL PROGRAMS: CONTINUING MARGINALITY

Accounts of the bilingual program experience that were mentioned in previous chapters reveal a pattern of marginality: classes held under stairwells or in broom closets, soft money funding that dooms programs when federal funds expire, teachers and education professors not placed on tenure tracks, and a range of other phenomena.

This pattern extends from Washington to the schoolhouse; the program's marginal existence is understood throughout the school establishment. The awareness of the marginality seems to seep through classroom walls. OBEMLA administers a $143 million budget with a small professional staff in fiscal year 1986. Most other program offices in the Department of Education have more staff and budget. Special education, vocational education, Pell grants, Chapter I, and guaranteed student loans have more funds and larger staffs. Only 8 percent of LEP students are able to participate in federally funded programs; a much greater percentage of eligible students in programs like special education and Chapter I are able to participate. In Washington the size of your budget and your position within the bureaucratic constellation are everything. OBEMLA has little money or clout and usually lives out its life on the sidelines, far from the education secretary's ear.

Less than half the states have bilingual laws. Others permit bilingual programs, while West Virginia prohibits them. The state bilingual program is usually coordinated by staffers from the foreign language or federal programs office; only a minority of states have distinct bilingual education departments or divisions. Bilingual or ESL teacher certification exists in about half the states.[14] In others any warm body can teach LEP students if the teacher shortage is severe enough at a given time. Some states with certification requirements frequently relax them in the face of these shortages. Only 20 states spend their own money on bilingual programs. As in Washington, bilingual sections within state departments of education usually play second fiddle. They have little chance of competing for power and influence with the more entrenched sections that control more funds, enjoy a higher status, and usually have greater access to the superintendent.

Local districts usually relegate bilingual programs to an ill-defined section dominated by larger compensatory programs. The bilingual director often ranks below the directors of other federal programs like Chapter I. Bilingual programs rarely receive regular line-item funding. The program depends almost entirely on federal and/or state dollars. The local district therefore has little stake in the success or failure of the program. The program was probably established in the first place in response to pressure exerted from the Hispanic community, the federal government, or the courts. As New Jersey state superintendent Fred Burke observed,

> Urban schools beset by the agonies of municipal overburden, antiquated and inadequate facilities and a declining tax base and governed by a non-Hispanic power structure, were little inclined to place a high priority on supporting public schools attended almost exclusively by Hispanic and black children; nor were they enthusiastic about budgeting for expensive bilingual/bicultural programs.[15]

The local district's bilingual staff is usually quite small and has to spend most of its time scurrying around trying to locate enough funds and other resources to keep the program afloat. The staff rarely has the time or energy to spend major amounts of time upgrading and monitoring the program.

Bilingual teachers and aides walk a tightrope. They must defer to principals who might not be ecstatic to have the program in their schools. They must also deal with regular teachers who may feel threatened by bilingual programs for fear that their jobs as non-bilingual teachers may be in jeopardy. Bilingual teachers and aides are the glue that keeps the program together; most are highly committed to the education of the students.

Ever since the Bilingual Education Act was promulgated and a puny $7.5 million dollars was appropriated for it, the program has had a decidedly marginal character in relation to the main decision-makers in education. While it has grown over the years, it still languishes on the sidelines, waiting for its turn to get into the big game.

14

The Model Minority Setup

The model minority myth especially hurts Asians from lower income families. . . . The stereotyping of Asian Americans as a "model minority" implies that other minorities can become "successful" if they only work harder. The model minority myth serves to relieve responsibilities for continuing to work to overcome racial inequalities still existent today. This pattern of pitting one minority group against another is not only found in the media, but extends to the admission process here at Brown as well as at other leading universities.[1]

> Asian-American Student Association,
> Brown University, 1984

The interaction between the staff and the Asian immigrants led not only to a stereotype of the Asians, but also to stereotyping images of the other groups when they were compared to the Asians.[2]

> Celia Reyes Hailey, on a Northern
> California elementary school, 1984

Politicians, the media, and educators designate certain minorities as having achieved success and try to induce other minorities to perform at the same level: "If only you could be like the___" (Japanese, Jews, Vietnamese, etc.). This model minority designation and its use in society is a thoroughgoing setup; both the allegedly successful and the allegedly unsuccessful minorities are stereotyped and treated not as individuals but as faceless ethnics who are preordained to succeed or fail. Then they are pitted against each other. In past years the model minorities were the Jews and the Japanese; currently it is Asian-Americans.

Curiously, early in the twentieth century, both the Jews and the Japanese were classified along with other recent immigrants as retarded. Psychologists tested Jews arriving at Ellis Island and labeled them feeble-minded. Tests were also administered to West Coast Japanese with similar results. The tests were exclusively in English. Psychologists somehow changed their minds in the 1920s and 1930s; the Jews and Japanese were now seen to have IQs higher than the Anglo-Saxons. This recategorization followed several decades of high academic achievement and attainment by members of both groups. It is said that Supreme Court justices make decisions based partly on the latest election returns. In a similar vein, psychologists conjure up categories of intelligence not based on inherited intellectual factors as they claimed, but based on what the psychologists perceived as evidence of academic performance, as well as mastery of English and test skills.[3]

The Jews and Japanese came to the United States literate in at least one language, educated, conversant with school culture, and possessing enough marketable skills to be able to eventually fill important slots in an expanding economy. Most other immigrants of the 1880-1924 period were poor, rural, uneducated, and possessed little awareness of school culture or formal learning processes. It is little wonder that they did not do as well as the Jews and the Japanese.[4]

THE CURRICULUM AND POPULAR CULTURE

Popular culture and the Anglocentric curriculum promoted the notion that model minority children should transform themselves into WASP facsimiles. World history courses taught children that Asia and Latin America were backward unimportant places in comparison to Northern Europe and the United States. The message was that

> man's most significant development occurred in Europe and later in the United States. The study of areas beyond Europe entered the vision of world history only peripherally, mainly when the areas were "discovered" by Europeans. Thus China was "discovered" by Marco Polo and Japan's history began with the opening by Commodore Perry.[5]

The Jews and the Asians learned the same curriculum as everyone else – the Anglo-Saxons control the past and the future, and if you want to be a part of it, adapt as best you can. As late as 1970, three of eleven commonly used textbooks portrayed Jews as contributing to the crucifixion of Jesus Christ.[6] As Father Timothy Healy, president of Georgetown University put it, the world history most children receive

> consists of the doings and misdoings of two great empires: the Roman and the British. These are followed by the American empire. . . . The fact that between the first and the second of these enterprises there occurred a third, as large and as influential as either would come as a surprise to many of our students. The entire world of Spanish exploration, colonization work and understanding is a closed one in American history.[7]

The Asia Society and other groups established a Committee on Teaching about Asia. The committee found that Japan and China were frequently confused in textbooks and that artwork and photographs of life in one country were often mistakenly attributed to the other. One text referred to Japan as having a semitropical climate, even though they recently hosted the winter olympics. They discovered that Commodore Perry was "shrouded in a somewhat messianic light, proffering the fruits of Westernization."[8] The committee concluded that

> It has been said by many that U.S. textbooks are the most beautiful textbooks in the world. Unfortunately, many, especially those in U.S. history, are among the most ethnocentric. This is especially disturbing in light of the fact that U.S. authors often have access to the best and most sophisticated information network in the world.[9]

Popular culture also has deeply embedded WASP-as-hero notions within it. The parents and grandparents of the current public school student population grew up with and transmitted warmed-over Horatio Alger myths ". . . in the form of Dink Stover of Frank Merriwell of Tom Mix and the Rover Boys and of an endless succession of pulp-novel and comic book characters who had blond hair, blue eyes and what was inevitably called 'an open countenance'. . . ."[10] World War II movies portrayed the Japanese as big-eyed yellow monsters. A whole generation of postwar children grew up watching films with this characterization.

Even those minority or immigrant people who achieved positions of importance in relation to popular culture tended to retread the well-worn path of portraying traditional cultural heroes or creating WASP facsimiles to fill these roles. Thus MGM's Louis B. Mayer, for example, took second generation Polish calendar models and turned them into a packaged product – Doris Kappelhoff became Doris Day, Bernie Schwartz became Tony Curtis, Margarita Carmen Cansino became Rita Hayworth and Dino Crocetti became Dean Martin and played out the myth of the mainstream.[11]

THE JEWS: KNOWLEDGE AS POWER

Jews struggled to get ahead in school for several reasons. First because learning was inextricably bound up with religion; one's reputation in the community depended on the amount of knowledge and piety one possessed. Second, because learning opportunities were denied them in Europe due to a quota system, and parents vowed to recify that situation here by having their children attend college. Third, because in order to advance into the professions, it was necessary to obtain academic certification. Fourth, because learning for its own sake was also a community value; schools provided an avenue to accumulate this valuable commodity. These reasons will be delineated after describing the mechanics and dynamics of the quest for academic success.

The Struggle to Succeed

The effort to prevail in the educational system was intense and protracted. Alfred Kazin was conditioned by his parents to revere his "glacially remote Anglo-Saxon principal." As a student in Brownsville, Brooklyn

> It was never learning I associated with that school: only the necessity to succeed, to get ahead of the others in the daily struggle to "make a good impression" on our teacher who grimly, wearily and often with ill-conceived distaste watched against our relapse into the natural savagery they expected of Brownsville boys.[12]

Very early on in this struggle, an observer of the New York Jewish community noted, "The poorest Hebrew knows – the poorer he is the better he knows it – that knowledge is power and power is the means for getting ahead in the world."[13] The U.S. Immigration Committee made an exhaustive study of newcomers in 1911 and reached the following conclusion about the Eastern European Jews: "The poorest among them will make all possible sacrifices to keep his children in school; and one of the most striking phenomena in New York City today is the way in which Jews have taken possession of the public schools."[14]

A small, but powerful community of German Jews had arrived in the U.S. many decades before the Eastern European Jews. The Germans established a large center in Manhattan known as the Educational Alliance to instruct and Americanize the recent arrivals. The newcomers flocked to the Alliance classrooms, but resented the disdain of the German Jews, who ridiculed their Old World ways. A German-Jewish publication, the *Hebrew Standard*, commented that "the thoroughly acclimated American Jew . . . has no religious, social, or intellectual sympathies with them. He is closer to the Christian sentiment around him than to the Judaism of these miserably darkened Hebrews."[15] The new arrivals defended themselves. They spoke out in street-corner meetings and in letters to the Yiddish newspapers. Some playwrights wrote dramas for the Yiddish theatre that compared the condescending attitudes of the German Jews to the imperious behavior of Russian and Polish officials. The German Jews got the point. Community leaders moved the Educational Alliance to the Lower East Side, where the immigrants lived, and allowed the free expression of immigrant Yiddish in classrooms and cultural performances.[16]

The immigrant Jews not only wrung educational concessions from German Jews. They also vigorously protested the 1917 imposition of the Gary Plan on the New York schools. The Gary Plan was an effort to reorganize the schools in the name of efficiency. As the plan was first implemented, it seemed to threaten the existence of neighborhood schools.

> For ten days the anti-Gary demonstrations continued breaking out in one locality after another. . . . Of thirty-five Gary schools, nineteen reported riots and demonstrations. . . . Most of the riots took place in poor immigrant neighborhoods; most of the boys arrested were Jewish. . . . There were widespread fears in the poor Jewish community, played on by street orators, that the Gary Plan would close the doors of opportunity.[17]

The Board of Education got the message and dropped the Gary Plan.

Another New York City dispute arose over the policies of Lower East Side district school superintendent Julia Richman. Richman, a German Jew, banned Yiddish and Italian from the school grounds and urged strict enforcement of the laws against pushcarts. Pushcarts were a mainstay of

Jewish economic life. Richman said that "if these poor devils cannot make a living without violating our laws . . . the immigration department should take them back to the country from which they came."[18] Community leaders were incensed and organized mass meetings to express their indignation at "this self-appointed censor of our morality and patron saint of the slum seekers."[19] Richman confined herself to less controversial matters after this.

Chicago Jews also asserted their educational needs. They formed a large chapter of the Workmen's Circle, a major fraternal and benevolent organization, and involved it in school issues. A prime focus was to try to ameliorate the generation gap that resulted when public schools promoted assimilation. The Workmen's Circle declared, "The American melting pot built a stone wall between the parents and the children. . . . This lack of understanding seriously disturbed the children's education."[20] The organization attended local and citywide school meetings and established its own schools in order to promote family unity.

Special schools run by the Educational Alliance, the Young Men's Hebrew Association, and the Baron de Hirsch Fund supplemented the public schools. Instructors prodded the youngsters to learn what was necessary to succeed and coached them to pass college and professional school entrance examinations. All this activity quickly led to the popular conception that the Jews were overly aggressive and pushy, the results of which will be seen later.

The Jews' Special Circumstances

Jews came to the United States as literate, multilingual, and skilled trade or business-oriented people. The literacy came from the early community-based religious training for the boys and sometimes for the girls. To be able to read was to partake in Jewish religion and culture. Parents' proudest moments occurred when their son began Hebrew school at age five or six and when he completed his bar mitzvah ceremony at age 13. Most Eastern European Jews spoke Yiddish as well as one or more of the local languages like Polish, Russian, German, Hungarian, Lithuanian, or Romanian. While few spoke English on arrival in the United States, it is much easier to learn a third language after you have learned a second and are literate in the first, than for those from other groups who were monolingual and illiterate in their native languages.

Landowning in Europe was severely restricted or forbidden to the Jews. Most Jews were artisans, middlemen, or small businessmen in the old country. When they reached the expanding economies of New York, Chicago, and Philadelphia, they encountered avenues of opportunities for their skills as tailors, carpenters, tinsmiths, shoemakers, painters, and jewelers. The needle trades (dress, hat, cap, glove, fur and suit making), the construction trades, cigarmaking, and other urban manufacturing and service industries contained many Jewish workers. The urban economies provided opportunities that allowed many of the newcomers to reach the upper levels of the working class and the lower levels of the middle class in a relatively short time, a remarkable achievement for recent immigrants. Then and only then did the children and grandchildren rise through the public schools and colleges into the professions. The oft-told story that the schools carried the Jews upward is a distortion of the facts. The schools were used to affirm and expand the family's economic foothold. The credentials earned at school helped families build on the economic successes by elevating the sons and sometimes the daughters into the ranks of teachers, doctors, lawyers, and accountants. Many newly certified accountants worked initially for their parents' small businesses.[21]

The entry into academia was laden with obstacles, however. While public colleges usually accepted most high school graduates, private colleges often resisted Jewish entry. The president of New York University in the 1920s looked back on the previous decade: "We were at that time threatened with nothing less than the complete disintegration of our college as it was then constituted at University Heights . . . our chief problem centered in students of Russian, Polish and Central European descent."[22] The president of Columbia University in 1914 accepted the children of German Jews whose families had lived in the United States for generations, but found the Eastern European Jews to be far less desirable. *The Nation* magazine editorialized in 1922 against the efforts of Jewish students to enter the Ivy League colleges: ". . . the infiltration of a mass of pushing young men with a foreign accent accustomed to overcoming discrimination by self-assertiveness would obviously change the character of any of these institutions and lessen its social prestige."[23] Jews were being penalized for having the nerve to think that they could enter and compete on an equal basis with the sons of the rich. College presidents countered the pressure to admit Jewish students by instituting quotas. These quotas were enforced by special interviews and psychological personality tests that were designed to weed out most of the Jewish students that applied.

Thus successful performances in school were a mixed blessing. The schools broadened the horizons of learning and provided opportunities for poor immigrants who made it a few rungs up the economic ladder to certify their children or grandchildren as degreed professionals. But the ethnocentrism of the schools rubbed off on the students and produced family splits, just as had occurred in other immigrant communities. The Jews got where they did by persistent collective and individual pressure on the educational system to let them in. They certainly did not fit the image of the docile, accommodating group that the perpetrators of the model minority myth seek to impose on current minorities through the use of flawed historical analogies.

THE JAPANESE: PERSISTENCE AND STRUGGLE

After the U.S. government prohibited further Chinese immigration in 1882, Japanese immigrants were sought by some West Coast and Hawaiian firms as replacement labor for the Chinese. Japan established universal education in the nineteenth century, and most of those who came to the United States were literate members of the urban and rural middle sectors of the economy, not the very poor. A study of California minorities concludes

> the Japanese were better prepared than the Chinese, indeed than most immigrant groups of that era, to adjust to the social and economic realities of early twentieth-century California. . . . the Japanese may well have been the best-educated immigrant group ever to come to America with over 90 percent of them literate in their own language. Adults averaged nearly eight years of schooling, a higher figure than for the average Californian. The new Japanese residents had long experience with education and believed it could promote their economic and social well-being. The values were passed to their children.[24]

San Francisco established segregated schools for Asians in the first few years of the twentieth century. Local luminaries led by Mayor James Phelan launched a campaign to halt Japanese immigration in the same period. They also protested the presence of the Japanese in San Francisco and tried to make life as difficult as they could for the newcomers. The San Francisco *Chronicle* editorialized against any special language training for Asian young people: "We deny either the legal or moral obligation to teach any foreigner to read or speak the English language. It is a reasonable requirement that all pupils entering the schools shall be familiar with the language in which instruction is conducted."[25]

Since U.S. laws did not permit the Japanese to become citizens, they were precluded from activity protesting against discrimination in education. They therefore turned to the Japanese government to defend their interests. Japan took up the cry against segregated schooling and elevated the situation to an international incident. A Tokyo newspaper exclaimed, "Stand up, our countrymen have been humiliated on the other side of the ocean. Our boys and girls have been expelled from the public schools by the rascals of the United States."[26] President Teddy Roosevelt helped calm things down by promising to intercede with San Francisco authorities to end segregation. He did so, and the segregation of Asian students in San Francisco schools eventually ended. The Japanese community also launched court suits to break down educational barriers elsewhere on the West Coast and in Hawaii. The community also established a network of after-school and weekend instruction in the native language and culture for the younger generation. Even these were attacked by the likes of California Governor William Stevenson and publisher Valentine McClatchy in the 1920s. The attacks were based on the assumption that somehow the instruction was subversive. The same mentality led to the forcible internment of West Coast residents with one-sixteenth or more Japanese ancestry during World War II.

By the 1930s, significant numbers of Japanese students were able to enter public and private universities on the West Coast. The problem was that once they graduated, no one would hire them. Discrimination was intense. Many law and medical school graduates ended up driving cabs, waiting on tables, or working in greenhouses or gardens. The World War II internment further impeded advancement. The internment camps, however, did not stop the learning process. The internees established their own schools, which were made as similar as possible to the schools they would have been attending in their home towns.[27] After the war, Japanese-American youth re-entered the schools and universities. To some the experience was terrifying.

> The entire first week of school in Pasadena was agony. It was so traumatic in fact that it was the start of a number of bad dreams I have had off and on relating to my racial "freakishness" . . . in a dream I witnessed the explosion of the A-bomb in Hiroshima in the middle of the terrifying mushroom cloud amid cries of death and destruction, appeared the weeping face of Jesus Christ. During that week I felt an inexpressible sense of futility and fear settle over me. . . .

The dream underscored the basic ambivalence I felt about myself and my Japanese heritage. Aggravated by innumerable painful experiences such as those I and my family encountered in Pasadena, this ambivalence caused what might be termed a mild case of schizophrenia in which my feelings swung wildly from one extreme to another. There were times when I cursed the Japanese for making me a cultural half-breed; but there were other times when I was happy to belong to the Japanese-American community and felt nothing but fury at white America for failing to accept me as I was, a Japanese-American Nisei.[28]

Frequently, Japanese-American students felt that they had to wear masks that disguised their feelings in order to get ahead. They felt that they had to show a great deal of deference to their Anglo teachers, and to act out a sort of assimilationist psychodrama. They were less vocal than the Jews, but just as persistent.[29]

MODEL MINORITIES VERSUS LOW-EXPECTATION MINORITIES

Immigrant and minority students have often been held up to the example of the Jews and Japanese and asked why they did not perform as well. A major part of the answer is that they did not come to school with the same skills or community support. Another part is that teachers' expectations shape what happens in class.

The great majority of the last European immigrant wave and the current Latin American wave come from poor rural illiterate backgrounds. Unlike the Jews and the Japanese, the parents descended from these waves had no familiarity with schools and could not guide their childrens' journey through the schoolhouse. While individuals from all groups have achieved academic success, other groups achieved less than the Jews and Japanese because the deck was stacked – group members did not come to the classroom with the same preparation or mindset.

Today many try to lump the prepared with the unprepared and compare them in a way that is unfavorable to the latter. The immigrants from India or Vietnam or Cuba or Korea are held up as exemplars of achievement. A recent investigation of immigrants in Queens, New York, sheds light on the different backgrounds that newcomers bring with them. The study revealed that Indians and Koreans come from the wealthiest and best-educated strata of their countries, Colombians and

Israelis come from middle sectors, and Greeks and Italians largely from the poorer strata. Only 20 percent of the Italians had some college experience, while 56 to 83 percent of the non-Europeans had college experience. Forty-four percent of the Koreans had a bachelor's degree or higher degree, a remarkable figure.[30]

These people arrived under the 1965 Immigration Law that allowed them to enter the country as either family members of U.S. citizens or as possessors of either investment capital or a skill in demand. The Koreans and Indians were investors, engineers, or health professionals. They did not have relatives in the United States to bring them over. The Colombians and Israelis came to join their families or as professionals. The Greeks and Italians were working-class relatives of families that had been in the United States for generations.[31]

Almost the entire upper echelon of Vietnamese society came here in the 1975 airlifts. The same was true of the Cubans who arrived from 1960 to 1965. Many of the Koreans, Indians, and Pakistanis who have arrived here are from the most privileged sectors of their societies. If the professional and business classes of Mexico and the Dominican Republic had come here instead of the farm workers and other poor people, the results in school would be quite different. Even though some of the more recent arrivals from Vietnam or Cuba are from the poorer classes, the tone was set during the entry of the more affluent refugees. Cubans in Miami and New Jersey and Vietnamese in southern California, Houston, and northern Virginia are expected to do well in school and normally do.

ACTING OUT EXPECTATIONS

Educators often assume that Asians are smarter than others and they act out this assumption in their day-to-day work. They set up classroom environments that virtually assure that this positive stereotype will become deeply embedded in school culture.

As an example, a northern California elementary school recently received an influx of Vietnamese students of Chinese descent and acted out a drama that led to Asian success and Hispanic failure. The school had significant Mexican-American and black populations. It established two bilingual education programs in the children's native languages. After several years it became apparent that most Spanish speakers were not learning enough English to be able to participate in English-only classes. The Asians had greater success. Below the surface was a network of unstated but powerful assumptions that predicted that the Asians would succeed and the Hispanics would not.[32]

The principal impoverished the Spanish-English bilingual program through a number of actions. She insisted that more English be used in the classroom. Soon almost all instruction was in English; the program no longer functioned as a bilingual program. The bilingual kindergarten teacher was assigned to team teach with another teacher who was openly hostile to bilingual education. The kindergarten teacher quit soon after she was assigned this teaching partner. The cluster pattern of rooms in the Spanish bilingual program was changed so that they were no longer in close proximity. Bilingual aides' jobs were cut from full to part-time. Some bilingual teachers quit and others went on extended leaves of absence.[33]

The Asian students received a much fuller instructional program, free from most of the internecine conflicts and pressure that hampered the Spanish program. The English as a Second Language staff was more receptive to the Asian students than to the Hispanics. Most of the staff expected the Asians to succeed, shaped the learning environment to ensure that this would happen, and then celebrated the proof of their expectations.[34]

Other minorities sometimes buy into this Asian success story. Black and Mexican-American parents and children in Stockton, California knew that Asian students at the elementary school were smarter than they were. Immigrant literature is replete with references to the Jews by other immigrants as smart and cunning and able to get ahead.[35]

THE CULT OF THE CELEBRATORY

Various commentators generalized these stereotypes into a myth of school as the savior of the newcomers and the minorities. It is a part of the Horatio Alger or American Dream syndrome that promotes the idea that society is supremely meritocratic. That means that people's position in life coincides with their native abilities. They celebrate the public schools as the agency of this upward mobility and ignore other factors. It is basically a status quo political position that says what is, is what ought to be. As former *Saturday Review* education editor Peter Schrag observed,

As always the winners wrote the history of the war. The WASPs and those sons of immigrants – usually Jewish – who used the system to get ahead touted its virtues: all those doctors who were sons of immigrant peddlers, all those lawyers whose fathers worked in sweatshops . . . celebrating immigrant mobility through the common school and hardly aware of the Irish, the Italians, the Poles, the Negroes, the Lithuanians, the Indians who remained in their precincts and ghettoes and barely moved at all. When the system worked, it worked only on WASP terms: you changed your name and named your children Lynn and Shelly and Morris and you didn't mind their growing contempt for your ethnicity. But often it didn't work at all and the casualties who disappeared from public reckoning collected in places called South Boston, Charlestown, Harlem, Daly City, Cicero and South Side Chicago. . . .[36]

THE UNDERSIDE OF THE SUCCESS STORY

While Asian-Americans seem to be riding a wave of success, there has been another, more gloomy side to the picture. Although the blatant discrimination that the Japanese and Chinese have experienced has receded, there are plenty of unsavory incidents of bigotry against Asians. Taken together, these incidents form patterns that warn us that the excesses of the past have not been permanently overcome.

Some of the worst problems have beset the H'mongs, hill people from Laos who worked with U.S. forces in Indochina. They have no written language and few people who are literate in any language. Several thousand were resettled in Philadelphia and almost all have since moved on. Low-income Philadelphia residents resented the presence of the H'mong because they were under the mistaken impression that the H'mong received special job training or actual jobs. There were many incidents of violence and other forms of hostility.[37]

Many of the H'mongs moved from their original resettlement sites to Minnesota and California. In California, most settled in the area around Fresno. School systems in this area are faced with a large influx of LEP students. In Minnesota, many settle in the Minneapolis-St. Paul area. Unemployment is high and resentment runs deep among other minorities who have been led to believe the same false rumors as the people in Philadelphia. There have been name-calling and rock-throwing incidents. A H'mong commented, "In Laos we were a minority people, but there was no crime, no prejudice and we were never treated as badly as we are here."[38]

Vietnamese fishermen and their families on the Texas gulf coast have suffered because of their economic success. Willing to work harder and longer hours, they have consistently out-earned Anglo fishermen. Incidents of violence and the entry of the Ku Klux Klan brought matters to a boiling point. Many Anglo and Vietnamese families have moved elsewhere. In Denver, Vietnamese and Chicano residents of a public housing project came into conflict over access to public housing and jobs as well as over cultural differences and other issues.

Some politicians and newspaper publishers have pushed the idea that Southeast Asian refugee admissions should be drastically reduced or cut off altogether. They claim that U.S. citizens are suffering from "compassion fatigue" and no longer welcome refugees. Further, they claim that refugees are trying to stay on welfare indefinitely and do not want to work. This is a strange twist in the model minority situation. At the same time some political forces are praising the refugees to the skies, others are questioning their morality and threatening to prevent the possibility of their families' joining them in this country.

Filipinos (or Pilipinos) born in the United States often still suffer harsh conditions; many still work in agriculture-related jobs on the West Coast or in Hawaii for minimal wages. They and the native Hawaiian people are at the bottom of the ethnic scale in Hawaii. Another group of more recently arrived Filipinos are part of the middle-class culture, having been trained in universities in their home country. Chinese-Americans and Japanese-Americans still confront discriminatory conditions, but not as bad as in the bad old days. Some observers fear that as economic warfare escalates between the U.S. and Japan, Asian-Americans will suffer from the backlash. As if to underscore this fear, in 1984 a Chinese-American was killed by people connected to the automobile industry in the mistaken belief that he was part of a Japanese conspiracy to put Detroit out of business.[39]

These and other incidents point to the negative aspects of the model minority syndrome. The rise of anti-Semitic incidents and neo-nazism in various parts of the courty is another indication. There is no absolute permanence to the Asian or model minority success story in a country that has deep-seated anti-minority traditions. When times get tough, minorities usually suffer the most.

RECOGNITION OF THE SETUP

Asians and others have become increasingly aware of the way their favored positions and achievements have been held over the heads of other minorities. At Brown University, the Asian-American Students Association protested moves by the administration that would have placed them in an antagonistic relationship with other minorities. They were concerned about minority admission, hiring practices, and a whole range of other campus activities in which minorities were involved. They refused to allow the positive stereotype of the model minority to be put forth on their behalf by the administration or by others.[40]

Asian-American intellectuals have been noting and analyzing the contradictory situation that is often set up between themselves and other minorities. Eugene Wong, for example, points out that in the case of Asian-Americans, the model minority is praised as the image of delayed gratification, thrift, and perseverance, while other minorities are denounced as lazy and lacking ambition. Wong says this process implies that Asians are racism-proof, that they do not suffer from discrimination. This reverse "blame the victim" theory can be turned into its opposite when Asians are seen as too competitive, as the Jews were. When this happens, the Anglos fear the loss of their societal prerogatives and may strike out at the supposed perpetrator of their loss of privilege.[41]

Ultimately this recognition of the setup and its pernicious effects can help to overcome the worst of the syndrome. Once myths can be cleared away, the prospects for positive change improve. Both the successful and the destined-to-fail minorities are victimized by the model minority setup. So is society as a whole. It is a diversion in the effort to achieve both equity and excellence in education.

15

Why Programs Fail

What is going on in 90 percent of the classrooms in this country is a joke in respect to what bilingual education ought to be. And if you're going to tell me that it doesn't work, I'll agree with you. It doesn't work.[1]

Bilingual teacher trainer,
Sacramento, 1985

Conventional wisdom has it that bilingual education does not work. Investigating programs across the country leads to partial agreement with this view. The real issue is, why is this true? Is there something inherent in the program that causes poor results or are there other reasons?

To answer this question it is necessary to look at the process of delivering services to the classroom. As outlined in earlier chapters, there are certain common factors that render the program weak on a national basis:

1. Near total reliance on federal funding, which thus far has never served more than 10 percent of LEP students, combined with a scarcity of local and state money.
2. Poor teacher training mechanisms leading to a severe scarcity of bilingual teachers, administrators, counselors, and other educational personnel.
3. Understaffing of state and local bilingual education offices. Leadership sometimes chosen as political payoffs rather than on merit.
4. Reluctance by school officials to acknowledge the size and needs of the language minority population.

5. Uneven and sometimes negligent efforts to enforce federal and state laws dealing with bilingual education as civil rights.
6. Discrimination against Hispanics and other language minorities, which often leads to low academic expectations, tracking into nonacademic programs, and other obstacles.
7. Reluctance by regular classroom teachers to accept bilingual personnel.
8. Bilingual education's marginal, isolated position as a consequence of the factors mentioned above.

Given these conditions it is important to focus on the actual processes by which bilingual educational services are delivered by local districts to the students. To do so it is useful to examine several districts in northern California and Massachusetts that have significant LEP populations. Children learn here, but not enough to stay abreast of their English-speaking peers; the mental withdrawal and physical dropout rates are quite high.

San Francisco's situation provides a case study. Local language minority parents, led by Chinese community activists, urged the local school system to institute special language instruction for their children. Dissatisfied with slow progress, they launched the *Lau* v. *Nichols* case, which became the landmark Lau Decision of the Supreme Court in 1974. In the twelve years since the decision the city has been beset by conflict over how to implement the decision. The battle lines were drawn between a school board-appointed citizens' task force, which wanted bilingual instruction in the several major languages of the children, and an administration that wanted a token expansion of the preexisting system, which was mainly English-as-a-Second-Language instruction for some LEP students and submersion for many others. The main antagonist was the assistant superintendent, who supervised bilingual education. He set up a bilingual office that provided little help to a corps of struggling teachers whose new mandate was to start teaching in Chinese, Spanish, Korean, Vietnamese, and Pilipino as well as English. The program expanded, but never reached more than a fraction of those who needed this instruction.[2]

As the LEP population grew, the program reached a smaller percentage. In 1984 over 47 percent of the city's student population came from non-English-background homes. Many students had acquired spoken English, but were far from proficient in writing or reading the language. Almost 5,000 new LEP students of a total school population of 60,000 entered the system each year. Most were literally right off the boat (or plane). They received an initial course of instruction in special newcomer centers, but many fell between the cracks. As a system it was completely inadequate to cover the needs of the students. Many administrators and school board members could not adapt to the fact that their district had become heavily language minority and, like the state as a whole, would soon see these language minorities become the majority. As the Chinese community activist Dr. L. C. Wang saw it,

> the short-term small gains in the long struggle for bilingual-bicultural education made by the Task Force and the minority communities in San Francisco should not be construed as a lasting victory . . . bilingual-bicultural education as effective and appropriate as it may be, will be rendered useless and given no chance to survive in an environment that is both intolerant and hostile to the needs and interests of the students of different language and cultural backgrounds.[3]

Nearby Oakland also has a long history of conflict over bilingual programs. About 20 percent of the students are language minorities, mostly Latins and Asians. Spanish-English and Chinese-English bilingual programs have existed for over a decade. They came into being as part of a consortium of several neighboring school districts that pooled their resources to bring in dual language instruction. Hispanic and Chinese parents took a number of steps to convince career bureaucrats in the central office to support a districtwide bilingual program that would cover all the LEP students, but always fell short in spite of the fact that one of the superintendents was a whole-hearted supporter of bilingual education. The careerists' inertia apparently defeated the superintendent's enthusiasm.[4]

The parents eventually tired of this bureaucratic gamesmanship and took the school district to court. The district counter-sued the parents in an effort to get them to drop their litigation. The countersuit demanded that the parents and their attorneys pay more than $4 million. After months of bitter wrangling, both sides agreed to a court-approved settlement, which required the school district to

1. Adequately test students for level of English proficiency and refer them to appropriate instructional programs.
2. Provide curriculum material for bilingual classes.
3. Hire 200 more certified bilingual teachers and ensure that the 100 bilingual teachers who were teaching in 1985 when the settlement occurred would take the necessary steps to obtain certification if they were not already certified.

4. Form self-contained bilingual classes at every elementary school that had 20 or more students from the same non-English language group.

To try to guarantee that these provisions would actually be carried out, the parents demanded and won the right to have an expert auditor employed by the district for three years. The auditor, a bilingual education professor, would be responsible for "reshaping and fashioning bilingual education in Oakland."[5] If the district disagreed with the auditor's findings, a court-appointed monitor would mediate between the two sides.

Early indications were that the district quickly reverted to form. A reporter found that instead of hiring qualified bilingual teachers, regular teachers were merely being told to promise to learn the students' languages and were reborn as bilingual teachers. One teacher signed up to learn Khmer (Cambodian) because she knew that no classes in Khmer were being given anywhere in the area and thus she would not really have to learn the language. In fact not a single certified Khmer-English bilingual teacher existed in the entire state of California, a state in which more than 40,000 Khmers have settled. But the schools' did turn out to have a large number of Chinese-speaking Vietnamese students and the same teacher was told to learn Chinese. She was shocked. "She was so angry her voice shook. 'But there are Chinese classes. I've got 3 kids. I'm 40 years old. I'm not about to go try to learn Chinese.'"[6]

A temporary solution was found. Bilingual teacher aides were employed at $5 an hour with no fringe benefits. A principal soon discovered that people fluent in the native language and in English were not going to work for such low wages for long. Thus the likelihood of further contention and controversy will continue to exist for the indefinite future.

Lynn, Massachusetts is an aging industrial city north of Boston. Hispanics comprise a significant minority of its public school population. Most are Puerto Ricans and Dominicans. Just after Massachusetts enacted the first state bilingual education law in 1971, Lynn began a small bilingual program. At first the classes were held in a school that served the physically and mentally handicapped. Later classes were held in a local church. A local observer describes that program as total chaos. Still Lynn expanded its program as parental pressure and the presence of an expanded LEP population induced a change from the old ways. But, as often happens, the change was one of form not of substance. There were only two ESL teachers in the entire district, and both were "grandfathered" in without being certified. The counseling staff had no bilingual counselor. No provisions were made to adapt special, remedial, or vocational education to the needs of the Spanish-speaking students. Students were not learning English, nor were they able to participate in or profit by the range of special services that were offered to the majority students. The dropout rate was quite high and caused a parents' committee to file suit against the local district in collaboration with a legal defense and advocacy group. But in this case they used Lynn as only one example of what was happening statewide. They also sued the state board of education for failure to provide the necessary services and for failure to induce local boards of education to offer a complete education to LEP students.[7]

The litigants cited the case of Francisco V., a newly arrived Dominican student in Lynn, as an example of educational dysfunction. The student had been earning A's in his content subjects that were taught in Spanish, but had not been taught enough English to survive in the overall educational process. He was seen as a prime candidate for dropping out. Other students were in similar circumstances. Most suffered from a lack of English instruction. A state school official agreed that the students were receiving little or no English instruction and that counseling services were insufficient. All signs pointed to a policy of benign neglect on the part of Lynn and state school authorities.

The assistant superintendent in San Francisco, the central school bureaucracy in Oakland, and the local officials in Lynn left education for LEP students on the back burner. They committed sins of omission, not commission. They did not chastise or beat children who spoke Spanish or Chinese; neither did they serve them adequately. The common thread uniting these cities is the absence of official support. Thus programs fail primarily because they are not supported by school officials. Central offices and school boards have not supported bilingual education, they have sent it adrift. Many of these programs have failed or only partially succeeded in teaching English and content subjects to LEP students. When they are castigated in the media or in the political realm, a lot of the real blame can be placed on the indifference of school officials. Many of these officials see programs for LEPs as just one more irritating special mandate that they can wait out until the pressure is off. Only parents, with the help of interested professionals, have the interest and the staying power to ensure the creation and survival of effective programs.

16

Language Minority Education Outside the United States

Why are French and English Quebeckers so badly divided on educational issues? . . . Language stands at the head of the list . . . because it has been increasingly employed as a weapon of political and cultural change.[1]

Montreal education professor

Industrialized countries have brought in language minorities since World War II to handle society's dirty work. A few like Canada have much older language minority communities that never "melted" into the dominant society. Schooling practices in these countries vary, but some common themes can be uncovered that are comparable to U.S. minority schooling. The industrial boom of the three decades after World War II led to a demand for semiskilled and unskilled labor in the seven countries under consideration: Sweden, Canada, Israel, France, Germany, Great Britain, and the Netherlands. The native-born birth rates dropped sharply. The newcomers came from several sources:

1. As immigrants from present or former colonies.
2. As guest workers under contract between the industrialized country and the native country.
3. As immigrants or refugees from countries outside former colonial areas.
4. As undocumented or illegal entrants.[2]

Single men frequently came first and later brought family members to join them. The worldwide oil crisis of the early 1970s retarded industrial

135

growth and reduced the need for immigrant labor. While many governments tried to induce the immigrants to return home, most stayed and continued bringing over their families. There is currently a substantial youth population, the children and even the grandchildren of the original immigrants, who were born in the new country and may never have seen the native country. They still live as immigrants in the host society. Most of the newcomers live in urban areas and overall make up 5 to 15 percent of the national population. Demographers estimate that by the year 2000 a third of the under-35 age groups will be made up of language minorities. The demographic dynamic can be viewed in the following article on Germany:

> The population of West Germany today is about 60 million people. But Germany has the lowest birthrate in the world, and so the German population already is declining modestly.
>
> According to official projections, the slow decrease will gain momentum in the years to come. By the year 2030 – not so far away – the German population will have gone down to about 35 million!
>
> Is this a problem? My sense is that it is – an enormous one – and not only for Germany. This nation is only the laboratory model of what's going on in the rest of the free, modern, Western world.
>
> The Germans have a total fertility rate of 1.4 children per woman. The U.S. rate is 1.8 – which is about the rate for the entire community of modern nations. But it takes 2.1 children per woman to keep a population stable over time. So population loss – already begun in Germany – is likely to be in store for the rest of us in years to come.
>
> In theory, the demographic shortfall could be changed by massive immigration. But Germany already has 5 million foreigners – mostly Turks. They are not very popular. Most Germans agree that Germany will not take 20 million more Turks. So population will go down. So what? So there will be a stark change in Germany and, by extension, in the rest of the modern world.[3]

The immigrants come predominatly from Mediterranean countries, especially Spain, Portugal, Italy, Turkey, Morocco, Algeria, Yugoslavia, and Greece. Another large group comes from southern Asia: India, Pakistan, and Bangladesh. Smaller numbers come from Hong Kong, Africa, nationalist China, Finland, Poland, Iran, and elsewhere in the Middle East and Vietnam. Many are minorities within their native countries (the Kurds of Turkey, the Berbers of Algeria, and the Jews of Morocco) and may not be fluent in the national language. Most are from worker or peasant backgrounds in the home countries and few have had much formal education. There are sectors within this population that come from better-educated middle-class backgrounds, but the majority work in blue-collar jobs in the new countries and hope that their children will become businessmen or professionals.

Some of the countries have highly centralized educational systems that are run from the Ministry of Education. Others are decentralized. Most have historically educated immigrants in the assimilationist-submersion mode. Some changes were made in the European countries when, in 1976-1977, the European Economic Community or Common Market issued directives urging member countries to use bilingual education methods in their schools. As we proceed on brief country-to-country surveys, schooling patterns will become clear.

SWEDEN

Sweden makes the most use of bilingual education, although the program is not universally applied. Large numbers of Finns regularly enter Sweden as part of a regional open borders policy. The Finns are generally poor and in search of better economic opportunities. A highly successful bilingual education program was set up in northern Sweden in the 1960s to serve these Finnish newcomers.

More recent immigrants include middle-class Chilean and Vietnamese political refugees. They also include larger numbers of poor Turks, Greeks, and Yugoslavs, as well as recent waves of Finns. The non-Swedish population is about 10 percent, and in 1978 one in four births came from this sector. Metropolitan Stockholm has a number of heavily immigrant enclaves. Most Swedish youth learn English, German, or French; very few learn Finnish, Turkish, or Greek.

Swedish education regulations require that bilingual education be put into effect for immigrant students, but this is not always done. Many of the newcomers experience frustration and alienation in Swedish schools, and their academic and vocational attainments lag behind those of the native-born. Some have merely been submerged in all-Swedish classes and have been expected to absorb the language and the content instruction by osmosis. A Finnish immigrant remembers:

> There was nobody to explain things, there were no interpreters, no Finnish teachers and no kind of teaching of the Swedish language . . . . When the others wrote in Swedish, I wrote in Finnish. From the time I first learned to spell it had given me pleasure to put sentences together on paper. But that was something that just couldn't be done. The teacher grabbed my pencil and

angrily shook his finger at me. In spite of everything I continued to fall back
on my mother tongue. There was a row at my desk. The teacher tore up my
paper and stamped on my words he had thrown on the floor . . . a Finnish
boy from an upper grade was brought in to tell me writing compositions in
Finnish was prohibited.[4]

Immigrant students were less likely to be admitted to the academic
secondary schools than Swedish speakers. They were more likely to be
in vocational courses and more likely to become dropouts. But the gap
between the immigrant and native-born communities is less than that
elsewhere.

FRANCE

France presents a pedogogical situation different from that of
Sweden. France has insisted that newcomers learn French and learn in
French. A heavy cultural overlay buttresses the widely held belief that
French language and culture are superior to every other, and that they
need to be taught or inculcated in the minds of the young in as strong a
way as possible.

France, unlike many of the other countries considered here, has had a
long history of immigration. Millions of Italians and other southern
Europeans entered France in the nineteenth and early twentieth centuries
as laborers. Others entered as political refugees from tsarist or Soviet
Russia, Franco's Spain, and from various colonized areas. Some of the
post-World War II newcomers are also refugees from places like Iran,
Vietnam, Lebanon, and other trouble spots, some of which were former
French colonies. The great majority are immigrants in search of better
economic opportunities from Portugal, Algeria, Morocco, and Senegal.
They consitute 8 to 10 percent of the overall population and a much
greater percentage in metropolitan areas like Paris, Lyon, and Grenoble.

Certain languages are taught commonly and favored in French
schools. These include English and Spanish. On the other hand, the
languages of the immigrants, especially Arabic and Portuguese, are rarely
taught in schools or given any credibility. Not surprisingly, the young
immigrants are one to several years behind the national academic norm.
Newly arriving students are often placed in classes of native speakers
who are several years younger than themselves. This may set the
newcomers up to be ridiculed or stigmatized and may lead to early

dropouts. Few newcomers advance far enough in the rigorous academic coursework in the college preparatory sequence to gain admission to prestigious universities. Most take a vocational course in secondary school, but few are able to use this course to obtain a good job. Unemployment is high among these young people. There is little social mobility among Portuguese or Algerian youth, the two main immigrant groups.

France began special classes in French as a foreign language in some areas within the last decade, and has a few truly bilingual classes. The latter were instituted in a few schools in and around Paris in response to the European Economic Community's call for the use of such instruction in 1976 and 1977. More commonly, France contracts with embassies to provide native language instruction. These native language classes are often held after regular school hours and rarely in conjunction with French-as-a-Second-Language instruction. The predominant mode remains submersion in French-only instruction undergirded by a strong French cultural nationalism.

THE NETHERLANDS

The Dutch situation parallels the French. A formerly Dutch-only language instructional pattern is slowly changing. Holland's non-native Dutch-speaking population includes people from the former Dutch colonies of Indonesia and Surinam and the current colonies of Aruba and Curaçao. The majority are newer arrivals from Mediterranean countries like Turkey and Morocco. The current 7 to 8 percent foreign population is expected to continue growing rapidly in light of the fact that the Dutch birth rate has been dropping 3 to 4 percent per year. Amsterdam, The Hague, Leyden, and Rotterdam have large immigrant populations.

Historically, Dutch education policy has assumed that everything must be subordinated to the interests of the Dutch language and culture. Recent media attention to the high dropout and unemployement rates among immigrant youth, coupled with complaints by immigrant parents, has led to some educational experimentation. A widely heralded bilingual school in Leyden is one example. It provides dual language instruction to newly arrived Moroccan and Turkish students. It is part of the regular Dutch school system and does not segregate the students as German schools often do. Teacher training colleges have also been buffeted by the winds of reform. One educator noted that the colleges "need to be adjusted to the fact that Dutch society has become a multicultural society."

The reality of the ethnic diversification of Dutch society only gradually permeates the consciousness of educators who in turn institute reforms very slowly. Dutch schooling, like French, still marches to the assimilationist tune.[5]

GERMANY

Germany, like the Netherlands and France, comes from a tradition of vehement assimilationism. But rather than resisting the winds of change as long as the other countries have, the Germans have, in the main, opted for a system of native-language instruction in semi-segregated schools.

Since Germany had no former colonies to draw labor from and since it did not seek permanent immigrants, it made contractual agreements with Italy, Turkey, Spain, and Yugoslavia to receive guest workers. Their stay in Germany was supposed to be temporary. As the Employers' Association stated, "The great advantage in employing foreign workers is that it puts at our disposal mobile manpower. It would be dangerous to restrict this mobility by a policy of settlement."[6]

In 1966 there were 1.3 million foreigners, mainly single men. The number had doubled by 1973, a time when the international oil crisis forced a sharp reduction in industrial activity. Recruiting of foreign workers stopped and the government hoped that most guest workers would return home. They offered them financial inducements to return; but most rejected the offer and continued to bring in their families. By 1980 there were five million guest workers among 60 million people in the country as a whole.

Most of the newcomers work in low-paid unskilled or semi-skilled sectors of the major industries: chemicals, textiles, foundries, and mechanical and service industries. Most live in older sections of the major industrial cities. Frankfurt has a particularly heavy foreign presence – over half the births are to foreign parents. There is large scale unemployment. There are all the ingredients for the existence of an isolated underclass.

A considerable cultural and social distance exists between the Germans and the immigrants. As a rule, contact with Germans is restricted to the workplace; private contact seldom amounts to more than the exchange of greetings. Closer contacts involving family or leisure time activities are found only within the small group of immigrant workers whose knowledge of German is very good . . . .

The most striking feature of the immigrants' existence is a fundamental insecurity, which seriously affects the way they live in West Germany and which makes any long-term planning more or less impossible. This situation naturally has an effect on the immigrants' motivation to learn German or take part in any teaching programme. The foreign workers' motivation as well as their consciousness vacillates between adaptation to the foreign society and commitment to a familiar form of life. Such a state of permanent suspense has a particularly negative effect on the education of the second generation.[7]

Until the 1960s, Germany educated its immigrant children in the submersion mode. This was the accepted practice until pressure for change was exerted among educators and language minorities. Today there are various types of education offered at the discretion of state education authorities. Preschool programs are offered to all youngsters and are crucial to the early mastery of the German language. Most guest-worker families, however, have a hard time participating because they are set up in such a way that parents must transport children several times during the day. Since most immigrant mothers work, they cannot participate in such an arrangement.

The two most common approaches at the elementary and secondary levels are the submersion mode and "bilingual" mode. Bilingual instruction here is taken to mean predominantly monolingual instruction in the native language. There have been some highly successful bilingual experiments, notably the Greek School in Munich, in which students gain proficiency in Greek and German. Much more common, however, is native language instruction offered by teachers under contract from the German educational authority through the embassies of the native country. This monolingual instruction produces children who lack fluency in either the native language or German.

Because there is no coordination of instruction in both languages, the learners are overtaxed and, depending on individual circumstances, they either settle on rapid language assimilation or adhere to the ghetto of the native language. Yet almost all the (Yugoslav, Greek and Turkish) learners have deficits in their command of German and the native language so that one can speak of a two-sided demi-lingualism.[8]

Immigrant children are thus siphoned off from the educational mainstream into what are frequently called national or ghetto schools. They rarely learn enough German to allow them to transfer to mainstream schools. Finally, significant percentages of immigrant children come from minorities within their home countries and do not speak the national language. This is especially true of the large Kurdish contingent among the Turks. Most speak Kurdish and have scant knowledge of Turkish, in spite of the fact that the Turkish government has banned Kurdish instruction for many decades. In classes taught by Turkish-speaking contract teachers hired by the Turkish embassy, the Kurdish children are lost. They often cannot understand Turkish and their parents resent the covert or overt anti-Kurdish themes that may emerge during the school day. Many Kurds left Turkey to escape the anti-Kurdish aspects of Turkish society.[9]

Thus the German version of bilingual schooling seems to parallel the German effort to get the immigrants to return home. It tells them, learn the native language so you can go back home soon, even though as children and grandchildren of immigrants you may have been born in Germany and may never have seen or want to see the family's native country. Predictabley, few immigrants reach neither the highly competitive academic institutions nor the top-level trade schools that lead to good skilled jobs. Most end up without high school diplomas and are relegated to filling the same sort of low-wage low-status jobs their parents held, or they end up unemployed.

GREAT BRITAIN

Great Britain's educational system is decentralized and major decisions affecting language minorities are made at local levels. Language minorities have emigrated to major British cities for over a century. Prior to World War II most came from Ireland, Wales, and Scotland. While some spoke English and others originally spoke native languages, most have partly or wholly integrated into the English mainstream. Since the war the major influx has come form South Asia (India, Pakistan, and Bangladesh). Most speak Urdu, Punjabi, Gujarati, or Hindi as mother tongues. Some South Asians had lived in areas of Africa that had expelled or oppressed them. Another major stream has come from Jamaica, Trinidad, and other West Indian countries; but these immigrants are English-speaking and are treated as racial groups rather than as language minorities. A third stream comes from southern and eastern Europe and Asia. All these groups live in Greater London or in the midlands or other industrial areas to the north of London. While some of the newcomers, especially South Asians, are from professional or business classes at home, only a small fraction have attained that status in

Britain. Most are working class and are trying to cope with falling levels of employment in major industries.[10]

Illustrative of this situation is the midlands town of Derby, the home of Rolls-Royce, British Celanese, and British Rail Engineering, Ltd., all of which have instituted large layoffs in recent years. In the heavily immigrant neighborhood of Normantown, a social worker reflected on the condition of the South Asian, West Indian, and Vietnamese residents:

> Whether we want to admit it or not, we live in a racist society, and in a recession it get worse rather than better. . . . The people who live here lose their jobs first, and most of them are trapped in a poverty cycle.
>
> Inevitably when you look behind the emotional and family problems, you find no jobs, poor jobs, bad housing. They live in claustrophobic conditions. . . . Many of them speak no English, so it's almost impossible for them to get their hands on the levers that could alleviate their problems a bit.[11]

British education is highly localized. Language minority schooling is characterized by low expectations and tracking practices that impede the aspirations and academic progress of language minorities and by an assimilationist mindset that says to minorities "you do not exist." Many educators are still bound up in racialist approaches to the issue of school performance. A West Yorkshire teacher, referring to South Asian students, stated his views in terms familiar to those who grew up in Mississippi or South Texas:

> Now the people you are talking about, their sons and daughters, finish up in this school in classes which are non-examination or bottom CSE. They rarely have sons or daughters who are going to be bright GCE candidates and it isn't the fault of the education system and it isn't the fault of western civilization, it's inherent in life."[12]

These attitudes help set the stage for tracking (or streaming) these students away from academic tracks. Counselors and teachers frequently try to convince South Asian youth to lower their expectations.

British school systems use submersion, English-as-a-Second-Language, or bilingual modes of instruction. Bilingual experimentation has spread rapidly since the European Economic Community's support of this approach. One notable experiment took place in Bedford, north of London, a city whose massive brick-making concern began importing Polish and Italian laborers in the 1950s. A later recruiting campaign brought hundreds of more Italians, largely poor country people from southern Italy and Sicily, as well as South Asians and West Indians. The city is more than a third immigrants, 80 percent of whom are Italians. The Italians were hired to fill "the desperate shortage of English labourers willing, in a time of affluence, to do the tough dirty work of the brick fields."[13] Landlords divided houses into tiny apartments "to pack in Italian families like bricks in a wall."[14] Most of the newcomers were illiterate and few had any experience with schooling that they could transmit to their children.

European Economic Community officials urged the local education authority to conduct Italian-English instructional programs and provided the initial funding. An elementary program and later a secondary program were established that were rated positively by several evaluators. Bedford never taught its native English speakers Italian, however; it concentrated on French. Bedford and nearby Bradford are also the sites of experiments in Punjabi-English instruction. Bradford College became a leader in the effort to train bilingual teachers. By 1984, several nationwide organizations had arisen to promote bilingual instruction and numbers of local education agencies had launched bilingual projects, especially at the preschool and early primary levels. A number of teacher training institutions had instituted a bilingual training course and had included multiculturalism as part of their general curriculum. Bilingual education appears to be on the rise in Great Britain.

CANADA

Canada's 25 million people include about 12 million Anglo-Canadians, 7 million French Canadians, and another 6 million who are not descended from these "founding peoples." They are the descendants of pre- and post-World War II immigrants from Ireland, Italy, Greece, Portugal, and Eastern Europe as well as recent arrivals from China, the West Indies, Latin America, South Asia, and Vietnam. Most are clustered in and around Toronto, with significant numbers in Montréal and Vancouver. Sixty percent of Toronto's public school population speaks a language other than English as their first language.[15]

Nowhere have language issues been more intense than in Canada, with many schoolhouses serving as battlegrounds. Ever since British troops vanquished the French on the Plains of Abraham in 1763, the two groups have battled over language rights. Canada is officially bilingual in English and French; but schools are conducted in English almost everywhere except the Fench stronghold of Québec, which has Montréal as its major city. Québec maintained separate English and French school systems prior to the 1960s when the Ministry of Education unified the two systems. About the same time the famous St. Lambert immersion program began in a suburb of Montréal. Here middle-class English-speaking parents promoted total French instruction in the early grades. By the upper levels of elementary school, children were introduced to English instruction, and by secondary school many children had attained dual fluency. Some parents wanted their children to learn French as a way to unify the French and English sectors of the nation; others wanted their children to be more competitive in the increasingly bilingual job market. This program coincided with the militant assertion of French language and political rights, as exemplified by the rise of René Lévesque's Parti Québécois and other factions that called for separation from Canada. The French immersion programs eventually spread to include over 250,000 English speakers throughout Canada and are actively promoted by a national group of parents.

Those who designed the program avoided immersing the French-speaking minority children in English. They contend that minority children placed in immersion classes in the majority language are likely to get lost in an atmosphere that undervalues their native language. They therefore proposed bilingual education as an alternative so that French could be preserved as English was learned. Bilingual education has become common in Québec and among French speakers in other provinces. Language wars continue, but at a lower level than previously, due in part to government recognition of French and other language minority rights as embodied in 1970s legislation that promotes multicultural and multilingual awareness in schools.

Multiculturalism and multilingualism have probably gone further in Canada than in the other countries described in this chapter. Education has come a long way from the nineteenth and early twentieth centuries, when Asians were forbidden to immigrate and immigrants were said to have faulty intelligence. The Toronto school superintendent characterized the Irish immigrants in the following manner:

> The physical disease and death which have accompanied their influx among us may be precursors of the worst pestilence of social insubordination and disorder. It is therefore of the last importance that every possible effort should be employed to bring the facilities of education within the reach of the families of these unfortunate people, that they may grow up in the intelligence and industry of the country and not in the idleness and paupering not to say mendacity and vices of their forefathers.[16]

Interestingly, Toronto has taken the lead in multicultural experimentation. Its Main Street School is built on the idea that children gain from sharing experiences and learning together. Its principal flatly rejected assimilationism as a goal: "The aim is not to assimilate these young people into our culture, but to integrate them."[17] Bilingual schools were started for the Italian, Greek, and Chinese communities as well. Vancouver established a system of bilingual instruction using English and several languages of the Indian subcontinent. Québec offers French bilingual schooling for Portuguese, Italian, and Greek speakers. Alberta offers English-Ukrainian programs and Manitoba and the Northwest Territories offer instruction in several of the languages of the North American Indian population in those provinces.

In spite of these innovations, language minorities confront school systems that put forth low expectations and a job market that offers limited horizons. Most are guided into vocational tracks and few get to academic tracks. Ethnocentric attitudes continue from the old days: "Administrators and teachers were suddenly required to alter long-held ethnocentric attitudes without any special preparation and had in a short time to begin accommodating a very different kind of new Canadian from Trinidad, Bangladesh, the Azores, Jamaica. . . . There were no educational policies; there were no guidelines to help devise programs, no instruments for the assessment and placement of atypical students. Furthermore the teachers themselves were never prepared . . . ."[18]

Bilingual and multicultural education may help ameliorate the learning process and promote academic progress, but they are not the panacea for social inequality.

ISRAEL

Israel's educational policy is derived from and driven by its founding and sustaining ideology, Zionism. Zionism is the modern nationalism of European Jews that arose in Central Europe in the nineteenth century and found its mass appeal in Eastern Europe early in the twentieth. A secular philosophy, Zionism promotes the use of Hebrew over Yiddish and other languages spoken by Jews.[19]

The Jews of Middle Eastern countries, the Sephardim, had very little contact with Zionism prior to Israeli independence in 1948. Zionism had been almost completely the property of European Jews, the Ashkenazim, as well as those descendants of European Jews who settled in the Americas and South Africa. The European Zionists set up settlements in Palestine in the late nineteenth and early twentieth centuries. Palestine was ruled at first by the Ottoman (Turkish) Empire and later by the British. Both colonial powers gave the Zionists the right to set up their own school system. Non-Zionist Jews (both Ashkenazim and Sephardim) also lived in Palestine. Their schools were usually conducted in major European languages. Zionists tried to convince them to Hebraicize their schooling and were partially successful.

The great mass of Sephardim came to Israel in the decade and a half after independence. They were brought in to settle the country. Most spoke Arabic, while others spoke French, Ladino (A Spanish-Hebrew language), Kurdish, or Italian. Once in Israel they were sent to separate and less prestigious resettlement areas than the Ashkenazim. Most were put in the new industrial towns in the interior far away from Tel Aviv and Jerusalem. Many Sephardim later drifted into these cities, primarily into decaying neighborhoods or shantytowns. Regardless of education or experience, Sephardim were geared to blue-collar occupations by the government, while most newly arriving Ashkenazim were placed in the professional, business, clerical, or semi-professional sectors. Schools and neighborhoods tended to be segregated; Hebrew was the sole medium of instruction. Most educators were Ashkenazi, and because almost none knew Arabic, they were unable to help their Arabic-speaking students make sense of the curriculum. The curriculum was built around the European Zionist ethos and contained almost nothing about Sephardic culture or its contributions to the building of the new state. As one Sephardim remembers it: "I learned about Bialik and Tchernichovsky, I studied Hebrew literature and Jewish history. I learned abaout every movement and counter-movement, Maskilim and Fundamentalists, Hassidim and Mitnugdim, but not one word about my people, about my culture."[20] Arabic was seen as an inferior language in a country striving hard to be a European bastion in the Middle East; students were often told to discard their Arabic and rely totally on Hebrew. Many Sephardim refused, as illustrated by the following example:

One day an 8-year-old said the Passover blessings in Hebrew instead of the family's traditional Arabic. The father asked him why. The youngster said that the teacher had told him that because they were in Israel they had to speak Hebrew. The father pointed to the door of the apartment and said, "Look at that door. Out there is Israel. In here is Morocco."[21]

Palestinian Arab students were placed in a separate Arabic-speaking school system and not provided with the advantages of the Ashkenazi schools. After the 1967 War, Arab students in the occupied territories of the West Bank and Gaza attended schools in a semi-autonomous system administered by the same officials who administered them prior to 1967. Arabs inside Israel have certain rights, but exist in a legal status inferior to that of Jews in a Jewish state. Some master Hebrew and are able to enter the major universities. A few become professionals and enter the Israeli mainstream, but most remain on the margins.

Sephardic students' school attainment has consistently lagged behind those of Ashkenazim. Educators often project low expectations for Sephardic youngsters, and there is a high rate of mental and physical withdrawal. Sephardim are frequently guided into nonacademic tracks, and relatively fewer complete college than do the Ashkenazim.

After a series of sporadic protests by the Sephardim in the 1950s and 1960s, school authorities instituted reforms designed to integrate the two Jewish groups and to remedy Sephardic underattainment. The reforms were based on the notion of cultural deprivation, namely that Sephardic culture was not up to European standards. Patronizing attitudes permeated the reform efforts. Sephardic attainment improved, more Sephardic teachers were hired, some aspects of Sephardic culture filtered into the curriculum, and there were some attempts at integration. But through all this Sephardim lagged as far behind the Ashkenazim as ever. Ashkenazi attainment had also risen.

Sephardim have since become the majority of Israeli Jews. They provided the margin of victory for Menachem Begin's triumphs in 1977 and 1981. But, according to Deputy Prime Minister David Levy, a Sephardi,

> The Zionist perception of one culture turned out to be a myth . . . (Sephardim) were treated differently. They were sprayed with DDT, sent off to poor housing in development towns, with their children given inferior educations. Their resentment, still burning, is a fundamental political and social fact in Israel now.[22]

This burning anger surfaces periodically on a range of issues, including education. The elite of Israel's decision-makers in business, the military academia, schools, and politics is still overwhelmingly Ashkenazi in spite of two terms under Begin. The schools remain Hebrew-only, and students learn English as a foreign language and not Arabic. The prospects for Sephardic advancement to parity with the Ashkenazim using the schools as the agency for upward mobility is extremely unlikely.

What can we conclude about the experiences of other industrialized countries in educating minorities? First, that most started treating foreign-language-speaking students in the submersion mode and later, under pressure, began to modify the situation by employing bilingual instruction as well as the national language-as-a-foreign language methodology. In most countries, submersion remains a major method of instruction; in Israel it remains virtually the only mode for its Jewish students. In some countries, bilingual education has made major pedagogical and even political inroads, especially in Sweden and Canada and increasingly in Great Britain. In others, notably Germany and France, what is called bilingual education is more than likely to be instruction in the native language only, which may be a cover for a policy of persuading guest workers to return home and which often leaves children in a state of nonproficiency in both the native language and the new language.

Second, in all the societies under consideration, language minorities remain on the slow track, as in the case of Israel, where Sephardim have become the numerical majority of the dominant group. Low expectations, cultural deprivation notions, nonacademic tracks, dropping out, and a host of other negative characteristics beset most language minority youth, even in countries in which instructional programs are advanced and enlightened. An ethnocentric cultural motif hangs heavily over these countries and pervades the education profession. There are surely cases of individual and small-group success among language minorities (many South Asians in England, for example), but overall the picture is bleak. Most language minority youth seem destined to fill the same dirty work slots their parents held, or, worse yet, become candidates for chronic unemployment.

Third, demographic projections and conventional wisdom suggest that the language minority presence is increasing rapidly as the native population's birth rate declines sharply. The implication is that language minority education will become an issue of greater significance in the future and that political battles over control and allocation of resources will be reflected in battles over schooling as they have been in Canada and Israel as well as in the United States.

Fourth, the foreigners' language is almost never taught as the prestige foreign language to native students. Swedes do not learn Finnish, they learn English. Germans do not learn Turkish or Arabic, they learn

English. French children eschew Portuguese and Arabic in favor of English, Spanish, or Swedish. Israelis learn English, not Arabic. Europeans are multilingual but rarely proficient in the languages of their immigrant populations; this reflects a Eurocentric view of the world.

Fifth, in order to enter and succeed in institutions of higher education, language minority students must master the dominant language, and to a certain degree at least, they must cast off their native languages and cultures and absorb or embrace the dominant ones.

How does all this compare to the case of U.S. Hispanics? In many ways, very closely. Hispanics also do the dirty work, are subject to layoffs and employment uncertainty and are treated as marginal even if they have lived in the country for generations. Their children rarely attain high levels of schooling or the vocational programs designed to prepare them for desirable blue-collar jobs. Most are directed into non-academic tracks and get little encouragement from teachers and counselors. Within the overall population are middle-class subgroups whose children frequently achieve higher levels of academic and vocational accomplishment, as is the case with many Cubans. Like language minorities abroad, Hispanic demographic growth brings with it actual or potential political clout and the possibility that more entrenched groups will resent the intrusion of the newcomers.

U.S. schooling trends tend to follow patterns similar to those elsewhere: a gradual move away from submersion toward a bilingual situation buttressed by teaching English as a second language. However, the movement is intermittent, is buffeted by conflicting local and national conditions, and is subject to frequent reversals. Furthermore, the mentality of many mainstream education personnel lingers in the era of the submersion mode, a fact that often causes deep rifts between them and the bilingual personnel. One major difference between the United States and other school systems flows from the question of which foreign languages are to be learned by majority students. Spanish is now the major foreign language studied in the United States, whereas in other countries the language of minorities is rarely used or even shunned, except in Canada.

Language minorities in the United States and elsewhere comprise peoples from all parts of the world:

1. Indians, Pakistanis, Koreans, Vietnamese, Pilipinos, Chinese, Indonesians
2. Black Africans

3. Northern Europeans (e.g., Finns and Poles)
4. Turks, Arabs, Kurds, Armenians, Afghans, and other Middle Eastern peoples
5. Southern Europeans, such as Greeks, Portuguese, Italians, Yugoslavs, and Spanish
6. Latin Americans
7. Polyglot peoples like the Surinamese and Arubans from present and former Dutch colonies in the Americas
8. Native peoples, especially in Canada and the United States
9. Other peoples of the Americas who are not of Spanish origin, like the Haitians

All have certain experiences in common; all are to one degree or another on the periphery of the host society and all have experienced discrimination in one form or another.

There are differences too. A Finn or a Pole can fit into the Swedish or British mainstream easier than a Turk or a Pakistani. Third-world immigrants find things more difficult than their European counterparts. Language minorities are not in the same position as those treated primarily on a racial basis, like U.S. blacks or British West Indians, who speak the mainstream language. Racism pervades the treatment of language minorities as well, but seems to take a more virulent form against the same-language racial groups mentioned above. The main thrust against language minorities seems to be a virulent nationalism or even xenophobia that sometimes surfaces as it did in the United States during and after World War I. This ultra-nationalism sometimes takes the form of seeking to preserve the purity of the native language against the onslaughts of the newcomer groups who want to challenge its sanctity with the threat of bilingualism.

17

Preschools and Teacher Shortages: Promise and Dilemma

A consensus is building among educators and a large segment of the public that early childhood education is valuable, especially for the children of minorities and the poor. Early experiments in nursery school education were not as well received. These experiments flowed from the attitude of noblesse oblige of the rich toward the poor. Philanthropists sought to remove children from what they assumed were the negative influences of their parents and communities. As the Boston philanthropist Annie Fields put it in the 1890s:

> Let us take the little child in the future from its possibly ignorant careless mother as soon as it can walk and give it three hours daily in the kindergarten where during that time it will be made clean, will enjoy light, color, order, music and the sweet influence of a living and self-controlled voice.[1]

Immigrant and working-class parents were suspicious of the motives of these wealthy do-gooders.

Unlike the elementary and secondary schools which were transformed from private or religious institutions into public ones, nursery schools are still largely privately run. There never has been a massive government effort to set up permanent nursery schools. During World War II, when women workers were needed in the factories, day-care centers were set up overnight. They were just as quickly dismantled when the war ended and the female workers were displaced by males. The 1960s and 1970s saw the onset of Head Start and other early intervention programs aimed at the poor. There were efforts to establish

152

federally subsidized day-care centers or nursery schools. But they fell victim to the claim that if Uncle Sam sponsored or aided these centers or schools, federal intrusion into the home and family life would result.

Recent studies of the effectiveness of Head Start programs provide evidence that Head Start graduates achieve at a higher level in elementary and secondary school than do children from similar backgrounds who have not been enrolled in Head Start. It seems reasonable to assume that early childhood education can help the children learn the rudiments of reading, writing, and arithmetic, and even science and social studies before they enter kindergarten or first grade. Perhaps, more importantly, they can learn about the culture of the school. They can understand the kind of discipline the teacher expects. They can adapt to classroom learning situations. They can be ushered into the public world of schooling and commune with, or become conversant with, the storehouse of knowledge and wonder and excitement that true learning provides.[2]

This is doubly important for language minorities. The public world they enter is not one of their parents' making, it is one constructed by the adherents of the majority culture. Making a smooth transition to this public world is all-important in school success. Youngsters who fail to make this transition often end up in the mental withdrawal syndrome described earlier, which almost guarantees school failure.

Public figures like New York Mayor Edward Koch, Texas Governor Mark White, computer magnate Ross Perot, New York Governor Mario Cuomo, South Carolina Governor Richard Riley, and Hunter College President Donna Shalala favor a vast expansion of early childhood education opportunities. Many have cited the high minority dropout rate as a key factor in their view that preschools help breed a climate of success.

Texas school reform law HB 72, enacted in 1984, embodies some of these ideas. Preschools are mandated for four-year-old LEP students and for special education students. Ross Perot, Mark White, and other Texas leaders believe that LEP students can learn a great deal of English in the year before kindergarten and will be able to enter school much better equipped than they were before.

Koch and Shalala also base their support for preschools partly on the need to serve language minority pupils. It is no accident that New York City, the dropout capital of the world, is in the forefront of these developments. The dropout rate has risen in recent years, and there is public discussion and debate on how to stem it. As the nation's media center, anything New York does gets national attention. If early childhood education is seen to work here on a large scale, the possibilities increase for its use by other areas.[3]

But what of cultural intrusion? Could preschool be just another spruced-up version of Anglo cultural invasion? The answer of course is, if left alone it could be. Parental vigilance and the willingness to struggle over the curriculum of the preschool may play an important role. Nothing is guaranteed. Early childhood education could be a tremendous boon to language minority young people; but it could also become an obstacle. A lot depends on how the political forces shaping the preschool movement are defined, and how they carry out their mission.

THE TEACHER SHORTAGE: THE PROGRAM'S ACHILLES HEEL

There never have been enough teachers for bilingual programs. The scarcity exposes the program's weakness; it demoralizes parents, children, and school people who want the program to succeed. The estimates of the teacher deficit vary from 20,000 to over 100,000 nationwide, with only 2,000 bilingual teachers graduating from college each year.

Houston's school system provides a case in point. In 1985 they needed 500 bilingual teachers, including those who will teach in the new state-mandated bilingual preschools. The entire state of Texas produced only 320 bilingual teachers in 1984. Houston already has 16 percent of its students in 1,000 bilingual classes. The Houston Independent School District went a step further than most districts in need of teachers; it advertised outside the United States. It placed advertisements in Mexican newspapers, although it did not expect a large supply from Mexico. It did achieve media attention and dramatized the problem. A school official stated,

> What we are seeing all across the Southwest is an increased need for bilingual education. We are not alone in our recruitment. . . . Schools are going about getting teachers all ways – offering them extra money, offering to pay for their moving expenses and offering tuition reimbursement.[4]

Los Angeles, with 130,000 students enrolled in 5,000 bilingual classes, also has a huge shortfall. It has resorted to several categories of waivers for teachers without bilingual training to allow them to teach bilingual classes provisionally. These nontrained teachers are of three types. Some are English-only speakers who work with native-language teacher aides. The English speakers have six years to gain bilingual certification. Another category consists of English-speaking teachers who team-teach with bilingual teachers. Finally there are bilingual college graduates who majored in fields outside education. A Los Angeles school official stated that even if all students currently enrolled in bilingual teacher training programs in all of California's colleges and universities were to enter the Los Angeles schools en masse, it would still not completely fill the shortage. San Francisco, Boston, Washington, D.C., Chicago, Seattle, Albuquerque, and other districts are experiencing similar shortages. New York City had to hire bilingual teachers from Spain and Puerto Rico. The Phoenix assistant superintendent stated that "we are almost desperate."[5]

Why is this so? Bilingual teacher training programs turn out far too few graduates because there are far too few of these programs. This is due in part to the reluctance of colleges of education to launch bilingual training programs until they know that federal money is guaranteed. Like elementary and secondary school officials, deans of schools of education are cautious and see bilingual education as a marginal program that they would prefer to have little to do with. They themselves rarely know anything about bilingual education or the needs of LEP students. There is nothing sexy or trendy about the field as there is in math or science or computer education. They frequently view professors of bilingual education as upstarts who are trying to push a new subdiscipline into the tried-and-true verities of teachers' college culture. For these reasons and more, the prospects for major improvement in the training of bilingual teachers are not promising.

Without a solid teacher corps to anchor its infrastructure, bilingual education will remain chronically weak. Model programs from Coral Way to the present have shown that this infrastructure could be bolstered if resources and energy were expended. It is not only a matter of money, but also of will, of determination. After the initial luster wears off, teachers, parents, and administrators often become discouraged. Bilingual education has not ushered in the millenium. Youngsters still do poorly and drop out in large numbers. In the face of this disheartening ebb tide, many are ready to give up, making bilingual education just one more frustration in the chain of well-intentioned programs that go awry.

Those who reject this defeatism and want to persevere in spite of the obstacles need to devise a teacher training agenda that speaks to retraining teachers from other fields, providing more support and a career ladder for bilingual teachers' aides, and expanded and improved teacher training in colleges of education. The focus of action has to be on pressuring the federal and state governments to act on this issue that has now reached crisis proportions. If such an agenda is not devised and acted on successfully, bilingual education is liable to dry up from its own internal contradictions.

18

Non-Hispanic Groups in the Bilingual Education Constituency

When we fail to keep our language and culture, we lose a part of ourselves. We can never do our best work if we are trying to be someone else.[1]

Ross Swimmer,
chief of the Cherokee Nation

Hispanics account for about 70 percent of the students involved in bilingual education programs; Asians for 10 to 15 percent. The remainder include a diverse group of other minorities and non-English speakers including the Cajuns, Haitians, and French-Canadians; Indians of various tribes; immigrants from Middle Eastern countries; and recent arrivals from countries that provided the bulk of immigrants in the 1880 – 1924 wave of immigration – Poland, Italy, Portugal, and Greece. Unlike the Hispanics, they are not at the center of the bilingual movement, and unlike the Asians, they are not considered model minorities. However, these groups are important members of the constituency whose support has helped to keep bilingual programs afloat, especially in regions and states that do not have a large Hispanic or Asian presence.

CAJUNS

The Cajuns of Louisiana are the descendants of the Acadians, French speakers who both left and were forced out of British-ruled Canada in the eighteenth century. They resettled in the then French territory of Louisiana. The territory was later sold to the United States. The Cajuns have preserved aspects of their language and culture ever since. They are centered in the southwest part of the state. Here the towns have names like Breaux Bridge, Thibodaux, Lafayette, and St. Martinville. Louisiana entered the union as a predominantly French-speaking state. Counties are called *parishes*, and aspects of the Napoleonic Code still prevail in the law. The state constitution makes several references to the importance of French language instruction in the schools.

Many Cajuns work in the oil and natural gas economy that is widely dispersed throughout the region. Therefore it is unnecessary to move to the larger cities to secure employment. Radio stations broadcast in French. Newspapers and magazines often publish in both languages. A local priest has recently published a dictionary of Cajun French. Several congressmen and Governor Edwin Edwards are Cajuns, and the ethnic group plays a major part in state politics.

Bilingual programs began in several school districts early in the 1960s and expanded to the rest of the Cajun parishes as well as to the Baton Rouge and New Orleans areas, both of which have significant Cajun populations as well as Hispanics and Asians. Louisiana educators are also actively promoting foreign language in the schools as a way to teach French to English-dominant Cajuns and to non-Cajuns. French-English bilingual programs imported teachers from Belgium, France, Québec, and Switzerland.

FRENCH-CANADIANS

The French-Canadians are closely related to the Cajuns. They too immigrated from Canada, but they came within the last one hundred years. They settled initially in Maine, Vermont, and New Hampshire towns near the Canadian border. About 30 percent of Maine residents are of French-Canadian descent. Many later moved to industrialized New England towns and cities like Bangor, Providence, Salem, Lowell, and Manchester. They and the Mexican-Americans are the only U.S. ethnic groups that live adjacent to their ancestors' native land.

Most came originally as farm laborers and mill workers. They have gradually become a part of all levels of the social structure. Several congressmen are of French-Canadian descent. The most well known is probably Rep. Ferdinand St. Germaine of Rhode Island, the chairman of the House Banking Committee.

Bilingual programs have honeycombed the northern New England region. Among them have been programs in Richford, Vermont; Berlin,

New Hampshire; and the St. John's Valley of Maine. Several branches of the University of Maine are actively engaged in training bilingual teachers to conduct these and other French-English projects.[2]

HAITIANS

The Haitians are also French speakers from a former French colony. Their dialect, like the distinct dialects spoken by the Cajuns and by the French-Canadians, is quite different from the French spoken in France. Most Haitians are recent emigres from the harsh economic and political conditions in their native country. They settle predominantly in the Miami and New York City areas, as well as in other East Coast cities. New York City's black congressmen and the Congressional Black Caucus have taken up the cause of the Haitians and have promoted the community's participation in bilingual education. Shirley Chisholm, former Brooklyn congresswoman was particularly active in this area as well as in defending bilingual education as a whole. The number of Haitian bilingual programs is rising, as is the awareness of the needs of Haitian children among educators in New York City, Miami, and elsewhere.

NATIVE AMERICANS

There are more than 200 tribes of Indians and other native peoples in the United States. Some live on reservations, some near former reservations, and others dispersed among the general popualtion in towns and cities. Most tribes maintain some aspects of their native language; a few, like the Lumbees of North Carolina, speak only English. Historically, Indian schooling has been carried out by the tribes themselves or by the U.S. Bureau of Indian Affairs (BIA), which is part of the Department of the Interior. Some tribes in the nineteenth century had a higher rate of literacy in their native language than the surrounding non-Indian populations. This was especially true of the Mississippi Choctaws and the Oklahoma Cherokees.

The BIA both operates schools and contracts out the operation of Indian schools. The federal Johnson-O'Malley Act, enacted in 1934, reimburses states that educate Indians in local school districts. The more recent Indian Education Act subsidizes some Indian schooling as does the federal Impact Aid law. The Bilingual Education Act provides money for about 90 bilingual programs, a multifunctional resource center that serves Indian education in western states, and various materials development projects that help develop texts and other instructional materials in Indian languages and in English. This crazy-quilt pattern of funding forces Indian educators to master the byzantine and often changing maze of federal laws and regulations.

The largest tribal group is the Navajo, who maintain a huge reservation in Arizona and surrounding states, which includes the famous Rock Point bilingual school.[3] Others active in the bilingual movement include the Hopi, Yaqui, and Papago of Arizona, the Cheyenne and Crow of Montana, the Zuni of New Mexico, the Sioux and Lakota of South Dakota, the Blackfeet of Idaho, the Choctaws of Mississippi, the Passamaquoddy of Maine, the Ojibway of Minnesota, and the Menominee of Wisconsin. There are also many cities like Chicago, Los Angeles, Albuquerque, Minneapolis, St. Paul, Tucson, and Seattle in which children from one or more language groups participate in bilingual or ESL programs.

The Cherokees are the second largest tribe and one of the most active. Centered in four northeastern Oklahoma counties, they present a rich history of persistence in their struggle to survive. In 1821 they published books in their native language and circulated them among tribal members. In 1836 the U.S. government forced them to move from their tribal homeland in Georgia, Tennessee, Alabama, and Mississippi to Oklahoma. Most had to march the entire distance. Over 4,000 people died on the infamous Trail of Tears.

Once resettled they devoted a tremendous amount of energy to educational endeavors. They conducted over 30 elementary schools and two higher education seminaries. All of the instruction was in the native tongue and most of the teachers were Cherokees. Their literacy rate was higher than the Anglo rate in Oklahoma and Arkansas; by the 1880s the Cherokee literacy rate reached 90 percent, a remarkable achievement for the period. As more Anglos moved into Oklahoma after 1889, the territorial and federal governments dissolved the Cherokee lands and school system. Cherokee youngsters had to attend the Anglo schools, in which all instruction was in English. They were punished for speaking the Cherokee language in school. Their literacy rate in the native language and in English declined sharply and the dropout rate surged.[4]

The Cherokees were among the first groups to take advantage of Title VII grants and used them to try to reconstruct the damage done to their education by providing dual-language instruction. Most of the Cherokees are poor and work in the food processing, lumber, and garment industries. The unemployment rate is about 25 percent. Many have intermarried with Anglos. Many Cherokees moved to nearby larger cities like Tulsa, but found that the discrimination was difficult to endure and moved back to the four northeast counties. The bilingual programs in the four counties involve nine elementary schools that enroll a total of 2,000 students, about two-thirds of whom are Cherokees. Most learn enough English to allow them to advance to the Anglo-dominated secondary schools of the region. Most also learn enough of their native culture and language to help reinforce their identity as Cherokees, which in turn helps them discover the positive values of education.[5]

Closely connected to Indian education is the education of other native peoples of Alaska and the Pacific. The Eskimos as well as the native peoples of Hawaii, Guam, and American Samoa have made good use of Title VII programs to try to provide their young people with increased opportunities. Many have used bilingual programs as a platform that has equipped them to go on to either local or distant institutions of higher education.

PORTUGUESE

Portuguese immigrants entered the United States as part of the last wave of European immigration. But they are coming over in significant numbers in the current wave of immigration as well. The recent arrivals are largely from the Azores, a group of islands in the Atlantic Ocean. They tend to settle in the same areas as the earlier Portuguese: New England, especially Rhode Island and Massachusetts, and to a lesser extent in Connecticut, New Jersey, and northern California. The Portuguese have historically been associated with maritime industries and still are. These include fishing, shipbuilding, stevedore and warehouse work, and import and export concerns. Bilingual programs have been under way in Providence, Fall River, New Bedford, and the Boston area for more than a decade.

Immigrants from Cape Verde, a newly independent former Portuguese colony, settle in some of the same areas and have several bilingual programs.

ITALIANS, GREEKS, AND POLES

Italians, Greeks, and Poles were major groups in the 1880 – 1924 stream of immigrants. The 1965 Immigration Law and the Refugee Act of 1980 liberalized immigration requirements, making it possible for hundreds of thousands of residents of these countries to come to the United States.

Poles have been entering the United States in recent years as refugees from Soviet-dominated Poland. Included in this group are a number of members and supporters of the organization Solidarity. Many Poles have settled in Chicago, the largest Polish city except for Warsaw, and in other areas of Polish settlement like Detroit, Buffalo, Cleveland, and Milwaukee. Chicago and Hamtramck, Michigan, among other jurisdictions, have sponsored Polish-English bilingual classes in the public schools.[6]

Greeks settled in the Northeast, the Midwest, and on Florida's west coast early in the twentieth century. More recent arrivals have followed similar patterns. Queens in New York City and the Tarpon Springs area of Florida have started Greek-English programs. Florida State University and several other institutions of higher education have established teacher training institutes for the preparation of educational personnel to work in these programs.

Italians also settled in the Northeast and, to a lesser extent, in the Midwest, California, New Orleans, and Tampa. Bilingual programs in Italian and English are functioning in New York City and parts of Massachusetts. Several congressmen of Italian descent have been supporters of bilingual education, including Rep. Silvio Conte of western Massachusetts and Rep. Mario Biaggi of New York City. It is no accident that Italian bilingual programs are located in these areas.

MIDDLE EASTERN IMMIGRANTS

People from Middle Eastern countries have come to the United States in recent years as both refugees and immigrants. The Armenians are both an old and new immigrant group. Early in this century Armenians settled in New England, the New York City area, and California. A number of recent Armenian refugees from the civil strife in Lebanon have settled in southern California. Los Angeles has dual language programs in several schools. The Chaldean community and other Christian and Muslim Arab communities are spread around the Detroit area, especially in Dearborn, Michigan. Dearborn, Hamtramck, and Detroit have had extensive Arab language bilingual programs. Arab communities in Brooklyn and Queens have also participated in these types of instructional programs.

Refugees from the upheavals in Iran and Afghanistan are also part of some bilingual programs. Iranians have been active in southern California, in the Washington, D.C. area and in the New York City area. Afghan youngsters have also participated in several programs in eastern cities, especially in the northern Virginia suburbs of Arlington and Fairfax counties and the city of Alexandria.

These groups together comprise only a small portion of the U.S. population, but their influence is broader than their numbers. When they organize politically they are able to become an important pillar of support for bilingual education. This occurs in three ways. First, a number of senators and representatives from districts without a significant Hispanic presence have been lined up as supporters. This is especially true of Indian areas like Oklahoma, Montana, and the Dakotas, French and Portuguese areas of New England, the Cajun section of Louisiana, and Euro-ethnic areas of the East and Midwest.

Second, the Bilingual Education Act requires OBEMLA to distribute its grants equitably across the country. This provision ensures that New York, California, and Texas will not monopolize the grants and that many will go to non-Hispanic areas. Third, Asians and the ethnic groups mentioned in this chapter give the bilingual education program the image of being more than just a Hispanic enterprise. While Hispanics will probably always have the majority of participants because of political and demographic considerations, all of the above-mentioned groups will share in the remaining 30 percent of program grants. The increasingly polyglot makeup of urban populations reflected in bilingual classes points to the fact that bilingual programs serve many populations, including the majority. No one has an exclusive franchise on them.

19

Congress and the Courts in the 1980s

The federal courts and Congress continue to provide a backdrop to the evolution of all federal education programs, including bilingual education.

THE COURTS

Hispanic students and their parents have filed two types of class action suits in seeking to advance their educational opportunities. The first type is suits initiated by language minorities demanding special language instruction and/or bilingual instruction. These suits started in the early 1970s after the Office of Civil Rights issued its May 25 Memorandum, which required districts to do something about Hispanic inability to speak English. The Lau, Serna, and Aspira cases outlined earlier were put forth and achieved limited gains. Bilingual programs were set up in many areas, some as a direct result of court decrees, others from Office of Civil Rights pressure. However, as noted earlier, many of these districts reverted to a business-as-usual stance when the glare of the federal judge's attention faded. These cases were seen as one-shot deals – the judge decided and the school district complied.

In longstanding desegregation cases, on the other hand, another set of circumstances has prevailed. Many judges have themselves seen the need for consistent monitoring and frequent re-intervention in the desegregation process after the initial decision. The logistics of desegregation are often seen as far more complex and time-consuming to carry out than is the case with other types of school litigation cases. Therefore, in those desegregation cases in which Hispanic communities have been admitted as aggrieved parties, the chances of consistent judicial monitoring are greater than in the one-shot type of case.

Denver's Keyes desegregation case began this process when, in 1974, the judge declared that Mexican-Americans were a distinct ethnic group and were entitled to participate in the desegregation proceedings. The judge ordered Denver to institute bilingual programs in five elementary schools as part of the effort to end discrimination in education. Several years later the judge ruled that the program must be expanded to 15 schools. In 1984 he ordered that 31 schools institute Spanish or Vietnamese programs.[1]

What changed in this time period? Demographics and consciousness. When the desegregation suits started in southern school districts in the 1950s and in northern and western districts in the following decade, blacks were the only recognized minority. The suits were based, after all, on the *Brown* v. *Board of Education* decision, which concerned blacks, as well as on the Fourteenth Amendment to the Constitution, which was passed to protect the rights of newly freed slaves.

But the Denver judge commented in 1984 that now Hispanics were the city's largest minority. By extending bilingual education to 31 of the city's 81 elementary schools he was showing awareness of both the demographic change and the change in consciousness that came about when he and other judges became fully cognizant of the rights of language minorities to be instructed in dual-language settings.

The longstanding Ross desegregation case in Houston shows some similarities. Hispanics there were not yet the largest minority group, but in 1984 represented 34 percent of the school system's population. Several Houston school officials stated that Hispanics would equal or overtake the 45 percent black population later in the 1980s. Houston's Hispanic growth is caused by several factors. First is the fact that Hispanic residents of Houston are younger than other populations and there are proportionately more women of childbearing age. Second is the migration to Houston of Hispanics from towns and smaller cities in Texas. Third is the immigration from Mexico and most recently from El Salvador and other parts of Central America.

The judge in the Ross case has supported bilingual education as a remedy for the discrimination that Hispanics suffered in the past. In 1984 he required the school system to hire many more Spanish-speaking aides than were currently on staff. As mentioned elsewhere, Houston is also faced with compliance with a new state law requiring bilingual preschool classes for LEP children, as well as with a severe shortage of bilingual teachers.[2]

San Jose's school system has also been the target of a desegregation suit. Its 30 percent Latin constituency lives in the poorer northern part of the city, while most of the Anglo children live in the wealthier southern part. The judge here is also monitoring the desegregation process to ensure that the rights of language minority children in the district were being institutionalized.[3]

Denver, Houston, and San Jose are southwestern cities with huge Hispanic communities, so it is natural that some of the major court desegregation decisions mandating bilingual education are being produced there. However, other parts of the country have seen similar suits. Milwaukee, Detroit, and Boston, for example, have witnessed the intervention of Hispanic communities in desegregation suits initiated by blacks. The trend of the 1980s seems to be that federal judges in desegregation cases are more and more likely to mandate bilingual education as a recognition of the rights of the growing Latin presence among the school districts's population.[4]

THE CONGRESSIONAL CONSTELLATION

Bilingual education did not drop from the sky full-grown. It had a socially constructed reality that followed a pattern not unlike that of other Great Society programs outlined in previous chapters. Bilingual advocates help keep it alive by enfolding it within the protective surroundings that are afforded all the enduring Great Society programs. This is revealed in three ways: First through the placement of Title VII in omnibus education bills at reauthorization time; second in bilingual provisions that have been placed in other federal education laws; third in the overlapping and mutual cooperation in lobbying activity.

Hours after Congress convened in 1983, Chairman Carl Perkins of the House Education and Labor Committee introduced House bill H.R. 11. He knew that his measure would get a low number that was easily recognizable as the major federal education measure. He also knew that his measure would gain momentum by being introduced months before the Reagan administration supporters in Congress could come up with their own federal education package. H.R. 11 contained the bilingual education reauthorization as well as adult education, Indian education, women's equity education, and similar measures. By embedding bilingual education within the protective mantle of the omnibus education package, Perkins and other leading education advocates hoped to keep it moving steadily through congressional twists and turns, rather than leaving it isolated and vulnerable to attack. After representatives Kildee and Corrada introduced and shepherded a separate, expanded bilingual bill through the House Education and Labor Committee, they eventually placed the new measure in Perkins' omnibus package for the rest of its journey through Congress. Perkins agreed to accept the Kildee-Corrada version as a substitute for his bilingual measure. This has been the pattern for all three of the Bilingual Education Act reauthorizations.[5]

Bilingual education is also a part of other federal education programs. Congress added bilingual provisions to these other education programs as a way of ensuring that Hispanics would participate. The vocational education program, for example, includes funding for training adults to acquire job skills using dual-language methodology. Hispanics have been trained as auto and airplane mechanics, chefs, and computer operators. Both the immigrant and migrant education programs make widespread use of dual-language instruction. Special education programs are sponsoring innovative approaches to the instruction of handicapped LEP students. A large segment of adult education program energies is devoted to aiding the establishment of English as a Second Language and naturalization classes. In states that give the high school equivalency examination in Spanish, adult education classes are also held bilingually. Refugee education and Indian education programs provide funds for school systems that frequently use bilingual instruction for these students. Chapter I, Head Start, the Job Corps, and many others use funds in similar ways. Almost all federal education, labor, and health laws contain provisions requiring them to serve historically underserved constituencies, which often brings them into contact with LEP students.

LOBBYING GROUPS

Washington's education lobbying groups can be classified into general and the specific types. General types can be further characterized by their main focus: higher education or elementary and secondary education. The latter include the National Education Association, the National School Boards Association, the Children's Defense Fund, the Council of Great City Schools, and the American Association of School

Administrators. Associations of governors, cities, labor unions, counties, and state legislatures also have lobbyists who work on general education issues. Specific groups concentrate primarily on a single program. They include the American Vocational Association, the Council for Exceptional Children, the Adult Education Association, and the National Indian Education Association.

NABE deals with both the specific and general education groups in mobilizing support for the Bilingual Education Act reauthorizations and funding issues. NABE may support other groups' primary issues as well. NABE also coalesces with ethnically based organizations such as the National Council of La Raza, the League of United Latin American Citizens, the Organization of Chinese Americans, Aspira, the National Puerto Rican Coalition, the Congressional Hispanic Caucus, the National American Indian Congress, and the Mexican-American Legal Defense and Education Fund.

Bilingual advocates have found it useful to cast their lot with the constellation of federal education programs. By acting in concert with supporters of this education package deal, they can best guide their program through dangerous waters. In relatively good years like the late 1970s, everyone gains; the education programs got funding increases and regulations more to their liking. In bleak years like 1981 and 1982 they all suffered; most had to absorb cuts of 15 to 25 percent and accept regulations that weakened their implementation efforts. In the mid-1980s, these federal programs are bobbing along, neither adequately funded nor wiped out. By sticking with them, bilingual education assures itself better chances at survival, but not dynamic advancement or growth.

20

Funding:
The Bottom Line

Ever since guns won out over butter during the Vietnam War, reporting about the federal funding of education has been one negative story after another – the annual fight against rescissions during the Nixon and Ford years; the generally stagnant funding that followed under Carter; the massive cuts during the first year of the Reagan Administration; and recent efforts to prevent a repeat of that debacle. Education's share of the total federal budget is so small that some policy makers, including some state governors, seem to believe that their energies would better be spent elsewhere.[1]

Anne Lewis, education analyst, 1985

Education programs live or die by the funds they can conjure up. Officials of programs like bilingual education with insecure funding patterns spend an inordinate amount of time (sometimes the majority of it) seeking money. The administering of the program may suffer. Secretarial and clerical support staff may be tied up in funding matters to the detriment of program matters. Principals and even teachers may be pulled away from their jobs to help write proposals or to lobby legislators or bureaucrats. As states and the federal government retrench, less money is available, and the squabble over scarce dollars intensifies.

The 16,000 U.S. school districts have vastly different funding patterns. The average district receives about half its funding from the state, about 40 percent locally, and just under 10 percent from Uncle Sam. Local funds are tied to property taxes. Obviously, poor districts have far less of a tax base to draw on than richer ones. The poorer districts must spend a greater proportion of their time going hat in hand,

169

to Washington and the state capitol seeking money. Moreover, the richer districts have better equipped federal or state program offices whose main duty is to secure grants and contracts. Therefore wealthier districts often pull in more money than poor ones, especially in categories like bilingual education in which the grants are discretionary. Discretionary grants are issued to those districts that complete laborious application forms and offer convincing plans on how they will use the proposed funding. Some districts do not find out about grant opportunities in time. Others have the applications filled out by the uninitiated, who don't understand the welter of tedious regulations, which may result in disqualification for a given grant. The paperwork involved in this process is enormous.

Federal funding is largely categorical; that means that it is targeted to specific types of programs. The largest federal education programs (those over $500 million annually) are

1. Chapter I (formerly Title I) for low-income children. It is distributed nationwide on the basis of numbers of children in a given district. $3.7 billion in 1985.
2. Guaranteed Student Loans and Pell Grants for college students. The grants are made to low-income students. The loans serve lower- and middle-income students or their families. $6 billion in 1985.
3. Special education for the physically or mentally handicapped regardless of income level. It is distributed by a numerical formula. $2.5 billion in 1985.
4. Vocational and adult education. Various kinds of grants, some formula-funded, some discretionary, for a total of over $800 million.
5. Impact aid. Aid to local districts for the education of the dependents of federal employees or military personnel. $685 million in 1985.
6. Chapter II (formerly Title II). Block grants to states for their use in various types of educational programs. $532 million in 1985.

The smaller federal education programs are:

1. Bilingual education – $143 million in 1985.
2. Migrant education – $7.5 million.
3. Science and math education – $100 million.
4. Refugee education – $16.6 million.
5. Indian education – $68 million.
6. Magnet schools – $75 million.
7. Immigrant education – $30 million.[2]

THE CONGRESSIONAL APPROPRIATIONS PROCESS

When a new law is enacted or an older law is reauthorized (extended), Congress sets the law's authorization level. This level is a ceiling, the maximum amount of funding allowable in a given year. The amount Congress actually spends or appropriates in a given year is usually lower than the maximum amount. In 1985, for example, bilingual education had a $176 million authorization level, but only received $143 million in actual appropriations. Some programs get de-funded – they receive no appropriations, and they die.

Annual appropriations decision-making is a circuitous and protracted process. First the president offers a budget for the entire federal government broken down into departments. Then the Senate and House Appropriations Committees consider the funding in subcommittees which specialize in one or more federal departments. The chairmen of the committees and subcommittees wield tremendous power. Almost all members of Congress come to them to seek funding for favored projects. The House committee chairman is Rep. Jamie Whitten, the longest-term member of the House and the father-in-law of OBEMLA director Carol Whitten. On the Senate side, Senator Lowell Weicker heads the subcommittee that controls the purse strings of the Labor, Education, and Health and Human Services departments. His attacks on Education Secretary William Bennett are described elsewhere.

The secretary of education and the assistant secretaries present the administration budget to the appropriations subcommittees of the House and Senate. The subcommittee members "mark up" or deliberate and decide on a money figure for each function of the department. Their recommendations are sent on to the full House and Senate appropriations committees and then to the floors of both chambers. Amendments can be offered at any time to raise or lower the money figures, and some of the amendments succeed. After both the House and Senate pass their appropriations bills, the bills are sent to a conference committee of members of both chambers to iron out differences. Then an agreed on measure goes back to each chamber for a final vote. The skillful legislative strategist knows when to have friendly Congress members offer amendments that will raise the dollars allotted. The bill arrives on the president's desk. If he signs it, it becomes law. If he vetoes, it, a two-thirds majority of members of both chambers is necessary to override the veto. If the veto is not overcome, both chambers have to start from scratch with new appropriations bills. The strategist who masters this network of details is in a good position to influence the eventual outcome.

The final stages of the congressional appropriations process usually occur at the end of one fiscal year (September 30) and the beginning of the next. Complicating the whole matter is the need to keep the government operating while the appropriations are finally decided. Congress usually deals with this problem by passing short-term continuing appropriations measures. These measures are grab-bags that also contain long-term pet projects that members of Congress would dare not offer in quieter times because they are often boondoggles to special interests. Congress and the president often accept these special interest measures in order to help finish the appropriations process, even if they would have voted against them if they had been brought up earlier in the session. Measures favorable to bilingual education have sometimes been passed this way. In 1984, the Immigrant Education Act appropriations were put into the continuing resolution by Rep. Jim Wright, the second highest-ranking House Democrat. The appropriations eventually passed. They contain provisions that mandate school districts to use bilingual education techniques with their immigrant children. The year before, the Immigrant Education measure was tacked on to a State Department authorization measure.

MIXING AND MATCHING

School districts must mix and match funds from various sources in order to educate LEP students. The Bilingual Education Act (Title VII) provides only a fraction of the funds necessary; its programs serve less than 10 percent of the more than 3.6 million LEP students nationwide. Chapter I funds serve many districts, as do vocational education, refugee, migrant, immigrant, and Indian funds if they can be secured. About 20 states provide some sort of funding for educating LEP students to local districts. The pattern is uneven; California, New York, and Illinois provide the most; some of the 20 states offer only a nominal amount. Some heavily LEP states like Florida provide no money at all. The majority of states are in this category, and West Virginia expressly forbids dual-language instruction. State funds at best supplement the federal dollars; local funds for educating LEP students are sparse.

There is little likelihood that most local districts with significant LEP populations will become independent of Uncle Sam any time soon.

SCRAMBLING FOR WASHINGTON'S DOLLARS

As many local districts receive greater numbers of LEP students, they try to find ways to get larger chunks of Title VII money. Some put themselves through contortions to better qualify for these funds. New York City, for example, began competing for federal funds not as one local district, but as 32 community school districts. These community districts were formed in response to various school-centered upheavals that hit the city in the 1960s and 1970s. But they are not fully autonomous – there is still one local education agency. Using the community district approach, over 80 percent of them received Title VII funds. The city as a whole received half as much Title VII money as the entire state of California, which has many more LEP students. New York City (114,000 LEP students) outpaced Los Angeles (143,000 LEP students) $7.2 million to $338,000 in Title VII funds in a recent year, according to a California congressman, who commented: "Unless the New York City Board of Education is uniquely adept at writing grant proposals, I really can't understand how it, even as the country's largest school district, can receive about 20 times more in Title VII funds than the second largest school district."[3] Clearly New York education officials are both adept grant writers and skillful politicians.

THE DEPENDENCE ON TITLE VII

Without federal Title VII funding there would be far fewer Title VII programs and far fewer students in those that continue to exist. Title VII funds accomplish several stated and unstated ends. They directly fund programs that serve 7 to 10 percent of the nation's LEP students and that produce most of the 2,000 bilingual teachers who graduate from college each year. They support the information and technical assistance network that helps districts overcome their deficiencies in bilingual curriculum, instructional material, and information on recent political and pedagogical developments and on funding sources. Finally, they give political direction to local and state education agencies, most of which would have no program to educate LEPs were it not for federal political leadership and civil rights enforcement.

This federal leadership and funding is deeply appreciated by, and relied on by school officials at all levels. Philip Runkel, Michigan's school superintendent, has had a difficult time wringing school funding from a legislature in a state beset by the decline of industrial capacity, a prime example of life in the "Rust Belt." Listen to his 1982 plea to Congress:

Title VII funds were an important incentive for establishing this successful program in Michigan and continue to supplement our efforts. Services from Title VII training and technical assistance have also been important in helping Michigan evolve the high quality programs of which we can justly be proud. In fact, acting upon one of the recommendations in the evaluation report, Michigan has applied for Title VII funding to establish a parent involvement project in addition to funds for basic programs for children. . . . In a year of retrenchment in education, the entire education community must stand united. Title VII is a successful program that fulfills a specific national need – teaching English and educating our nation's limited English proficient children. . . .[4]

Bristol, Rhode Island is a small industrial town near Providence. It has had a bilingual education program since 1977 that was largely federally funded. Bilingual director Maria Lindia characterizes the program for a congressional committee:

From the first whaling ship that brought back new deck hands from the Azores until the present, there has been a steady influx of Azorian Portuguese into Bristol, Fall River, Massachusetts, New Bedford, Massachusetts, and many other smaller cities. This immigration continues and so there are newly arriving students all year round. . . .

Our bilingual program has quietly begun to turn around what has been a vicious pattern of school failure, dropout, unemployment, and crime which we all know far too well. Because our program only began in 1977, we are just now able to see comparisons which might serve to elucidate the drama that is unfolding and the real impact the program is making on our students.

During the last three years 217 students have dropped out of Bristol High School. Of these 26 percent are Portuguese speaking students with a limited English proficiency. This number is six times that of the regular Bristol dropout. We have focused on our elementary school children and have served 200 students in grades one through four. The average length of time each student needs to be mainstreamed is about three years. . . . The first group of these students is turning sixteen now and the cycle is beginning to be broken. . . .

We must allow our newly arriving students to tie into the history that has brought us into our third century and not restrict their capacities, energies and dreams.[5]

Superintendent James Loughridge of Folsom, California, near Sacramento, also faces a heavy influx of LEP students and relies on Title VII to add to what the state can provide. Most of his LEPs are Southeast Asian refugees who speak five different languages. He uses Title VII funds for in-service education to equip his teachers and principals to deal with the newcomers. Some are taught English as a Second Language methodology; most are taught to be aware of the cultural and linguistic backgrounds of the newcomers. Textbooks and audio-visual materials are also provided by Title VII, as are a range of other all but indispensable services.[6]

The pattern is clear. Local school systems need federal bilingual funds to expand and begin to serve all the LEP students within their jurisdictions. They also use other federal money, state funds when available, and some local funds if possible. They have to scramble with one another and tread through difficult federal regulations in order to obtain grants. The ability to get funded, not the actual performance of students, is the ultimate measure of success or failure in bilingual programs. Those who fail to understand the funding imperatives, fail to recognize the foundation on which bilingual education is built.

Conclusion

This journey through the evolution of bilingual education reveals a complicated and often contradictory panorama. The program began as an afterthought of the War on Poverty – as a symbolic gesture to the Hispanic community. It was replete with assumptions about poverty-induced pathology and cultural deprivation and came into being only after the Hispanic community began a series of protests. Some community activists and educators saw bilingual education as the path to liberation; others were not so sure.

The federal government entered the bilingual education-as-civil-rights arena only after the wave of protests intensified. The Office of Civil Rights enforced the policy unevenly and made major tactical errors. The Carter administration also made major errors when it issued the Lau Regulations in 1980. The opposition took advantage of these errors and managed to consign the new regulations to the trash can. Successive administrations from Johnson onward have been less than enthusiastic about bilingual education. Most have exhibited a deep-seated ambivalence about the progam – about its pedagogical value; about providing a measure of decision-making power to Hispanics; about melting pot versus pluralism; about the growing Latin presence and its political repercussions; about the preservation of the anglocentric curriculum. Liberal senators and congressmen expanded the program and rescued it from most administration attempts to weaken or defund it. Most members of Congress seem to view bilingual education as both an education improvement and as a measure of Hispanic empowerment.

Statehouses, local boards of education, and schools themselves became arenas of struggle between

1. Latins and Anglos. Latins seeking to wrest a share of power from entrenched Anglo bureaucracies.
2. The American Federation of Teachers and the National Education Association.
3. English-as-a-Second-Language and bilingual teachers.
4. Different ethnic and class groups within the Hispanic community, each vying for power and control.
5. School officials and federal civil rights authorities.
6. Local media and bilingual advocates over whether the program was a pedagogical advancement or a political power play.

Community, federal, or judicial pressure brought most of the bilingual programs into being and led to their expansion beyond skeletal proportions. The programs that resulted were hastily conceived and poorly implemented, at least in their early stages. They were full of cultural deprivation notions and were decidedly marginal to school system operations. There was almost no experience or in-place infrastructure to draw on. It was not surprising that the programs merely limped along. Teachers and aides struggled to hold programs together, but could only do so much in light of all the surrounding political realities.

Bilingual programs did not fundamentally improve the socioeconomic conditions of poor Hispanic communities. They did not create hundreds of thousands of new jobs. They did not produce overwhelming success as measured by standardized test scores.

What the programs did do was to establish exciting learning environments. These were places in which students and parents felt a part of the schools. This helped to defeat or at least reduce the mental withdrawal-dropout syndrome. The programs did teach students to become proficient in English and, at the same time, to retain their Spanish and not to become ashamed of their native language, family, and culture. At their best, the programs unified majority and language minority students in integrated curricular settings in which both languages and cultures were valued. The programs went a long way toward diminishing the influence of the anglocentric curriculum.

Things never stay static, and bilingual advocates and supporters of pragmatic or philosophical pluralism must formulate and enact a reform package or risk the drift backward toward the sink-or-swim period. The package must contain both long- and short-range objectives and it must be aimed at federal, state, and local levels of school decision-making. It must transform what is into what should be.

This transformational strategy should aim to expand transitional bilingual programs into high-quality integrated programs in which all students could participate. Majority children should learn Spanish (or other major world languages) and basic aspects of Hispanic and other cultures. Language minority children should learn to become proficient in reading and writing their native language while they are learning English. Textbooks should present a true picture of the multi-ethnic nature of the building of U.S. society, not the exclusive Anglo-American view. Majority and minority students should be integrated to learn cultural, linguistic, and content subjects together whenever possible. Magnet schools and other creative devices should be used to attract majority youngsters if they do not live in the school's neighborhood. It has been demonstrated that many English-speaking parents want their children to attend school with Hispanics and to learn to speak Spanish. This is true not only in California, Florida, and Texas, but also in Buffalo, Detroit, Cincinnati, New York, Boston, Milwaukee, Chicago, and hundreds of other places. Programs must be designed to enhance this positive integration.

At the school district and state levels the struggle to centralize and institutionalize the program must be waged. Bilingual education must no longer be viewed as a vestige of the 1960s or as a program solely reliant on federal soft money. The bilingual office must be placed in the bureaucratic mainstream, the program must be funded as a regular line item.

Much of the same holds true at the federal level. But here, the funding question is more serious, even in this period of governmental austerity. Without a much greater federal monetary commitment, state and local increases may just barely keep the program afloat. Federal money is necessary for it to flourish. What is needed is formula funding, a given amount of dollars provided each year per number of LEP students. Special education and low-income educational programs are funded this way; language minority programs are just as important. Local experimentation in program design should be encouraged with the provisos that submersion is totally unacceptable and that language minority parents would be empowered to bring suit rapidly in federal courts against school districts that fail both to teach their children English and to keep them on grade level in their content subjects.

This formula funding would provide a floor for program continuation and would give educators the leeway to experiment without having to be constantly under the cloud of survival anxiety. This formula-funded bill should be part of a national language learning and international studies legislative package that would stimulate major reforms in language learning, area studies, geography, and history and would encourage all students to become bilingual or multilingual. At the same time the current Bilingual Education Act could be used to strengthen the bilingual infrastructure, especially in the areas of teacher training and the development of curricula and instructional materials.

None of this reform activity ensures that creative programs will result. Parental and advocacy involvement and pressure are the necessary ingredients in this sphere. Nor does the reform package guarantee upward mobility to language minorities. This would come about through economic expansion, public and private training and retraining programs and greater public sector employment, especially in building and maintaining the nation's physical infrastructure and its knowledge base.

The key to educational reform is political debate over the curriculum. Ways must be found to involve the public in the debate over the nation's language and other intellectual deficits and the way that the sink-or-swim and cultural deprivation policies have contributed to these deficits. Fair-minded people can be convinced that language minorities are here to stay, do not present a threat to them, and can be educated with instructional programs that serve the interests of both majority and minority language students. Those who are not fair-minded can be out-organized and out-voted.

As a nation we can begin to understand and act on the axiom that

education is a mirror held up against the face of a people; nations may put on blustering shows of strength to conceal political weakness, erect grand facades to conceal shabby backyards and profess peace while secretly arming for conquest, but how they take care of children tells unerringly who they are.[1]

Notes

INTRODUCTION

1.   Fred Burke, "Bilingual/Bicultural Education: An Adventure in Wonderland," *Annals of the American Academy of Political and Social Sciences* 454 (1981):174.
2.   R. Freeman Butts, *Public Education in the United States* (New York: Holt, Rinehart and Winston, 1978); David Tyack, *The One Best System* (Cambridge, MA: Harvard University Press, 1974).
3.   Milton Gordon quoted in Butts, *Public Education*, p. 25.
4.   Tyack, *The One Best System*; James Brooke, "A City's Blight: Riots, Crime, Golf in the Streets," New York *Times*, August 23, 1984, p. A-1.
5.   Heinz Kloss, *The American Bilingual Tradition* (Rowley, MA: Newbury House, 1977).

CHAPTER 1   MILITARY-STYLE ASSIMILATION, 1880-1945

1.   Carey McWilliams, *Brothers under the Skin*, p. 207-8 (Boston, MA: Little, Brown, 1948).
2.   Quoted in Diego Castellanos, *The Best of Two Worlds*, p. 31 (Trenton, NJ: New Jersey State Department of Education, 1983).
3.   Quoted in Charles Aaronson, "The Involvement of the Federal Government in Providing Public Instruction for Non-English-Speaking Pupils from 1800-1980," p. 6 (Ph.D. dissertation, Virginia Polytechnic Institute, 1980).
4.   Marion Brown, "Is There a Nationality Problem in Our Schools?" *National Education Association Proceedings* (1900):585.
5.   Ibid., p. 590.
6.   Elwood Cubberley, *Changing Conceptions of Education*, p. 15 (Boston, MA: Houghton Mifflin, 1909).
7.   Guadalupe San Miguel, "Endless Pursuits: The Chicano Educational Experience in Corpus Christi, Texas, 1880-1960," p. 65 (Ph.D. dissertation, Stanford University, 1978).
8.   David Tyack, *The One Best System,* pp. 198-216 (Cambridge, MA: Harvard University Press, 1974).
9.   Paul Taylor, *Mexican Labor in the United States*, vols. 1-7 (Berkeley, CA: University of California Press, 1928-1934).
10.   Quoted in Meyer Weinberg, *A Chance to Learn*, p. 146 (New York: Cambridge University Press, 1977); see also Paul Taylor, *Mexican Labor* and *An American-Mexican Frontier* (Chapel Hill, NC: University of North Carolina Press, 1934).
11.   Mario Garcia, *Desert Immigrants* (New Haven, CT: Yale University Press, 1981); Ricardo Romo, "Mexican-American Workers in the City: Los Angeles, 1915-1930" (Ph.D. dissertation, University of California-Los Angeles, 1975).

12. Virginia S. Korrol, "Settlement Patterns and Community Development Among Puerto Ricans in New York City, 1917-1948" (Ph.D. dissertation, State University of New York-Stony Brook, 1981).

13. Joseph Monserrat, testimony, U.S. Commission on Civil Rights, *Hearing in New York City, February 14-15, 1971*, p. 43 (Washington, D.C.: U.S. GPO, 1972).

14. Salvatore LaGumina, "American Education, The Italian Immigrant Response," in *American Education and the European Immigration*, edited by B. Weiss, pp. 61-77 (Champaign, IL: University of Illinois Press, 1982); Humbert Nelli, *The Italians in Chicago*, pp. 39-95 (New York: Cambridge University Press, 1970); Leonard Covello, *The Social Background of the Italo-American School Child* (Leiden: E. J. Brill, 1967); J. B. Maller, "Economic and Social Correlatives of School Progress in New York City," *Teachers College Record* 34 (1933):660-68.

15. "Interview with Leonard Covello," *The Urban Review* 3 (1969):59.

16. Selma Berrol, *Immigrants at School, New York City, 1898-1914* (New York: Arno Press, 1978).

17. Gerd Korman, *Industrialization, Immigrants and Americanizers* (Madison, WI: State Historical Society of Wisconsin, 1968); Tyack, *The One Best System*; Robert Carlson, *The Quest for Conformity* (New York: John Wiley, 1975).

18. Gilbert Gonzalez, "The System of Public Education and Its Function in the Chicano Community, 1920-1930" (Ph.D. dissertation, University of California-Los Angeles, 1974); C. R. Tupper, "The Use of Intelligence Tests in a Small City," in *Intelligence Tests and School Reorganization*, edited by L. Terman, pp. 92-102 (Yonkers, NY: World Book, 1923); Sol Cohen, ed., *Education in the United States*, vol. 5, p. 2933 (New York: Random House, 1973).

19. Tyack, *The One Best System*; Carlson, *The Quest*.

20. Gonzalez, "The System of Public Education"; Weinberg, *A Chance* , pp. 140-77.

21. Paul Wrobel, "Becoming a Polish American, A Personal Point of View," in *White Ethnics*, edited by J. Ryan, p. 55 (New York: Prentice Hall, 1973).

22. Leonard Covello, *The Heart Is the Teacher,* pp. 30-31 (New York: McGraw-Hill, 1958).

23. Irene Ramirez, testimony to U.S. Commission on Civil Rights, *Hearings, San Antonio, Texas, December 9-14, 1968*, pp. 28-87 (Washington, D.C.: U.S. GPO, 1969); Selma Berrol, "The Open City: Jews, Jobs, and Schools in New York City, 1880-1915," in *Educating an Urban People*, edited by D. Ravitch and R. Goodenow, p. 106 (New York: Teachers College Press, 1981).

24. Tyack, *The One Best System*, p. 109.

25. Hubert Humphrey, "U.S. Policy in Latin America," *Foreign Affairs* 42 (1964):601.

26. Weinberg, *A Chance*, pp. 140-77; Thomas Simmons, "The Citizen Factories: The Americanization of Mexican-American Students in Texas Schools, 1920-1945" (Ph.D. dissertation, Texas A&M Unversity, 1976).

27. Michael Kane, *Minorities in Textbooks* (Chicago, IL: Quadrangle Books, 1970); Abraham Hoffman, "Where Are the Mexican Americans? A Textbook Omission Overdue for Revision," *The History Teacher* 6 (1972):143-50.

28. Tyack, *The One Best System*, p. 202.

29. Korrol, "Settlement Patterns"; Maria Canino, "An Historical Review of the English Language Policy in Puerto Rico's Education System, 1848-1949" (Ed.D. dissertation, Harvard University, 1981); Weinberg, *A Chance*, pp. 140-77, 230-59.

CHAPTER 2   MISSIONARY-STYLE ASSIMILATION, 1945-1968

1. Charles Wollenberg, *With All Deliberate Speed*, p. 122 (Berkeley, CA: University of California Press, 1976).
2. Herbert Gans, *The Urban Villagers*, p. 143 (New York: Free Press of Glencoe, 1962).
3. Wollenberg, *With All Deliberate Speed*; Meyer Weinberg, *A Chance to Learn* (New York: Cambridge University Press, 1976).
4. Charles Abrams, "How to Remedy Our Puerto Rican Problem," *Commentary* 19 (1955):395.
5. Weinberg, *A Chance*, pp. 240-59.
6. Ibid.; see also the New York City school system's journal, *High Points:* 29 (November 1947):58-62; 31 (May 1949):60-66; 32 (March 1950):27-30; and 33 (January 1951):32-42; I. Lorge and F. Mayans, "Vestibule vs. Regular Classes for Puerto Rican Migrant Pupils," *Teachers College Record* 55 (1954):231-37.
7. Clara Rodriguez, "The Structure of Failure II, A Case in Point," *The Urban Review* 7 (1974):215-16.
8. J. Cayce Morrison, *The Puerto Rican Study, 1953-1957* (New York: Board of Education, City of New York, 1958).
9. Judith Krugman, "Cultural Deprivation and Child Development," *High Points* 38 (1956):5-20; Norman Friedman, "Cultural Deprivation: A Commentary on the Sociology of Knowledge," in *Toward A Sociology of Knowledge*, edited by J. Beck, C. Jenks, N. Keddie, and M. Young, pp. 120-33 (New Brunswick, NJ: Transaction Books, 1978).
10. Colman Brez Stein, Jr., "A Policy Study of Bilingual Education, 1953-1983" (Ph.D. dissertation, University of Maryland, 1983).
11. Quoted in remarks of Andrew Greeley in M. Ridge, ed., *The New Bilingualism*, p. 208 (New Brunswick, NJ: Transaction Books, 1981).
12. Tucson Public School System, "The Safford Exploratory Project," in *Educating the Culturally Disadvantaged Child,* edited by L. Crow, L. Murray, and H. Smythe, pp. 184-86 (New York: David McKay, 1966).
13. Celia Heller, *Mexican American Youth at the Crossroads*, pp. 33-34 (New York: Random House, 1966).
14. Harold Allen, *The Teaching of English as a Second Language* (Washington, D.C.: TESOL, 1978); Steve Darian, *English as a Second Language: History, Development and Methods of Teaching* (Norman, OK: University of Oklahoma Press, 1972); James Alatis, "Teaching Standard English as a Second Language or Dialect," in *Teaching English as a Second Language*, edited by R. Fox, p. 43 (Washington, D.C.: National Council of Teachers of English, 1973).
15. Diego Castellanos, *The Best of Two Worlds*, pp. 63-70 (Trenton, NJ: New Jersey State Department of Education, 1983); Alfredo Lanier, "Teaching with Subtitles," *Chicago* vol. 33, no. 4 (June 1984):163-65, 191.

16.   Iris MacCrae, testimony to National Advisory Council on Bilingual Education, *Hearings, Philadelphia, Pennsylvania, October 16, 1975*, mimeo., pp. 136-45; see also testimony of Raquel Spence of Reading, Pennsylvania, schools at the same hearing on pages 48-72; Lanier, "Teaching with Subtitles."

17.   Quoted in William Madsen, *The Mexican-Americans of South Texas*, p. 107 (New York: Holt, Rinehart and Winston, 1964).

18.   Quoted in ibid., p. 106.

19.   Castellanos, *The Best*, pp. 185-86; Paul Simon, *The Tongue-Tied American* (New York: Continuum, 1980).

20.   Joe Bernal, testimony to U.S. Commission on Civil Rights, *Hearing in San Antonio Texas, December 9-14, 1968*, pp. 256-58 (Washington, D.C.: U.S. GPO, 1969); John Ogbu, *Minority Caste and Class* (New York: Academic Press, 1978).

21.   Theodore Parsons, "Ethnic Cleavage in a California Town," p. 387 (Ph.D. dissertation, Stanford University, 1965).

22.   Jane Mercer, "Current Retardation Procedure and the Psychological and Social Implications on the Mexican-Americans," (Arlington, VA: ERIC Document Reproduction Service ED 052 848, 1970) and *Labelling the Mentally Retarded* (Berkeley, CA: University of California Press, 1973); California Advisory Committee to the U.S. Commission on Civil Rights, *Evaluation of Educable Mentally Retarded Programs in California* (Washington, D.C.: 1970).

23.   Robert Coles, *Children of Crisis*, vol. 4, p. 380 (Boston, MA: Little, Brown, 1977); see also Robert Rosenthal and Lenore Jacobson, *Pygmalion in the Classroom* (New York: Holt, Rinehart and Winston, 1968).

24.   Richard Rodriguez, *Hunger of Memory* (New York: Norton, 1983).

25.   Richard Gambino, *Blood of My Blood*, p. 99 (Garden City, NY: Doubleday, 1974); Clara Rodriguez, "The Structure of Failure"; Coles, *Children*, p. 247.

26.   Norman Podhoretz, *Making It*, pp. 7-8 (New York: Random House, 1967).

27.   Ibid., pp. 10-11.

CHAPTER 3   REINVENTING BILINGUAL EDUCATION

1.   Heinz Kloss, *The American Bilingual Tradtion* (Rowley, MA: Newbury House, 1977); Steven Schlossman, "Is There An American Tradition of Bilingual Education? German in the Public Elementary Schools, 1840-1919," *American Journal of Education* 91 (1983):139-86; Selwyn Troen, *The Public and the Schools: Shaping the St. Louis School System, 1838-1920* (Columbia, MO: University of Missouri Press, 1975).

2.   Sources for this section are W. Mackey and V. N. Beebe, *Bilingual Schools for a Bicultural Community* (Rowley, MA: Newbury House, 1977); J. L. Logan, "Coral Way: A Bilingual School," *TESOL Quarterly* 1 (1967):50-54; G. Cancela "Bilingual Education in Dade County," in *Introduction to Bilingual Education*, edited by L. Ortega, pp. 47-60 (Long Island City, NY: L A Publishing, 1975).

3.   Julie Jeffrey, *Education for the Children of the Poor*, pp. 8-20 (Columbus, OH: Ohio State University Press, 1978); Morris Krugman, "The Culturally Deprived Child in School," *NEA Journal* 50 (1961):22-27; Sophie Elam, "Acculturation and Learning Problems of Puerto Rican Children," *Teachers College Record* 61 (1960):258-64.

4.   Frank Reissman, *The Culturally Deprived Child* (New York: Harper and Row, 1962); Benjamin Willis, "Compensatory Education in Chicago's Public Schools," in *Educating the Culturally Disadvantaged Child*, edited by L. Crow, L. Murray, and H. Smythe, pp. 202-28 (New York: David McKay, 1966).

5.   See J. McVicker Hunt, ed., *The Challenge of Incompetence and Poverty* (Urbana, IL: University of Illinois Press, 1969).

6.   Carl Brauer, "Kennedy, Johnson and the War on Poverty," *Journal of American History* 69 (1982):98-119.

7.   "Interview with Sargent Shriver" in *Project Headstart*, edited by E. Zigler and J. Valentine, pp. 49-67 (New York: Free Press, 1979); Jeffrey, *Education for the Children*, pp. 8-35.

8.   Hugh Graham, "The Transformation of Federal Education Policy, The Kennedy and Johnson Years," National Institute of Education Project no. 80-0139, (mimeo.), Washington, D.C., 1983; Samuel Halperin, "ESEA: Five Years Later," printed in *Congressional Record*, September 7, 1970, p. 30918.

9.   Quoted in Graham, "The Transformation," p. 138.

10.   Graham, "The Transformation," pp. 138-47; Halperin, "ESEA," pp. 30916-19.

11.   Quoted in Merle Miller, *Lyndon: An Oral Biography*, p. 409 (New York: Putnam's, 1980).

12.   E. Eidenburg and R. Morey, *An Act of Congress*, pp. 82-95, 180-82 (New York: W. W. Norton, 1969); Jeffrey, *Education for the Children*, pp. xi-3.

13.   Milbrey McLaughlin, *Evaluation and Reform* (Santa Monica, CA: Rand Corporation, 1975).

14.   Quoted in Jeffrey, *Education for the Children*, p. 90.

15.   Eidenburg and Morey, *An Act of Congress*, pp. 2-63, 232-33; William Wayson, "The Negative Side," *Phi Delta Kappan* 57 (1975): 156.

16.   Raymond Castro, "Assumptions Underlying Bilingual Education in the United States" (Ph.D. dissertation, Harvard University, 1976).

17.   See W. Moquin and C. Van Doren, eds., *A Documentary History of the Mexican-Americans*, pp. 471-93 (New York: Bantam Books, 1972).

18.   Meyer Weinberg, *A Chance to Learn*, pp. 170-74, 251-52 (New York: Cambridge University Press, 1977).

19.   Jeffrey, *Education for the Children*, pp. 5-20.

20.   National Education Association, *The Disadvantaged American*, p. 11 (Washington, D.C.: The National Education Association, 1962).

21.   Oscar Lewis, *La Vida* (New York: Random House, 1966).

22.   Joseph Monserrat, testimony at U.S. Senate Special Subcommittee on Bilingual Education, *Hearings on Bilingual Education, 1967*, p. 78 (Washington, D.C.: U.S. GPO).

23.   Francesco Cordasco, "The Puerto Rican Family and the Anthropologist," *Urban Education* 3 (1967):32-37; Eleanor Leacock, ed., *The Culture of Poverty: A Critique* (New York: Simon and Schuster, 1971).

24.   Thomas McFeeley, statement to U.S. House of Representatives Committee on Education and Labor, General Subcommittee, *Hearings on Bilingual Education Programs, 1967*, pp. 520-21 (Washington, D.C.: U.S. GPO).

25. United States Commission on Civil Rights, *Hearings, San Antonio, Texas, December 9-16, 1968* (Washington, D.C.: U.S. GPO, 1969).

26. Richard Margolis, *The Losers*, p. 8 (New York: Aspira, 1968).

27. Castro, "Assumptions Underlying Bilingual Education," pp. 1-62; Elliott Judd, "Factors Affecting the Passage of the Bilingual Education Act of 1967" (Ph.D. dissertation, New York University, 1977).

28. Jose Vega, *Education, Politics and Bilingualism in Texas* (Washington, D.C.: University Press of America, 1983).

29. National Education Association, *Third National NEA Conference on Civil and Human Rights in Education: "New Voices in the Southwest" October 30-31, 1966, Tucson, Arizona* (Washington, D.C.: National Education Association, 1967).

30. "Remarks of Senator Ralph Yarborough," *Congressional Record*, January 17, 1967, p. 600.

31. Ibid.

32. Maria Eugenia Matute-Bianchi, "What is Bilingual Bicultural Education?" *The Urban Review* 12 (1980):89-106; Judd, "Factors Affecting," p. 140.

33. John Molina, "Bilingual Education in the USA," in *Proceedings of the First Inter-American Conference on Bilingual Education*, edited by R. Troike and N. Modiano, p. 28 (Arlington, VA: Center for Applied Linguistics, 1975).

34. Castro, "Assumptions Underlying Bilingual Education," pp. 12-73; Judd, "Factors Affecting," pp. 76-170; Senator Ralph Yarborough, "Remarks," *Congressional Record*, September 27, 1967, pp. 27053-54.

35. Graham, "The Transformation," p. 294; Carl Kaestle and Marshall Smith, "The Federal Role in Elementary and Secondary Education, 1940-1980," *Harvard Education Review* 52 (1982):394-99.

36. Judd, "Factors Affecting," pp. 133-72.

37. Quoted in Graham, "The Transformation," pp. 261-62.

38. Senator Ralph Yarborough, "Remarks," *Congressional Record*, March 6, 1968, p. 5460.

39. Senator Ralph Yarborough, testimony at U.S. Senate Select Committee on Equal Education Opportunity, *Hearings, August 18-21, 1970*, Part 4, p. 2534.

40. Graham, "The Transformation," p. 28.

41. Castro, "Assumptions Underlying Bilingual Education," pp. 153-58.

42. Quoted in Graham, "The Transformation," p. 331.

CHAPTER 4   CREATING A PROGRAM OUT OF THIN AIR, 1968-1980

1. Maria Medina Swanson, "Bilingual Education as a Profession," in *Perspectives on Bilingualism and Bilingual Education*, edited by J. Alatis and J. Staczek, p. 253 (Washington, D.C.: Georgetown University Press, 1985).

2. Julie Jeffrey, *Education for the Children of the Poor*, pp. 104-85 (Columbus, OH: Ohio State University Press, 1978).

3. Quoted in Jeffrey, *Education for the Children*, p. 170.

4. Jeffrey, *Education for the Children*, p. 178.

5.   Quoted in Ernest House, *The Politics of Educational Innovation*, pp. 207-08 (Berkeley, CA: McCutchan, 1974).

6.   Ibid.

7.   Quoted in Theodore Andersson, "Bilingual Education, the American Experience," *Modern Language Journal* 51 (1971):433-34.

8.   Ibid.

9.   U.S. Government Accounting Office, *Bilingual Education: An Unmet Need*, pp. 27-28 (Washington, D.C.: U.S. GPO, 1976).

10.   Vera John, "Letter from the Southwest on Bilingual Education," *Urban Review* 7 (1974):43-45.

11.   R. Kjolseth, "Bilingual Programs in the United States: For Assimilation or Pluralism?" in *Bilingualism in the Southwest*, edited by P. Turner, pp. 3-29 (Tucson, AZ: University of Arizona Press, 1973).

12.   James Gambone, "Bilingual Bicultural Civil Rights: The May 25th Memorandum and Oppressive School Practices," pp. 1-6 (Ph.D. dissertation, University of New Mexico, 1973); Peter Roos, "Bilingual Education: The Hispanic Response to Unequal Educational Opportunity, *Law and Contemporary Problems* 42 (1978): 111-40.

13.   Gambone, "Bilingual Bicultural Civil Rights," p. 2.

14.   Roos, "Bilingual Education."

15.   Quoted in United States Commission on Civil Rights, *A Better Chance to Learn*, pp. 207-08 (Washington, D.C.: U.S. GPO, 1975).

16.   Ibid.

17.   Susan Schneider, "The 1974 Bilingual Education Amendments: Revolution Reaction or Reform" (Ph.D. dissertation, University of Maryland, 1975), and "The 1978 Bilingual Education Act," *Education Libraries* 4 (1979):53-54, 66-67; Arnold Leibowitz, *The Bilingual Education Act: A Legislative Analysis* (Rosslyn, VA: National Clearinghouse for Bilingual Education, 1980).

18.   Josué Gonzalez, *Toward Quality in Bilingual Education*, p. 4 (Rosslyn, VA: National Clearinghouse for Bilingual Education, 1979).

19.   Christine Paulston, *Bilingual Education Theories and Issues* (Rowley, MA: Newbury House, 1980).

20.   Maria Eugenia Matute-Bianchi, "The Federal Mandate for Bilingual Education," in *Bilingual Education and Public Policy in the United States*, edited by R. Padilla, pp. 25-30 (Ypsilanti, MI: Eastern Michigan University, 1979).

21.   Stephen Rosenfeld, "Bilingualism and the Melting Pot," Washington *Post*, September 27, 1974, p. A-14; Howard Hurwitz, "Dual Language School System: Disservice to Students," *Human Events*, December 21, 1974; Albert Shanker, "Bilingual Education: Not Why But How," New York *Times*, November 3, 1974, p. E-11; Tom Bethell "Why Johnny Still Can't Read," *Harper's*, November 1979; Noel Epstein, *Language, Ethnicity and the Schools: Policy Alternatives for Bilingual Education* (Washington, D.C.: George Washington University, 1977).

22.   Quoted in Abigail Thernstrom, "Language Issues and Legislation," in *Harvard Encyclopedia of American Ethnic Groups*, edited by S. Thernstrom, p. 623 (Cambridge, MA: Harvard University Press, 1980).

23.   Joseph Califano, testimony to U.S. House Committee on Appropriations,

Subcommittee on Departments of Labor and HEW, *Hearings, February 21, 1978,* Part 2, pp. 69, 126 (Washington, D.C.: U.S. GPO).

24.   Quoted in Joseph Califano, *Governing America*, p. 313 (New York: Simon and Schuster, 1981).

25.   Iris Berke, "Evaluation Into Policy, Bilingual Education, 1978," pp. 80-111 (Ph.D. dissertation, Stanford University, 1978).

26.   Quoted in ibid., pp. 114-15.

27.   Quoted in Califano, *Governing*, pp. 313-14.

28.   M. Danoff, *Evaluation of the Impact of ESEA Title VII Bilingual Education Programs*, vols. I-IV (Palo Alto, CA: American Institutes of Research, 1977-78); Keith Baker and Adriana DeKanter, eds., *Bilingual Education: A Reappraisal of Federal Policy* (Lexington, MA: Lexington Books, 1983).

29.   Joshua Fishman and Gary Keller, eds., "Introduction," to their *Bilingual Education for Hispanic Students in the Untied States*, pp. ix-x (New York: Teachers College Press, 1982).

30.   *Federal Register* 45, no. 152, August 5, 1980, pp. 52052-76.

31.   Castellanos, *The Best*, pp. 219-28; "Education Associations Mobilize Against Lau Regulations," *Department of Education Weekly*, August 25, 1980, p. 3.

32.   "Debate Intensifies on Bilingual Education Proposals," *Education Daily*, September 11, 1980.

33.   Ibid.; Cecil Clift, "School Districts Resent Intrusion on Bilingual Rules," San Antonio *Express*, September 10, 1980, p. 5.

CHAPTER 5   THE FIGHT FOR POWER

1.   Alfredo Lanier, "Teaching with Subtitles," *Chicago*, June 1984, p. 65.

2.   Paul Sandoval, "Gut Level Politics," in *Chicanos in Higher Education*, edited by H. Casso and G. Roman, pp. 68-78 (Albuquerque, NM: University of New Mexico Press, 1976).

3.   Jose Vega, *Education, Politics and Bilingualism in Texas* (Washington, D.C.: University Press of America, 1983).

4.   Alfredo Benavides, "A Bilingual Community and Its Schools," in *Bilingual Education and Public Policy in the United States*, edited by R. Padilla, pp. 212-28 (Ypsilanti, MI: Eastern Michigan University, 1979).

5.   Lois Steinberg, "The Bilingual Education Act and the Puerto Rican Community" (Ph.D. dissertation, Fordham University, 1978); Isaura Santiago, "Aspira vs. Board of Education of the City of New York: A Historical and Political Analysis" (Ph.D. dissertation, Fordham University, 1978).

6.   David Savage, "Shanker Out Front Again in Push for School Reform," article reprinted in *Education Week*, July 27, 1983, p. 51.

7.   Quoted in David Vidal, "Bilingual Education Stirs Debate in New York City," New York *Times*, June 21, 1976, p. 35. See also Arnold Lubasch, "New York Schools Found in Contempt," New York *Times*, October 27, 1976, p. 32; and Herbert Teitelbaum, "Bilingual Education Here," New York *Times*, May 26, 1975, p. 15.

8.   "Bilingual Danger," New York *Times*, November 22, 1976, p. 24.

9.   Vidal, "Bilingual Education."

10.   J. Shockley, *Chicano Revolt in a Texas Town* (Notre Dame, IN: University of Notre Dame Press, 1974); Alfred Steinberg, *Sam Johnson's Boy*, pp. 259-62 (New York: Macmillan, 1968).

11.   E. Bilbao and M. Gallart, *Los Chicanos: Segregacion y Educacion* (Mexico City: Editorial Nuevo Imagen, 1981); W. Smith and D. Foley, "Mexicano Resistance to Schooled Ethnicity," *Education and Urban Society* 10 (1978):145-76; Donald Post, "Ethnic Competition for Control of Schools in Two South Texas Towns" (Ph.D. dissertation, University of Texas, 1974).

12.   Bilbao and Gallart, *Los Chicanos.*

13.   Juan Guzman, "Community Conflict: A Case Study of the Implications of a Bilingual Education Program" (Ph.D. dissertation, Oregon State University, 1978).

14.   Beverly Hall, "The Bilingual Bicultural Schools," *The Nation,* November 20, 1976, pp. 519-22.

15.   Diego Castellanos, "The History of Bilingual Education in New Jersey," p. 242 (Ed.D. dissertation, Fairleigh Dickinson University, 1979).

16.   Ibid., pp. 150-320; Fred Burke, "Bilingual Bicultural Education: An Adventure in Wonderland," *Annals of the American Academy of Political and Social Sciences* 454 (1981):172-80.

17.   Castellanos, "History," pp. 160-310.

18.   John Ogbu, *The Next Generation* (New York: Academic Press, 1972).

19.   Sonia DeHunt, testimony to National Advisory Council on Bilingual Education, *Hearing in Portland, Oregon, May 3, 1983,* mimeo., pp. 46-56.

20.   Sarah Melendez, "Hispanos, Desegregation, and Bilingual Education: A Case Analysis of the Role of 'El Comite de Padres' in the Court-Ordered Desegregation of the Boston Public Schools" (Ed.D. dissertation, Harvard University, 1981); B. MacDonald, C. Adelman, S. Kushner, and R. Walker, *Bread and Dreams* (Norwich, England: University of East Anglia Centre for Applied Research in Education, 1982).

21.   Ibid.

CHAPTER 6   THE BLUNDERBUSS APPROACH TO FEDERAL ENFORCEMENT

1.   Barbara Deane and Perry Zirkel, "The Bilingual Education Mandate: It Says Schools Must Do Something," *American School Board Journal* 63 (1976):24-34.

2.   Betsy Levin, "An Analysis of the Federal Attempt to Regulate Bilingual Education," *Journal of Law and Education* 12 (1983):37.

3.   Gene Maeroff, *Don't Blame the Kids,* pp. 26-28 (New York: McGraw-Hill, 1982).

4.   Norman Jones, "A Survey of Student, Parent and Staff Attitudes Toward and A Description of Nashville's ESL/Bilingual Program," pp. 1-4 (Ed.D. dissertation, Vanderbilt University, 1981); Aida Waserstein, "Organizing for Bilingual Education: One Community's Experience," *Inequality in Education* 19 (1975):23-30.

5.   Angela Lupo-Anderson, "A Legal and Administrative Study in Bilingual Education" (Ph.D. dissertation, Florida State University, 1980).

6.   Rodrigo Garreton, "The State of Bilingual Education in the State of Ohio: An Exploratory Study," pp. 152-58, 176-94 (Ph.D. dissertation, Miami University, 1979).

7. University of Texas, Lyndon B. Johnson School of Public Affairs, "Federal Policy for Equal Education Opportunity: Conflict and Confusion," (Arlington, VA: ERIC Document Reproduction Service, ED 159 258, 1977).

8. V. Ochoa, "Bilingual Desegregation: School Districts' Responses to the Spirit of the Law Under the Lau vs. Nichols Supreme Court Decision," p. 242 (Ph.D. dissertation, University of Massachusetts, 1978).

9. Douglas Lee, "Pluralism and Public Policy in Education," in *Pluralism, Racism and Public Policy*, edited by E. Clausen and J. Bermingham, p. 157 (Boston, MA: G. K. Holt, 1981).

10. Paul Martinez, "Serna vs. Portales: The Plight of Bilingual Education Four Years Later," *Journal of Ethnic Studies* 7 (1979):108-16.

11. Lois Steinberg, "The Bilingual Education Act and the Puerto Rican Community," pp. 110-25, 190-230 (Ph.D. dissertation, Fordham University, 1978).

12. U.S. Commission on Civil Rights, *Hearings, Denver, Colorado, February 17-19, 1976*, p. 223 (Washington, D.C.: U.S. GPO, 1976).

13. Ibid., pp. 43-44.

14. U.S. Commission on Civil Rights, *Hearing, Corpus Christi, Texas, August 17, 1976*, pp. 16-17 (Washington, D.C.: U.S. GPO, 1976).

15. Wisconsin Advisory Committee to the U.S. Commission on Civil Rights, *Falling Through the Cracks: An Assessment of Bilingual Education in Wisconsin* (Madison, WI: 1982).

16. California Advisory Committee to the U.S. Commisison on Civil Rights, *State Administration of Bilingual Education* (Sacramento, CA: 1976).

CHAPTER 7   BUSINESS AS USUAL: THE MISSIONARY STYLE REVISITED

1. Quoted in California Advisory Committee to the U.S. Commission on Civil Rights, *State Administration of Bilingual Education*, p. 33 (Sacramento, CA: 1976).

2. New Hampshire Advisory Committee to the U.S. Commission on Civil Rights, *Shortchanging the Language Minority Student* (Concord, NH: 1982).

3. Martha Montero, "An Ethnography of Teachers' Perspectives in Bilingual Classrooms: Implications for the Pedagogy of Culture and Meaning" (Ph.D. dissertation, Boston University, 1981); Marcel Ringawa, "Bilingual/Bicultural Teacher Needs and Attitudes" (Ed.D. dissertation, University of Massachusetts, 1980).

4. Maria Eugenia Matute-Bianchi, "What is Bilingual Bicultural Education?" *The Urban Review* 12 (1980):89-109.

5. W. Zaher, "The Mexican-American Child and the Public School" (Ph.D. dissertation, Stanford University, 1973).

6. Shirley Achor, *Mexican-Americans in a Dallas Barrio* (Tucson, AZ: University of Arizona Press, 1978).

7. Irene Blea, "Bessemer: A Sociological Perspective of a Chicano Barrio" (Ph.D. dissertation, University of Colorado, 1981).

8. Josué Gonzalez, "Research Needs, Issues and Capabilities," in National Institute of Education, *Conference Report-Desegregation and Educational Concerns of the Hispanic Community*, p. 15 (Washington, D.C.: U.S. GPO, 1977).

CHAPTER 8   CREATIVE PROGRAMS AND THE
POLITICS OF PLURALISM

1.   Quoted in L. Larew, "English Speaking Students Predominate in Bilingual Multicultural Program in Buffalo," *Hispania* 65 (1982):98-99.
2.   Robert Carlson, *The Quest for Conformity*, pp. 120-28 (New York: John Wiley, 1975).
3.   N. Montalto, "Multicultural Education in the New York Public Schools, 1919-1941," in *Educating an Urban People*, edited by D. Ravitch and R. Goodenow, pp. 67-83 (New York: Teachers College Press, 1981); Louis Adamic, *My America* (New York: Harper and Brothers, 1938); Carey McWilliams, *North From Mexico*, pp. 239-43 (New York: Greenwood Press, 1968, originally published 1948).
4.   Leonard Covello, *The Heart Is the Teacher* (New York: McGraw-Hill, 1958).
5.   Robert Peebles, "Leonard Covello: A Study of an Immigrant's Contribution to New York City" (Ph.D. dissertation, New York University, 1967); Leonard Covello, *The Social Background of the Italo-American School Child* (Leiden: E. J. Brill, 1967).
6.   Peebles, "Leonard Covello: A Study"; "Interview with Leonard Covello," *The Urban Review* 3 (1969):56-63.
7.   Mary Farmer, "Bilingual Integration in San Diego," *Hispania* 65 (1982):427-29.
8.   Larew, "English Speaking Students."
9.   Fred Hechinger, "Combating Lingui-chauvinism: A Biracial Bilingual Experiment," *Saturday Review*, March 8, 1975, pp. 46-47.
10.   John Gersuk, "Southboro Elementary School," *Palm Beach Post,* September 26, 1983, reprinted in Florida Department of Education, *Bilingual Education Newsletter* 8 (Fall 1983):4.
11.   *FOCUS* 13 (Rosslyn, VA: National Clearinghouse for Bilingual Education, February 1984); *Today's Education*, 1984-1985 Annual Edition, pp. 21-23.
12.   Lois Steinberg, "The Bilingual Education Act and the Puerto Rican Community" (Ph.D. dissertation, Fordham University, 1978).
13.   Virginia Collier, "A Sociological Case Study of Bilingual Education and Its Effects on the Schools and the Community" (Ph.D. dissertation, University of Southern California, 1980); Patricia Ohmans, "'European-Style' School is Model of Bilingual Instruction," *Education Week*, March 2, 1983, pp. 1, 18.
14.   Susan Grubb, "'Back of the Yards' Goes Bilingual," *American Education* vol. 12, no. 2, (March 1976):15-18.
15.   C. Cazden, R. Carrasco, A. Maldonado-Guzman, and F. Erickson, "The Contributions of Ethnographic Research to Bilingual Bicultural Education," in *Georgetown University Round Table on Language and Linguistics 1980*, edited by J. Alatis, p. 67 (Washington, D.C.: Georgetown University Press, 1980);Sally Reed, "Bilingual Classes: A Bilateral Conflict, New York *Times*, August 21, 1983.
16.   B. MacDonald, C. Adelman, S. Kushner, and R. Walker, *Bread and Dreams*, p. 216 (Norwich, England: University of East Anglia Centre for Applied Research in Education, 1982).
17.   Soledad Arenas, "Innovations in Bilingual/Multicultural Curriculum Development," *Children Today* 9 (1980):17-20.

18.   Terry LaCroce, "Teaching the Bilingual Gifted Child," *NJEA Review* 53 (1980):16-17.

19.   *FOCUS* 13 (Rosslyn, VA: National Clearinghouse for Bilingual Education, February 1984).

20.   National Advisory Committee on Bilingual Education, *Sixth Annual Report* (Washington, D.C.: 1981); S. Elliot and E. Berlin, "Hamtramck, Michigan: From Polish to Pluralistic," *NABE News* 5 (September 1981):9.

21.   Wallace Lambert, "An Overview of Issues in Immersion Education," in *Studies in Immersion Education* (Sacramento, CA: California State Department of Education, 1984).

22.   Ibid.; "Spanish as a Learning Tongue," *Newsweek*, December 3, 1984, p. 92; E. Howe, "The Success of the Cherry Hill Spanish Immersion Program in Orem, Utah," *Hispania* 66 (1983):592-96; "Grass Roots Organization Backs Bilingual Education for All," *Bilingual Journal* vol. 8, no. 3, (Spring 1984):4.

23.   L. Larew, "Primary Approach to Languages," *Hispania* 66 (1983):92.

24.   House Subcommittee on Postsecondary Education, *Hearings on National Security and Economic Growth Through Foreign Language Improvement, July 14-15, 1981* (Washington, D.C.: U.S. GPO, 1981).

25.   "Louisiana Lengthens School Day for Foreign Language Study," *Education Week*, March 7, 1984.

CHAPTER 9   THE REAGAN YEARS

1.   Abigail Thernstrom, "E Pluribus Plura: Congress and Bilingual Education," *The Public Interest* 60 (1980):3-22; Neil Pearce, "English as the Only Language," *Philadelphia Inquirer*, May 30, 1983, p. A-11; Robert Rossier, "Bilingual Education, Training for the Ghetto," *Policy Review* 25 (1983):36-45.

2.   Nathan Glazer in M. Ridge, ed., *The New Bilingualism* (New Brunswick, NJ: Transaction Books, 1981).

3.   S. I. Hayakawa, testimony to U.S. House of Representatives Subcommittee on Elementary, Secondary and Vocational Education, *Hearings on Bilingual Education, March 28, 1984*, pp. 63-64 (Washington, D.C.: U.S. GPO).

4.   Quoted in *Congressional Record*, April 22, 1985, p. S4452.

5.   Wallace Lambert, "An Overview of Issues in Immersion Education," in *Studies on Immersion Education*, p. 26 (Sacramento, CA: California State Department of Education, 1984).

6.   Eduardo Hernandez-Chavez, "The Inadequacy of English Immersion Education as an Educational Approach for Language Minority Students in the United States," in *Studies on Immersion Education*, pp. 144-83 (Sacramento, CA: California State Department of Education, 1984); R. Gersten, "Structured Immersion for Language Minority Students: Results of a Longitudinal Evaluation," *Educational Evaluation and Policy Analysis* 7 (Fall 1985):187-96.

7.   Stanley Elam, "The National Education Association: Political Powerhouse or Paper Tiger?" *Phi Delta Kappan* 63 (November 1981):169-74; Stephen Chapman, "NEA Seizes Power: The Teachers Coup," *New Republic*, October 1, 1980, pp. 9-11.

8.   Christine Paulston, *Bilingual Education Themes and Issues*, p. 75 (Rowley, MA: Newbury House, 1980).

9. James Alatis, "The Role of ESL in Bilingual Education," *NABE Journal* 3 (1979):27-37; Gladys Nussenbaum, "Cooperation Between Bilingual and ESL Teachers," *NABE News*, January 1983, pp. 6, 11.

10. James Alatis, president, Joint National Committee for Languages, "Statement presented to National Advisory Committee on Bilingual Education, Washington, D.C., January 28, 1982," mimeo.

11. Eileen White, "ED Finds Bilingual Resources Low, but Recommends Cut of 25 Percent," *Education Week*, December 15, 1982, p. 10; Thomas Toch, "The Emerging Politics of Language," *Education Week*, February 8, 1984, pp. 1, 12-16.

12. *Report on the Education of the Disadvantaged*, August 16, 1982, pp. 5-6; October 29, 1982, p. 3; and December 24, 1982, p. 4.

13. Quoted in Dan Balz, "Administration Backs Off on Budget Cuts, Will Continue to Fund Bilingual Education," Washington *Post*, March 7, 1981.

14. Dan Balz, "As the Hispanic Vote Emerges, Republicans Seek to Christen It," Washington *Post*, July 11, 1981, p. A-3.

15. Colman B. Stein, Jr., *The Bilingual Education Act of 1984* (Rosslyn, VA: National Clearinghouse for Bilingual Education, 1985).

16. "MEMO on the 98th Congress," (Rosslyn, VA: National Clearinghouse for Bilingual Education, December 1984).

17. Stein, *The Bilingual Education Act of 1984*.

18. *Congressional Record*, June 20, 1984, p. H6109-28.

19. Diego Castellanos, *The Best of Two Worlds*, pp. 254-57 (Trenton: New Jersey State Department of Education, 1983).

20. U.S. Department of Education Reform 88 Coordinating Committee, "Response and Implementation Plan Addressing the Recommendations of the President's Private Sector Survey on Cost Control Task Force Report on the Department of Education," draft, Washington, D.C., 1984.

CHAPTER 10 THE STRUGGLE FOR CONTROL OF THE DEPARTMENT OF EDUCATION

1. Elizabeth Kastor, "Bidding Bell Farewell," Washington *Post*, December 19, 1984.

2. Donald Warren, *To Enforce Education* (Detroit, MI: Wayne State University Press, 1974).

3. Hugh Graham, *The Uncertain Triumph* (Chapel Hill, NC: University of North Carolina Press, 1984).

4. Quoted in Donna Engelgau, "Protecting Education from Stockman's Cuts," *Chronicle of Higher Education*, November 20, 1984.

5. John Hanrahan and Julie Kosterlitz, "School for Scandal," *Common Cause* 9, no. 5 (September 1983):16-25.

6. Quoted in Stephen Engelberg, "Lesson in Hard Knocks for Education Secretary," New York *Times*, May 2, 1985.

7. Fred Hechinger, "Conflicting Messages from Administration," New York *Times*, May 7, 1985.

8. Robert Pear, "Reading, Writing, Roping Liberals," New York *Times*, December 4, 1984.

9. Quoted in George Will, "My Son and Life's Lottery," Washngton *Post*, April 22, 1985.

10. Ibid.

11. Howard Kurtz, "Liberal Republican Foils Budget-Cutters," Washington *Post*, April 25, 1985.

12. Ibid.

13. Ibid.

14. Ibid.

15. The author attended these hearings.

16. Quoted in Engelberg, "Lessons in Hard Knocks."

17. "Correspondence Between Sen. Weicker and Bennett," *Education Week*, April 24, 1985, p. 10.

18. Quoted in George Archibald, "Education Press Spokesman Reportedly Forced to Resign," Washington *Times*, April 24, 1985.

19. James Hertling, "Bilingual Panel in its Final Act, Recommends Federal Cutback," *Education Week*, May 8, 1985.

20. "Gardner Says Bauer's Confirmation, Bennett's Reputation Paramount Concerns," *Education Daily*, May 1, 1985.

21. "Further Philosophical Reflections," Washington *Post*, April 20, 1985.

22. Ibid.

23. "The Antibodies Strike Back," *Wall Street Journal*, April 22, 1985.

24. Ibid.

25. Haynes Johnson, "A Cruel Month in Politics," Washington *Post*, April 21, 1985.

26. Ibid.

27. "Bennett Endorses Concept of Two-Track High Schools," Washington *Post*, May 12, 1985.

28. Engelberg, "Lessons in Hard Knocks."

29. Ibid.

30. "Education Secretary is Warned That Controversy Overshadows Education Issues," *Education Times*, April 29, 1985.

31. Ibid.

32. Carol Innerst and George Archibald, "Roche Quits Council, Blasts Policy," Washington *Times*, May 28, 1985.

33. Burton Pines and Paul Weyrich, "Bill Bennett Flunks His First Test," Washington *Times*, May 14, 1985.

34. Ibid.

CHAPTER 11 THE LATIN PRESENCE AND OPPORTUNITY STRUCTURE

1. Terrel Bell, "The Importance of Language Competence in Education," *TESOL Newsletter* 18 (August 1984):1.

2. Quoted in David Vidal, "Living in Two Cultures: Hispanic New Yorkers," New York *Times*, May 13, 1980, p. A-14.

3. National Commission for Employment Policy, *Hispanics and Jobs: Barriers*

to Progress, p. 9 (Washington, D.C., 1982).

4.   Ibid., pp. 9-24.

5.   U.S. Commission on Civil Rights, *Unemployment and Underemployment Among Blacks, Hispanics and Women* (Washington, D.C.: U.S. GPO, 1982).

6.   Quoted in Jane Seaberry, "Jobless Rate Dip Said Masking Bigger Woes," Washington *Post*, August 19, 1983, pp. D-8, D-9.

7.   Torsten Husen, "Are Standards in U.S. Schools Really Lagging Behind Those in Other Countries?" *Phi Delta Kappan* 64 (1983):455-61.

8.   Robert Politzer, "Social Class and Bilingual Education: Issues and Contraditions," California State University-Los Angeles Bilingual Education Paper Series, vol. 5, no. 2, 1981; R. Acuna, "Mixing Apples With Oranges," *Integrated Education* 13 (1975):12-17.

9.   Randy Fitzgerald, "The Teacher They Call 'The Champ,'" *Readers' Digest* (August 1983):119-24.

10.   Hispanic Policy Development Project, *The Hispanic Almanac* (New York, 1984); C. Davis, C. Haub, and J. Willette, "U.S. Hispanics: Changing the Face of America," *Population Bulletin* (special issue) 38 (June 1983):1-45; Cheryl Russell, "The News About Hispanics," *American Demographics* 5 (1983):15-25; U.S. Bureau of the Census, "Condition of Hispanics in America Today," paper presented to the House Subcommittee on Census and Population Hearings on Hispanics in America, September 13, 1983, mimeo.; "Fertility of Hispanic Women is Evaluated," New York *Times*, December 18, 1984, p. A-26.

11.   Ibid.

12.   Ibid.

13.   Luis Salces, "Changes in the Racial and Ethnic Composition of Public School Students in Chicago," (Arlington, VA: ERIC Document Reproduction Service, ED 224 640, 1983); Douglas Massey, "A Research Note on Residential Succession: The Hispanic Case," *Social Forces* 61 (1983):825-34.

14.   David Heer, "Intermarriage," in *Harvard Encyclopedia of American Ethnic Groups*, edited by S. Thernstrom, pp. 513-21 (Cambridge, MA: Harvard University Press, 1980).

15.   "Many Hispanics Nurture Identity, Survey Shows," *Education Week*, September 19, 1984, p. 8; Susan Foster, "Study Suggests Wide Support Exists for Bilingual Education," *Education Week*, August 24, 1983, p. 8; David Vidal, "Living in Two Cultures; Hispanic New Yorkers," four-part series, New York *Times*, May 11-14, 1980.

16.   Dorothy Waggoner, "The Minority Language Population from the 1980 Census," *FORUM*, National Clearinghouse for Bilingual Education 7 (October-November 1984):2, 6; "The New Urban Demography," *Education and Urban Society* (special issue) 16 (August 1984):395-520; National Center for Education Statistics, *The Condition of Schooling for Hispanic Americans* (Washington, D.C.: U.S. GPO, 1980).

17.   Ibid.

CHAPTER 12 THE POLITICS OF PROVINCIALISM: THE LEGACY OF THE ANGLOCENTRIC CURRICULUM

1.   American Association of Universities, *Beyond Growth: The Next Stage in Language and Area Studies*, p. 58 (Washington, D.C., 1984).

2.   Quoted in *USA Today*, May 12, 1985, p. 8A.

3.   Lynne Reer, testimony to National Advisory Committee on Bilingual Education, *Hearing, Portland, Oregon, May 3, 1983*, p. 37, mimeo.

4.   Robert Levenson, statement to House Subcommittee on Postsecondary Education, *Hearings on National Security and Economic Growth Through Foreign Language Improvement, July 12-15, 1981*, p. 224 (Washington, D.C.: U.S. GPO, 1981).

5.   Moorhead Kennedy, testimony to House Subcommittee on Postsecondary Education, *Hearings on National Security and Economic Growth Through Foreign Language Improvement, July 12-15, 1981*, p. 116 (Washington, D.C.: U.S. GPO, 1981).

6.   Admiral Bobby Inman, testimony to House Subcommittee on Postsecondary Education, *Hearings on National Security and Economic Growth Through Foreign Language Improvement, July 12-15, 1981*, p. 108 (Washington, D.C.: U.S. GPO, 1981).

7.   Ibid.

8.   American Association of Universities, *Beyond Growth*, pp. 58-65; Rep. Leon Panetta, "International Education and National Security," *Congressional Record*, May 3, 1983, p. E2005.

9.   T. Shabad, "Geography a Lost Art," New York *Times*, January 16, 1985, p. C-1; "Geography Illiteracy Assailed by 2 Groups," New York *Times*, December 14, 1984, p. A-28.

10.   Quoted in *Foreign Language Annals*, April 1981, p. 125.

11.   Tony Martin, testimony to House Subcommittee on Elementary, Secondary and Vocational Education, *Hearings on the Bilingual Education Improvement Act of 1983, July-August 1983*, pp. 100-01 (Washington, D.C.: U.S. GPO, 1984).

12.   Quoted in *Congressional Record*, April 28, 1983, p. E1918.

13.   Quoted in *ACTFL Public Awareness Network Newsletter*, New York, March 1984, p. 5.

14.   Quoted in *Foreign Language Annals*, New York, April 1981, p. 118.

15.   Quoted in *ACTFL Public Awareness Network Newsletter*, New York, November 1982.

16.   "One American History for All: Myth or Reality," *Education Daily*, August 24, 1984, p. 5; Ruth Charnes, "U.S. History Textbooks: Help or Hindrance to Social Justice? *Interracial Books for Children Bulletin* 15 New York, (1984):3-8; Howard LaFranchi, "History Slighted in the 1970's, Comes Back," *Christian Science Monitor*, October 1, 1984, pp. 27-28.

17.   R. Freeman Butts, *Public Education in the United States* (New York: Holt, Rinehart and Winston, 1978); David Tyack, *The One Best System* (Cambridge, MA: Harvard University Press, 1974); Meyer Weinberg, *A Chance to Learn* (New York: Cambridge University Press, 1977); Guadalupe San Miguel, "Endless Pursuits: The

Chicano Educational Experience in Corpus Christi, Texas, 1880-1960" (Ph.D. dissertation, Stanford University, 1978); Charles Wollenberg, *With All Deliberate Speed* (Berkeley, CA: University of California Press, 1976).

CHAPTER 13 THE STATE OF THE SCHOOLS

1. John Ogbu, "Minority Status and Schooling in Plural Societies," *Comparative Education Review* 27 (1983):170-78, and *Minority Caste and Class* (New York: Academic Press, 1970); Robert Coles, *Children of Crisis,* vol. 4 (Boston, MA: Little, Brown, 1977).

2. Josue Gonzalez, "Research Issues, Needs and Capabilities," National Institute of Education, *Conference Report-Desegregation and Education Concerns of the Hispanic Community*, p. 11 (Washington, D.C.: U.S. GPO, 1977).

3. Hispanic Policy Development Project, *Make Something Happen*, vols. I-II, (New York, 1984); Howard La Franchi, "The Kids We Can't Afford to Waste," *Christian Science Monitor*, December 12, 1984.

4. Michael Olivas, "Federal Higher Education Policy: The Case for Hispanics," *Educational Evaluation and Policy Analysis* 4 (1982):302-11; S. Hill and J. Froomkin, "Characteristics of the Hispanic Post Secondary Students," (Arlington, VA: ERIC Document Reproduction Service, Ed 198 986, 1980).

5. Michigan Department of Education, *Hispanic School Dropouts and Hispanic Student Performance on the MEAP Test* (East Lansing, MI, 1984); Hispanic Policy Development Project, *Make Something Happen*, (New York, 1984).

6. "Hunter's President Brands School System 'Rotten,'" New York *Times*, October 29, 1984, p. B-3; Sidney Schanberg, "The Poverty Divide," New York *Times*, January 22, 1985, p. A-25.

7. Council of Great City Schools, *Federal Education Budget Policy, 1980-1984* (Washington, D.C., 1984).

8. Quoted in Alfredo Mathews, Jr., "Perceived Barriers," in National Institute of Education, *Conference Report-Desegregation and Education Concerns of the Hispanic Community*, p. 49 (Washington, D.C.: U.S. GPO, 1977).

9. Gene Maeroff, "Frequent Moves Affect Schoolwork," New York *Times*, November 27, 1984, pp. C-1, C-7.

10. Hispanic Office of Planning and Evaluation, *Hispanic Youth in Boston: In Search of Opportunity and Accountability* (Boston, MA, 1984).

11. Lester Golub, "Teacher Participation in Bilingual Education," in *Theory in Bilingual Education*, edited by R. Padilla, pp. 389-409 (Ypsilanti, MI: Eastern Michigan University, 1980).

12. Craig Richards, "Desegregation Bilingualism and Hispanic Staffing in the Public Schools" (Stanford University Institute for Research on Educational Finance and Governance, 1982); Michael O'Malley and Dorothy Waggoner, "Public School Teacher Preparation and the Teaching of ESL," *TESOL Newsletter* 18 (June 1984):1, 18-22.

13. Ibid.

14. U.S. Department of Education, *The Condition of Bilingual Education in the Nation, 1984* (Rosslyn, VA: National Clearinghouse for Bilingual Education, 1984).

15. Fred Burke, "Bilingual Education: An Adventure in Wonderland," *Annals of the American Academy of Political and Social Sciences* 454 (1981):174-75.

CHAPTER 14 THE MODEL MINORITY SETUP

1. Asian-American Student Association, "Asian-American Admission at Brown University," *Integrated Education* 22 (January 1985):35.

2. Celia Reyes Hailey, "Demographic Shifts, Social Class Status and Bilingual Education in California," paper presented to American Educational Research Association Annual Meeting, New Orleans, LA, 1984, p. 18.

3. Charles Wollenberg, *With All Deliberate Speed* (Berkeley, CA: University of California Press, 1976); David Tyack, *The One Best System* (Cambridge, MA: Harvard University Press, 1974); Russell Marks, "Testers, Trackers and Trustees: The Ideology of the Testing Movement in the United States, 1900-1954" (Ph.D. dissertation, University of Illinois, 1972).

4. Ibid.

5. Seymour Fersh, "Orientals and Orientation," *Phi Delta Kappan* 53 (1972):317.

6. Michael Kane, *Minorities in Textbooks* (Chicago, IL: Quadrangle Books, 1970).

7. Timothy Healy, "The CUNY Experience," in *Individualizing the System*, edited by D. W. Vermilye, pp. 171-75 (San Francisco, CA: Jossey Bass, 1976).

8. *Focus on Asian Studies* (a publication of the Asia Society), no. 50 (August 1980):1-2.

9. Ibid.

10. Peter Schrag, *The Decline of the WASP*, p. 38 (New York: Simon and Schuster, 1970).

11. Ibid.

12. Alfred Kazin, *A Walker in the City*, p. 17 (New York: Harcourt, Brace, 1951).

13. Hutchins Hapgood, *The Spirit of the Ghetto* (New York: Harper & Row, 1902).

14. Quoted in M. Hindus, *The Old East Side*, p. 19 (Philadelphia, PA: Jewish Publication Society of America, 1971).

15. Quoted in Moses Rischin, *The Promised City*, p. 97 (Cambridge, MA: Harvard University Press, 1962).

16. Ande Manners, *Poor Cousins* (New York: Coward, McCann, and Geoghegan, 1972).

17. Diane Ravitch, *The Great School Wars*, p. 225 (New York: Basic Books, 1974); see also M. Bonner, "The Introduction of the Gary Plan to the New York City School System" (Ph.D. dissertation, Rutgers University, 1978).

18. Quoted in Manners, *Poor Cousins*, p. 240.

19. Quoted in Rischin, *Promised City*, p. 101.

20. Quoted in Stanley Feldstein, *The Land That I Show You*, pp. 170 (Garden City, NY: Anchor Press/Doubleday, 1978).

21.   Selma Berrol, "Jews Jobs and Schools," in *Educating an Urban People*, edited by Diane Ravitch and Ronald Goodenow, pp. 101-15 (New York: Teachers College Press, 1981); Rischin, *Promised City*.

22.   Quoted in Feldstein, *The Land*, p. 246.

23.   Quoted in Stephen Steinberg, *The Academic Melting Pot*, p. 25 (New York: McGraw-Hill, 1974).

24.   Wollenberg, *With All Deliberate Speed*, pp. 51-52; also see W. Caudill and G. DeVos, "Achievement, Culture and Personality: The Case of the Japanese Americans," in *School Children in the Urban Slum*, edited by J. Roberts (New York: Free Press, 1967).

25.   Quoted in Wollenberg, *With All Deliberate Speed*, p. 54.

26.   Ibid., p. 26.

27.   Yamato Ichihashi, *Japanese in the United States* (Stanford, CA: Stanford University Press, 1932); Jeanne Wakatsuki Houston, *Farewell to Manzanar* (Boston, MA: Houghton Mifflin, 1973).

28.   Daniel Okimoto, *American in Disguise*, pp. 69-70 (New York: Walker/Weatherhill, 1979).

29.   Reed Ueda, "The Americanization and Education of Japanese Americans," in *Cultural Pluralism*, edited by E. Epps (Berkeley, CA: McCutchan, 1974).

30.   Geraldine Grant, "Six Immigrant Groups in Queens: A Pilot Study," (Arlington, VA: ERIC Document Reproduction Service, ED 237 598 and Ed 237 599, 1984).

31.   Ibid.

32.   Reyes Hailey, "Demographic Shifts."

33.   Ibid.

34.   Ibid.

35.   John Ogbu, *The Next Generation* (New York: Academic Press, 1972).

36.   Peter Schrag, *The Decline*, pp. 28-29.

37.   W. Robbins, "Violence Forces Hmong to Leave Philadelphia," New York *Times*, September 17, 1984.

38.   Quoted in B. Downing et al., "H'mong Resettlement," (Arlington, VA: ERIC Document Reproduction Service, Ed 245 015, 1984).

39.   Vietnamese residents of Boston were the victims of at least 12 racial attacks in early 1985 according to the June 10, 1985, Washington *Times*. Los Angeles incidents were reported in M. Ingwerson, "Asians, Blacks Work to Heal Rifts in L.A. Community," *Christian Science Monitor*, June 13, 1985.

40.   Asian-American Students Association, "Asian-American Admissions"; see also M. Winerup, "Asian Americans Question Ivy League's Entry Policies," New York *Times*, May 30, 1985.

41.   Eugene Wong, "Asian-American Middleman Minority Theory. The Constructional Framework of an American Myth," (Arlington, VA: ERIC Document Reproduction Service, Ed 241 654, p. 23, 1984); see also M. Wong, "Model Students? Teachers' Perceptions and Expectations of Their Asian and White Students," *Sociology of Education* 53 (1980):236-46.

CHAPTER 15 WHY PROGRAMS FAIL

1.   Cynthia Gorney, "The War of the Words," Washington *Post*, July 8, 1985.
2.   Information on San Francisco comes from L. C. Wang, "Lau vs. Nichols: History of a Struggle for Equality and Quality Education," in *Asian-Americans: Social and Psychological Perspectives*, vol. II, edited by R. Endo, S. Sue, and N. Wagner, pp. 190-223 (New York: Science and Behavior Books, 1980); see also San Francisco Unified School District, Bilingual Education Department, "Fact Sheet, November 1984."
3.   Wang, pp. 215-16.
4.   Information on Oakland comes from Cynthia Gorney, "The War of the Words," series in Washington *Post*, July 7-9, 1985; G. Guthrie, *A School Divided* (Hillsdale, NJ: Lawrence Erlbaum, 1985); and *Education Week*, June 19, 1985.
5.   *Education Week*, June 19, 1985.
6.   Gorney, "The War," July 8, 1985.
7.   Information on Lynn comes from the transcript of *Lynn Hispanic Advisory Committee v. Lawson*, U.S. District Court for the District of Massachusetts, Civil Action no. 85-2475-K, July 1985, and from *Education Daily*, July 23, 1985.

CHAPTER 16 LANGUAGE MINORITY EDUCATION OUTSIDE THE UNITED STATES

1.   Roger Magnuson, "Gallicism, Anglo-Saxonism and Quebec Education," *Canadian Journal of Education* 9 (Winter 1984):1-2.
2.   The major sources for this chapter are the following anthologies: *World Yearbook of Education 1981* (New York: Nichols, 1981); J. Bhatnagar, ed., *Educating Immigrants* (New York: St. Martin's, 1981); and C. Bagley and G. Verma, eds., *Multicultural Childhood* (Aldershot, England: Gower, 1984).
3.   Ben Wattenburg, "Population Decline Begins in Germany," Washington *Times*, July 25, 1985.
4.   Quoted in T. Skuttnab-Kangas, *Bilingualism or Not: The Education of Minorities* (Clevedon, England: Multilingual Matters, 1981).
5.   L. Berg-Eldering, F. De Rijcke, and L. Zuck, eds., *Multicultural Education, A Challenge for Teachers* (Dordrecht, The Netherlands: Foris, 1983); N. Altena and R. Apell, "Mother Tongue Teaching and the Acquisition of Dutch by Turkish and Moroccan Immigrant Workers Children," *Journal of Multilingual and Multicultural Development* 3 (1982):315-82.
6.   Quoted in I. Gutfleisch and B. Rieck, "Immigrant Workers in West Germany: Teaching Programs for Adults and Children," in *World Yearbook of Education 1981*, p. 342 (New York: Nichols, 1981).
7.   Ibid., p. 344.
8.   J. Smolicz, "Culture, Ethnicity and Education: Multiculturalism in a Plural Society," in ibid., p. 33.
9.   Skuttnab-Kangas, *Bilingualism or Not*; M. Malhotra, "The Educational Problems of Foreign Children of Different Nationalities in West Germany," *Ethnic and Racial Studies* vol. 8, no. 2 (April 1985):291-307.

10. P. Tansley and A. Craft, "Mother Tongue Teaching and Support," *Journal of Multilingual and Multicultural Development* vol. 5, no. 5 (1984).

11. R. Apple, "The Home of the Rolls-Royce Joins the Down and Out," New York *Times*, July 29, 1985.

12. Quoted in G. Verna and B. Ashworth, "Education and Occupational Aspirations of Young South Asians in Britain," in *World Yearbook 1981*, p. 250.

13. A. Tosi, *Immigration and Bilingual Education*, pp. 43-44 (Oxford, England: Pergamon Press, 1984).

14. Ibid., p. 47.

15. A. Andersen and J. Frideres, *Ethnicity in Canada: Theoretical Perspectives* (Toronto, Canada: Butterworths, 1981); Magnuson, "Gallicism"; California State Department of Education, *Studies in Immersion Education* (Sacramento, CA, 1984).

16. Quoted in J. Bhatnagar, "Multicultural Education of Immigrants in Canada," in *Educating Immigrants*, edited by J. Bhatnagar, p. 78.

17. Quoted in ibid., p. 78.

18. J. Bhatnagar and A. Hamalian, "Educational Opportunity for Minority Group Children in Canada," *World Yearbook 1981*, pp. 230-31.

19. Colman Brez Stein, Jr., "Israeli Policy Toward Sephardi Schooling," *Comparative Education Review* vol. 29, no. 2 (May 1985):204-15.

20. Quoted in ibid., p. 213.

21. Quoted in ibid., p. 212.

22. Quoted in ibid., p. 214.

CHAPTER 17 PRESCHOOLS AND TEACHER SHORTAGES: PROMISE AND DILEMMA

1. Quoted in M. Lazerson, *Origins of the Urban School*, p. 49 (Cambridge, MA: Harvard University Press, 1971).

2. L. Schweinhart and D. Weikart, "Evidence That Good Early Childhood Programs Work," *Phi Delta Kappan* (April 1985):545-48.

3. "Hunter's President Brands City School System 'Rotten,'" New York *Times*, October 29, 1984.

4. J. R. Sirkin, "Houston Schools Turn to Mexico for Bilingual Teachers," *Education Week*, February 27, 1985, pp. 1, 28.

5. Ibid.; see also C. Pesce, "Schools Scramble for Bilingual Teachers," *USA Today*, February 22, 1985; G. Maeroff, "Bilingual Aid in Schools Insufficient, Study Finds," New York *Times*, October 25, 1985.

CHAPTER 18 NON-HISPANIC GROUPS IN THE BILINGUAL EDUCATION CONSTITUENCY

1. Quoted in G. Ezzell and W. Young, *Cherokee Education Program*, p. 4 (Rosslyn, VA: National Clearinghouse for Bilingual Education, 1984).

2. Francis Von Maltitz, *Living and Learning in Two Languages* (New York: McGraw-Hill, 1975).

3. P. Rosier and W. Holm, *The Rock Point Experience: A Longitudinal Study of a Navajo School Program* (Washington, D.C.: Center for Applied Linguistics, 1980); L. Vorih and P. Rosier, "Rock Point Community School: An Example of a Navajo-English Bilingual Elementary School Program," *TESOL Quarterly* vol. 12, no. 3 (September 1978):263-69.

4. Ezzell and Young, *Cherokee Education.*

5. Ibid.

6. Sally Reed, "The New Pluralism," New York *Times*, August 21, 1983.

CHAPTER 19   CONGRESS AND THE COURTS IN THE 1980S

1. A. Branscombe, "Court Approves City Schools' Bilingual Proposal in Lawsuit," Denver *Post*, August 18, 1984.

2. "Desegregation Pact Advanced by Houston Schools, MALDEF," *Education Daily*, September 6, 1984, p. 7.

3. "San Jose School Officials Urge Court to Review Desegregation Case," *Education Daily*, March 14, 1985, p. 5.

4. T. Baez, R. Fernandez, and J. Guskin, *Desegregation and Hispanic Students: A Community Perspective* (Rosslyn, VA: National Clearinghouse for Bilingual Education, 1980); see also articles on Oakland and Massachusetts case in *Education Week*, June 19, 1985.

5. Colman Brez Stein, Jr., *The 1984 Bilingual Education Act* (Rosslyn, VA: National Clearinghouse for Bilingual Education, 1985).

CHAPTER 20   FUNDING: THE BOTTOM LINE

1. Anne Lewis, "Washington Report," *Phi Delta Kappan* 66 (May 1985):585.

2. *Department of Education Weekly*, October 15, 1984, pp. 2-3.

3. U.S. House of Representatives, Committee on Education and Labor, *Hearing on H.R.11 and H.R.5231*, p. 103 (Washington, D.C.: U.S. GPO, 1984).

4. Philip Runkel, statement, U.S. House of Representatives, Committee on Education and Labor, *Hearings on the Bilingual Education Amendments of 1981*, pp. 227-28 (Washington, D.C.: U.S. GPO, 1982).

5. Maria Lindia, testimony, ibid., pp. 207-08, 213.

6. James Loughridge, statement, U.S. House of Representatives, Committee on Education and Labor, *Hearings on the Bilingual Education Improvement Act of 1983*, p. 158 (Washington, D.C.: U.S. GPO, 1983).

CONCLUSION

1. George Bereday, *Comparative Methods in Education*, p. 5 (New York: Holt, Rinehart and Winston, 1963).

Bibliography

Baker, Keith and Adriana DeKanter, eds. *Bilingual Education: A Reappraisal of Federal Policy*. Lexington, MA: Lexington Books, 1983.

Berke, Iris. "Evaluation Into Policy, Bilingual Education, 1978." Ph.D. dissertation, Stanford University, 1980.

Burke, Fred. "Bilingual/Bicultural Education: An Adventure in Wonderland." *Annals of the American Academy of Political and Social Science* 454 (1981):164-77.

Carter, Thomas and Roberto Segura. *Mexican-Americans in School: A Decade of Change*. New York: College Entrance Examination Board, 1979.

Castellanos, Diego. *The Best of Two Worlds*. Trenton, NJ: New Jersey State Department of Education, 1983.

___. "The History of Bilingual Education in New Jersey." Ph.D. dissertation, Fairleigh Dickinson University, 1979.

Epstein, Noel. *Language, Ethnicity and the Schools: Policy Alternatives for Bilingual-Bicultural Education*. Washington, D.C.: George Washington University, 1977.

Gonzalez, Josue. "The Coming of Age of Bilingual/Bicultural Education: A Historical Perspective." *Inequality in Education*, no. 19 (February 1975).

Judd, Elliott. "Factors Affecting the Passage of the Bilingual Education Act of 1967." Ph.D. dissertation, New York University, 1977.

Kloss, Heinz. *The American Bilingual Tradition*. Rowley, MA: Newbury House, 1977.

Korrol, Virginia Sanchez. "Settlement Patterns and Community Development Among Puerto Ricans in New York City, 1917-1948." Ph.D. dissertation, State University of New York at Stony Brook, 1981.

Levin, Betsy. "An Analysis of the Federal Attempt to Regulate Bilingual Education." *Journal of Law and Education* 12 (1983):23-60.

Matute-Bianchi, Maria Eugenia. "The Federal Mandate for Bilingual Education." In *Bilingual Education and Pubic Policy in the United States*, edited by R. Padilla, pp. 21-31. Ypsilanti, MI: Eastern Michigan University, 1979.

___. "What is Bilingual Bicultural Education?" *Urban Review* 12 (Summer 1980):89-106.

Roos, Peter. "Bilingual Education: The Hispanic Response to Unequal Educational Opportunity." *Law and Contemporary Problems* 42 (1978):111-40.

Schneider, Susan. "The 1974 Bilingual Education Amendments: Revolution, Reaction or Reform." Ph.D. dissertation, University of Maryland, 1975.

Stein, Jr., Colman Brez. "A Policy Study of Bilingual Education, 1953-1983." Ph.D. dissertation, University of Maryland, 1983.

___. *The Bilingual Education Act of 1984.* Rosslyn, VA: The National Clearinghouse for Bilingual Education, 1985.

___. "Hispanic Students in the Sink or Swim Era, 1900-1960." *Urban Education* 20 (July 1985):189-98.

___. "Israeli Policy Toward Sephardi Schooling." *Comparative Education Review* 29 (May 1985):204-15.

Steinberg, Lois. "The Bilingual Education Act and the Puerto Rican Community." Ph.D. dissertation, Fordham University, 1978.

Tyack, David. *The One Best System.* Cambridge, MA: Harvard University Press, 1974.

Weinberg, Meyer. *A Chance to Learn.* New York: Cambridge University Press, 1977.

Wollenberg, Charles. *With All Deliberate Speed.* Berkeley, CA: University of California Press, 1976.

GOVERNMENT DOCUMENTS AND REPORTS

Congressional Record, 1967-1970, 1973-1974, 1977-1978, 1984.

Federal Register, 1980-1985.

National Advisory Council on Bilingual Education: *Annual Reports,* 1975-1985.

National Center for Education Statistics:
Selected Statistics on the Education of Hispanics, 1982.
The Condition of Education, 1978-1982.
The Condition of Education for Hispanic Americans, 1980.

National Commission for Employment Policy: *Hispanics and Jobs: Barriers to Progress*, 1982.

President's Commission on Foreign Languages: *Strength through Wisdom*, 1979.

Public Papers of the President of the United States, 1967-1970.

Select Commission on Immigration and Refugee Policy: *U.S. Immigration Policy and the National Interest*, 1981.

U.S. Bureau of the Census: "Condition of Hispanics in America Today," statement presented to House Subcommittee on Census and Population, September 13, 1983, mimeo.

U.S. Commisison on Civil Rights:
  A Better Chance to Learn: Bilingual Bicultural Education, 1975.
  California Advisory Committee, *State Administration of Bilingual Education – Si or No*, 1976.
  Civil Rights Issues of Euro-Ethnic Americans, Hearings:
    San Antonio, December 9-14, 1968
    New York City, February 14-15, 1972
    Denver, February 17-19, 1976
    Tampa, Florida, March 29-31, 1976
    Corpus Christi, Texas, August 17, 1976.
  Illinois Advisory Committee, *Bilingual Education, A Privilege or a Right*, 1976.
  Mexican American Education Study, 6 volumes, 1971-1974.
  New Hampshire Advisory Committee, *Shortchanging the Language-Minority Student*, 1982.
  Puerto Ricans in the Continental United States, 1976.
  Unemployment and Underemployment Among Blacks, Hispanics, and Women, 1982.
  Wisconsin Advisory Committee, *Falling Through the Cracks: An Assessment of Bilingual Education in Wisconsin*, 1982.

U.S. Congress:
  House Committee on Education and Labor, General Subcommittee on Education, *Hearings on Bilingual Education*, 1967.
  Senate Committee on Labor and Public Welfare, Special Subcommittee on Bilingual Education, *Hearings*, 1967.
  Senate Select Committee on Equal Educational Opportunity, *Hearings*, Parts 4 and 8, 1970.
  Senate Committee on Labor and Public Welfare, General Subcommittee on Education, *Hearings*, 1973-1978.
  House Committee on Labor and Education, Subcommittee on Elementary and Secondary and Vocational Education, *Hearings*, 1973-1984.

Senate Committee on Appropriations, Subcommittee on Labor and HEW, *Hearings*, 1973-1979.

House Committee on Appropriations, Subcommittee on Labor and HEW, *Hearings*, 1973-1979

Senate Committee on Labor and Human Resources, Subcommittee on Education Arts and Humanities, *Hearings on Bilingual Education Amendments of 1981*, 1981.

House Committee on Education and Labor, Subcommittee on Postsecondary Education, *Hearings on National Security and Economic Growth Through Foreign Language Improvement*, 1981.

House Committee on Post Office and Civil Service, Subcommittee on Census and Population, "Hearings on the Hispanic Population," 1983, mimeographed testimony in possession of author.

U.S. Department of Education:

Office of Inspector General for Audit, "Review of Federal Bilingual Programs" in 6 Texas School Districts; in files of National Clearinghouse for Bilingual Education, Rosslyn, Virginia.

Testimony at Regional Hearings on Lau Regulations, 1980. Mimeographed, in files of U.S. Office of Civil Rights, Washington, D.C.

The Condition of Bilingual Education in the Nation – A Report from the Secretary of Education, 1979, 1982, and 1984.

U.S. Government Accounting Office: Report to the Congress by the Comptroller-General of the United States, *Bilingual Education: An Unmet Need*, 1976.

Definitions

Bilingual education. Instruction in two languages.

English as a Second Language. Instruction in learning to speak, read, and write English, given in English only.

Hispanic or Latin. Person of Spanish origin.

Immigrant or ethnic. Used here broadly to refer to immigrants and their descendants who arrived in the United States from Europe 1885-1924, Latin America 1880-present, or from other regions.

Language minority. Ethnic group members whose first language is other than English. Usually applied to speakers of Spanish, Asian languages, Native American languages, Portuguese, and Haitian Creole.

Mexican, Mexican-American, Chicano. Terms used here to denote residents of the Untied States whose ancestry can be traced to Mexico; includes most residents of the Southwest when the U.S. acquired the region in 1848.

Puerto Rican. Person whose ancestry is Puerto Rican, whether residing on the U.S. mainland or in Puerto Rico.

Special language education. A program or set of practices to instruct non-English-proficient students in the use of English. English as a Second Language and bilingual education are its two major thrusts.

Abbreviations

AFT   American Federation of Teachers

BE   Bilingual education

BEA
or Title
VII   Bilingual Education Act

ED   U.S. Department of Education (also known as English to Speakers of Other Languages as ESOL)

ESL   English as a Second Language

ESEA   Elementary and Secondary Education Act

HEW   U.S. Department of Health, Education and Welfare

LEP
student Limited English proficient student

NABE   National Association for Bilingual Education

NEA   National Education Association

OE   U.S. Office of Education

TESOL Teachers of English to speakers of other languages

Appendix

TABLE A.1
CHRONOLOGICAL RELATIONSHIP BETWEEN FEDERAL AND STATE LEGISLATION FOR BILINGUAL EDUCATION

Year Enacted	Federal Legislation for Bilingual Education	State Legislation for Bilingual Education
1968	Bilingual Education Act of 1968 P.L. 90-247 (Amendment to Title VII of the Elementary and Secondary Education Act of 1965)	(year first enacted)
1969		
1970		
1971		Massachusetts, Oregon
1972		Alaska, Virgin Islands
1973		Arizona, Guam, Illinois, New Mexico, New York, Texas
1974	Bilingual Education Act* P.L. 93-380	Michigan, Rhode Island
1975		Colorado, Louisiana, New Jersey, Wisconsin
1976		California, Indiana
1977		Connecticut, New Hampshire, Minnesota, Maine, Utah
1978	Bilingual Education Act* P.L. 95-561	
1979		Kansas, Washington
1980		Iowa
1981		
1982		
1983		
1984	Bilingual Education Act* P.L. 98-511	

*Reauthorization of the original Bilingual Education Act.

Sources: The Fourth Annual Report of the National Advisory Council on Bilingual Education, InterAmerica Research Associates, Rosslyn, VA, 1979. "State Education Agency Information 1983-84," National Clearinghouse for Bilingual Education, Rosslyn, VA, 1985 (photocopy).

TABLE A.2
SAN FRANCISCO UNIFIED SCHOOL DISTRICT, BILINGUAL EDUCATION DEPARTMENT FACT SHEET, NOVEMBER 1984

A) 30,042 out of 63,215 students in the district have a home language which is other than English. (47.5%)

B) English language proficiency of students having a home language other than English (October 1984):

	Non- and Limited English Proficient	Fluent- English Proficient	District Total
All lang GPS	18,669	11,373	30,042
Chinese	7,217	4,639	11,856
Spanish	5,566	2,784	8,350
Vietnamese	1,798	470	2,268
Pilipino (Filipino)	1,749	1,639	3,388
Other	2,339	1,841	4,180

C) Growth in the numbers of non- and limited-English proficient students over the past 6 years:

1979-80	7,844
1980-81	11,829
1981-82	13,797
1982-83	16,166
1983-84	17,513
1984-85	18,669

continued

Table A.2, Continued

D) Number of newcomer students* processed by the intake center:

	000	100	200	300	400	500	600	700	800	900
Jul 83	██████████████
Aug 83	███
Sep 83	█████████████████████████████████████
Oct 83	███████████████
Nov 83	███████████████
Dec 83	███████████████
Jan 84	█████████████████████████████
Feb 84	██████████████████████
Mar 84	████████████████████████████████████
Apr 84	███████████████████████████
May 84	███████████████████
Jun 84	█████████████████

*The total number of newcomer students processed each year ranges from 4,500-5,000.

Source: San Francisco Unified School District, 1984.

TABLE A.3
BILINGUAL EDUCATION IN CALIFORNIA

1. **Number of LEP pupils in California:**

   1975   233,520
   1985   524,082

2. **Primary language groups of pupils served, 1985:**

1.	Spanish	72.6%	6.	Korean	1.8%
2.	Vietnamese	5.7%	7.	Lao	1.7%
3.	Cantonese	3.6%	8.	Mandarin	1.3%
4.	Pilipino/		9.	Japanese	0.7%
	Tagalog	2.3%	10.	Portuguese	0.5%
5.	Cambodian	2.0%		All Others	7.7%

Source: California State Department of Education, 1985.

TABLE A.4
STATE TEACHER CERTIFICATION REQUIREMENTS

Teacher/Adm. Certification	State	1979-80	1980-81	1981-82	1982-83
Code:	AL	N	N	N	N
	AK	N	N	N	N
N = None	AZ	R	BE	BE	BE
UD = Under Dev.	AR	N	N	N	N
R = Required	CA	R	BE	BE	BE
BE = Bilingual	CO	R	N	N	N
Ed. required	CT	UD	N	N	ESL;BE-UD
ESL = ESL required	DE	R	BE,ESL	BE,ESL	BE,ESL
	DC	R	BE,ESL	BE,ESL	BE,ESL
	FL	UD	UD	BE,ESL	BE,ESL
	GA	N	N	N	N
	HI	N	ESL	ESL	ESL**
	ID	UD	N	UD-ESL	UD-ESL
	IL	R	BE	BE	BE
	IN	R	BE	BE	BE;ESL-UD
	IA	UD	N	N	BE-UD
	KS	N	N	BE-UD;ESL-UD	BE-UD
	KY	N	UD,ESL	ESL-UD	ESL-UD
	LA	R	ESL	ESL	ESL
	ME	UD	N	N	N
	MD	UD	N	N	ESL-UD
	MA	R	BE,ESL-UD	BE,ESL-UD	BE-ESL
	MI	R	BE	BE	BE
	MN	UD	N	N	BE,ESL
	MS	N	N	N	N
	MO	N	N	N	N
	MT	N	N	N	N
	NE	N	ESL	ESL	ESL
	NV	N	ESL	ESL	ESL
	NH	R	BE,ESL	BE,ESL	BE,ESL
	NJ	R	BE,ESL	BE,ESL	BE,ESL
	NM	R	BE,ESL	BE,ESL	BE,ESL
	NY	UD	BE,ESL*	BE,ESL*	BE,ESL
	NC	UD	ESL	UD-ESL	ESL
	ND	N	N	N	N
	OH	UD	BE,ESL	BE,ESL	BE,ESL
	OK	UD	N	N	N
	OR	N	N	N	N
	PA	N	N	N	N

continued

Table A.4, Continued

Teacher/Adm. Certification	State	1979-80	1980-81	1981-82	1982-83
	RI	R	BE,ESL	BE,ESL	BE,ESL
	SC	N	N	N	N
	SD	N	N	N	N
	TN	UD	N	ESL-UD	ESL***
	TX	R	BE,ESL	BE,ESL	BE,ESL
	UT	UD	ESL	ESL	N/A
	VT	UD	N	N	BE
	VA	N	N	ESL	ESL
	WA	UD	BE	BE	BE
	W.VA	N	N	N	N
	WI	R	BE,ESL	BE,ESL	BE,ESL
	WY	N	N	N	N
	Am. Samoa	N	BE	BE	BE
	Guam	N	N	BE,ESL,N	BE
	Mariana Is.	UD	N	N	N
	PR	UD	ESL	BE-UD;ESL	ESL;BE-UD
	TT	UD	N	N	N
	VI	N/A	N	N	BE-UD

* Effective 9/83

** At secondary level

*** Effective 9/84

Source: U.S. Department of Education, *The Condition of Bilingual Education in the Nation, 1984,* p. 14.

TABLE A.5
1980 ESTIMATE OF U.S. MINORITY LANGUAGE POPULATIONS AND SCHOOL-AGE MINORITY LANGUAGE POPULATIONS

State	Total population	Minority language population	Percent	Total population 5-17	Minority language population 5-17	Percent
Total	226,361	34,637	15.3	47,494	8,034	16.9
Alabama	3,892	152	3.9	868	39	4.5
Alaska	401	74	18.5	92	20	21.9
Arizona	2,715	727	26.8	579	202	34.9
Arkansas	2,285	85	3.7	496	22	4.5
California	23,657	6,915	29.2	4,685	1,665	35.5
Colorado	2,887	402	13.9	594	122	20.5
Connecticut	3,106	637	20.5	639	134	20.9
Delaware	594	55	9.2	125	13	10.1
District of Columbia	638	70	11.0	109	12	10.8
Florida	9,738	1,634	16.8	1,795	316	17.6
Georgia	5,459	277	5.1	1,236	72	5.8
Hawaii	964	360	37.4	198	73	36.9
Idaho	943	88	10.5	214	23	11.0
Illinois	11,418	1,805	15.8	2,407	395	16.4
Indiana	5,486	318	7.0	1,201	96	8.0
Iowa	2,912	174	6.0	606	41	6.7
Kansas	2,362	185	7.8	469	44	9.3

continued

217

Table A.5, Continued

State	Total population	Minority language population	Percent	Total population 5-17	Minority language population 5-17	Percent
Kentucky	3,658	132	3.6	802	34	4.3
Louisiana	3,881	568	14.6	972	175	18.0
Maine	1,123	187	16.7	244	42	17.4
Maryland	4,214	415	9.8	896	96	10.3
Massachusetts	5,734	1,074	18.7	1,155	216	18.7
Michigan	9,254	954	10.3	2,068	205	9.9
Minnesota	4,073	374	9.2	867	77	8.9
Mississippi	2,519	100	4.0	602	28	4.7
Missouri	4,912	270	5.5	1,011	64	6.4
Montana	786	71	9.0	167	16	9.7
Nebraska	1,569	124	7.9	325	26	8.1
Nevada	799	134	16.8	160	28	17.3
New Hampshire	920	41	4.4	196	33	1.6
New Jersey	7,360	1,594	21.7	1,531	339	22.1
New Mexico	1,302	618	47.4	303	171	56.4
New York	17,546	4,514	25.7	3,560	936	26.3
North Carolina	5,878	274	4.7	1,256	69	5.5
North Dakota	652	119	18.2	137	25	18.0
Ohio	10,790	814	7.5	2,308	104	4.5
Oklahoma	3,023	212	7.0	623	53	8.6
Oregon	2,629	227	8.6	526	53	10.1

Pennsylvania	11,856	1,293	10.9	2,380	255	10.7
Rhode Island	947	224	23.7	187	43	23.0
South Carolina	690	84	12.2	148	20	13.4
South Dakota	3,120	157	5.0	706	43	6.0
Tennessee	4,588	179	3.9	975	46	4.7
Texas	14,218	3,802	26.7	3,143	1,062	33.8
Utah	1,460	184	12.6	350	50	14.4
Vermont	511	58	11.4	110	13	12.2
Virginia	5,343	392	7.3	1,114	96	8.6
Washington	4,128	422	10.2	834	105	12.5
West Virginia	1,949	81	4.2	414	19	4.5
Wisconsin	4,703	438	9.3	1,013	90	8.9
Wyoming	469	51	10.8	101	13	12.6

Source: National Clearinghouse for Bilingual Education, *Forum* October/November, 1984, Vol. 7, No. 5, p. 6.

219

TABLE A.6
HISPANIC POPULATION IN PROFILE
(Hispanics in America: 1982)

- Largest subgroup: Mexican (62.9 percent)

- Median age: 23.7 years

- Family size: 3.89 people

- Married couples: 73.0 percent of families

- Finished high school: 45.9 percent (25 years and older)

- Unemployment rate: 13.4 percent

- Percent of families residing in metropolitan central cities: 49.6

- Percent of families below poverty level: 24.0

- Most common occupational category: operatives (19.0 percent). Includes meat cutters, metalworkers, packers, dressmakers, precision machinists, and similar occupations in manufacturing and nonmanufacturing industries. Excludes transport operatives (bus drivers, etc).

Source: U.S. Department of Commerce, Bureau of the Census, *Data User News,* May, 1985, Vol. 20, No. 5, p. 1.

Population Growth

(Percent Change 1970 to 1980)

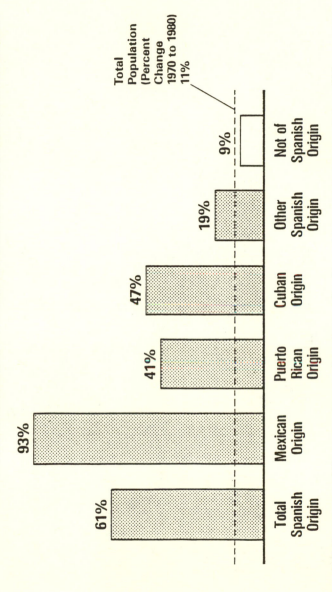

Source: U.S. Department of Commerce, Bureau of the Census, *Condition of Hispanics in America Today*, 1983.

Occupation Distribution: 1982

Base — Persons of Spanish origin and not of Spanish origin 16 years old and over, employed in the civilian labor force.

Note: Based on 1970 occupation classifications.

Source: U.S. Department of Commerce, Bureau of the Census, *Condition of Hispanics in America Today,* 1983.

Educational Attainment

(Persons 25 to 34 Years Old)

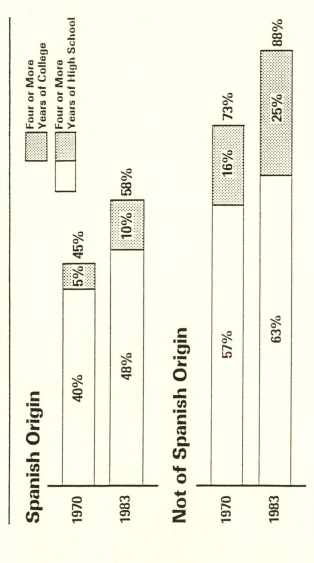

Base — Total persons of Spanish origin and not of Spanish origin 25 to 34 years old.

Source: U.S. Department of Commerce, Bureau of the Census, *Condition of Hispanics in America Today,* 1983.

FIGURE A.4

Age: 1980

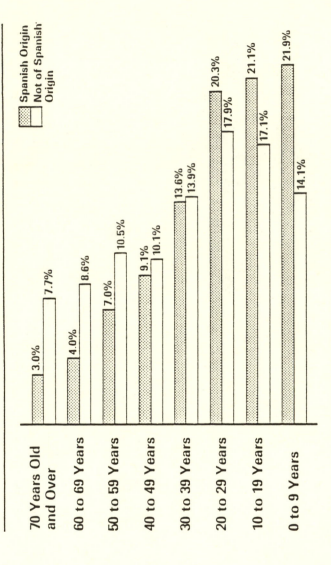

70 Years Old and Over — 3.0% | 7.7%
60 to 69 Years — 4.0% | 8.6%
50 to 59 Years — 7.0% | 10.5%
40 to 49 Years — 9.1% | 10.1%
30 to 39 Years — 13.6% | 13.9%
20 to 29 Years — 20.3% | 17.9%
10 to 19 Years — 21.1% | 17.1%
0 to 9 Years — 21.9% | 14.1%

Spanish Origin / Not of Spanish Origin

Base — Total population of Spanish origin and not of Spanish origin.

Source: U.S. Department of Commerce, Bureau of the Census, *Condition of Hispanics in America Today,* 1983.

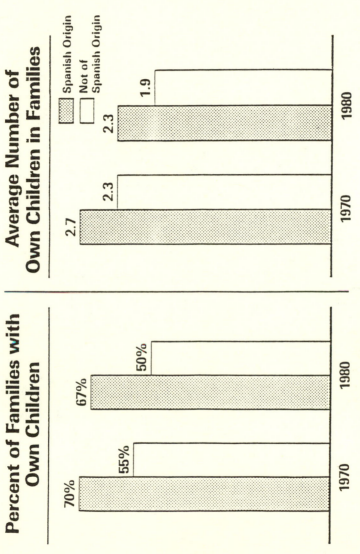

Percent of Families with Own Children

70%
55%
67%
50%

1970
1980

Average Number of Own Children in Families

Spanish Origin
Not of Spanish Origin

2.7
2.3
2.3
1.9

1970
1980

Base — Families of Spanish origin and not of Spanish origin.

Source: U.S. Department of Commerce, Bureau of the Census, *Condition of Hispanics in America Today*, 1983.

FIGURE A.6

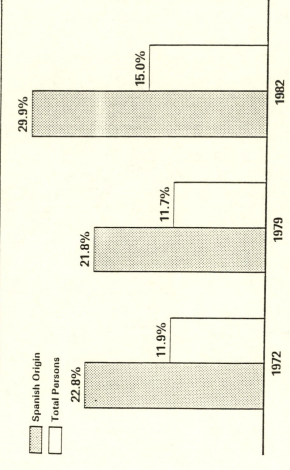

Poverty Rates of Persons

Spanish Origin

Total Persons

22.8%

11.9%

21.8%

11.7%

29.9%

15.0%

1972

1979

1982

Base — Total, all persons and persons of Spanish origin for whom poverty status is determined.

Source: U.S. Department of Commerce, Bureau of the Census, *Condition of Hispanics in America Today,* 1983.

Median Family Money Income

(In 1982 Dollars)

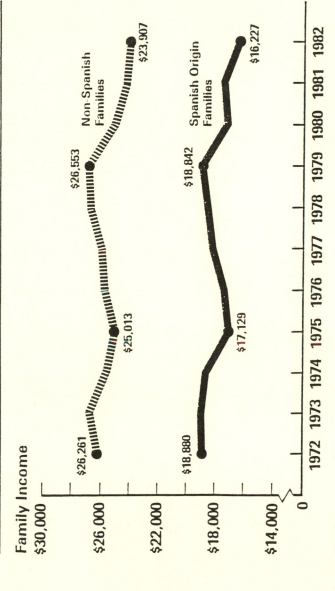

Source: U.S. Department of Commerce, Bureau of the Census, *Condition of Hispanics in America Today,* 1983.

Median Family Income in 1982

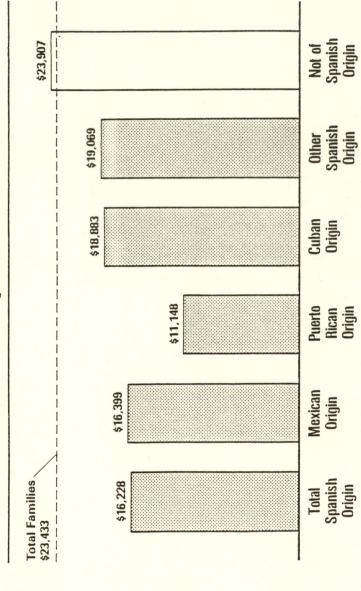

Source: U.S. Department of Commerce, Bureau of the Census, *Condition of Hispanics in America Today*, 1983.

Unemployment Rates
(Annual Averages)

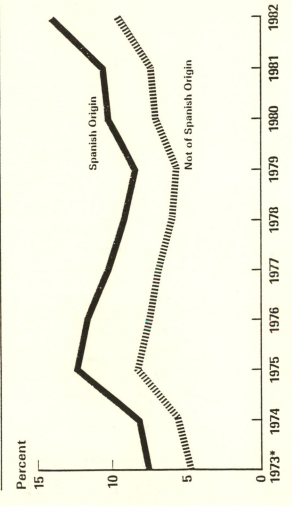

Percent

15

10

5

0

1973* 1974 1975 1976 1977 1978 1979 1980 1981 1982

Spanish Origin

Not of Spanish Origin

*First year for which data are available.

Base — Persons of Spanish origin and not of Spanish origin 16 years old and over in the civilian labor force.

Source: U.S. Department of Commerce, Bureau of the Census, *Condition of Hispanics in America Today,* 1983.

229

Percent Spanish Foreign Born: 1980

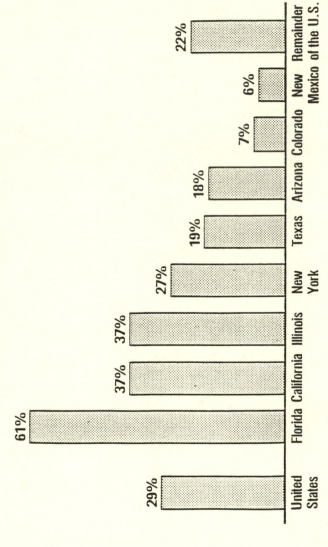

Base — Total Spanish origin population in each area.

Source: U.S. Department of Commerce, Bureau of the Census, *Condition of Hispanics in America Today*, 1983.

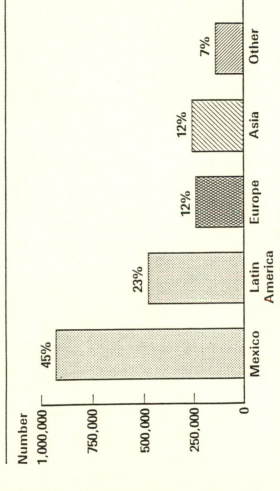

Area of Birth of Undocumented Aliens* Counted in the 1980 Census

(Estimates)

*The estimate of the undocumented alien population was derived using the 1980 census count of aliens and Immigration and Naturalization Service data on legal aliens in the United States.

Source: U.S. Department of Commerce, Bureau of the Census, *Condition of Hispanics in America Today,* 1983.

Legal Immigration by Area of Origin

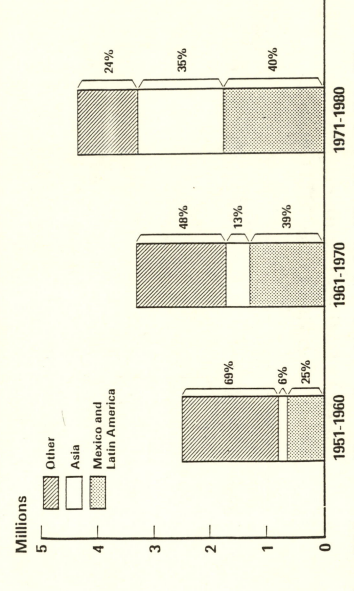

Millions

Other

Asia

Mexico and
Latin America

1951-1960   69%   6%   25%

1961-1970   48%   13%   39%

1971-1980   24%   35%   40%

Source: U.S. Department of Commerce, Bureau of the Census, *Condition of Hispanics in America Today,* 1983.

FIGURE A.13

Metropolitan-Nonmetropolitan Residence: 1980

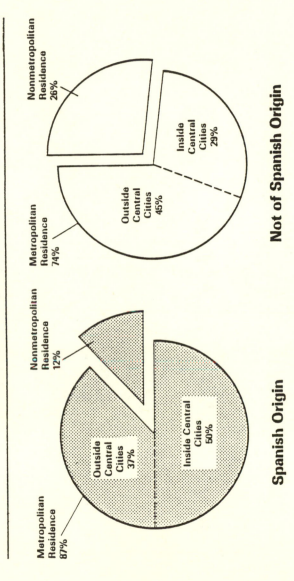

Spanish Origin

Not of Spanish Origin

Base — Total persons of Spanish origin and not of Spanish origin.

Source: U.S. Department of Commerce, Bureau of the Census, *Condition of Hispanics in America Today*, 1983.

Distribution of the Spanish Population by State: 1980

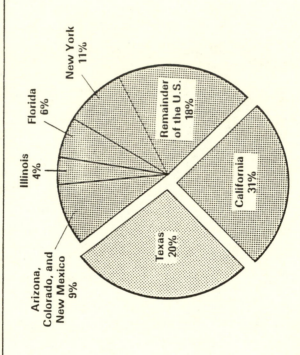

Base — Total persons of Spanish Origin in the United States.

Source: U.S. Department of Commerce, Bureau of the Census, *Condition of Hispanics in America Today*, 1983.

Index

About the Author

Colman Brez Stein, Jr., obtained a Ph.D. in education from the University of Maryland in 1983. He formerly served as research analyst at the National Clearinghouse for Bilingual Education and currently works as senior research analyst in the Washington, D.C., area. His publications include an analysis of the Bilingual Education Act of 1984 and articles on education policy issues in the Washington *Post*, *Comparative Education Review*, and *Urban Education*.